✳

Golden State, Golden Youth

✳

Golden State, Golden Youth

The California Image

in Popular Culture,

1955–1966

by KIRSE GRANAT MAY

THE UNIVERSITY OF NORTH CAROLINA PRESS
CHAPEL HILL AND LONDON

© 2002

THE UNIVERSITY OF NORTH CAROLINA PRESS
All rights reserved
Manufactured in the United States of America

This book was set in Adobe Garamond by Robert Slimbach, Matrix Inline
Script by Emigre and Adobe Officina Sans by Erik Spiekerman.

Book design by Eva Roberts

The paper in this book meets the guidelines for permanence and durability
of the Committee on Production Guidelines for Book Longevity of the
Council on Library Resources.

The title of Chapter 3, "Come Along and Sing Our Song," is taken from
"Mickey Mouse March," words and music by Jimmie Dodd.
© 1955 Walt Disney Music Company. All rights reserved, reprinted with
permission.

The title of Chapter 5, "Wish They All Could Be California," is taken
from "California Girls," words and music by Brian Wilson,
Mike Love. © Irving Music, Inc. (BMI). International copyright secured,
all rights reserved, reprinted with permission.

Library of Congress Cataloging-in-Publication Data
May, Kirse Granat.
Golden state, golden youth : the California image in popular culture,
1955–1966 / by Kirse Granat May.
    p. cm.
Includes bibliographical references and index.
ISBN 0-8078-2695-2 (cloth: alk. paper)
ISBN 0-8078-5362-3 (pbk.: alk. paper)
1. California—Civilization—20th century. 2. California—Social life and
customs—20th century. 3. Popular culture—California—History—20th
century. 4. Mass media—Social aspects—California—History—20th
century. 5. Youth—California—Social life and customs—20th century.
6. Baby boom generation—California—History. 7. Popular culture—United
States—History—20th century. 8. Mass media—Social aspects—United
States—History—20th century. 9. Mass media and youth—United States—
History—20th century. 10. Baby boom generation—United States—History.
I. Title.
F866.2 .M23 2002
979.4′053—dc21   2001053191

cloth   06 05 04 03 02   5 4 3 2 1
paper   06 05 04 03 02   5 4 3 2 1

∗ *Contents*

✳ *Illustrations*

✳   *Acknowledgments*

I must first thank Professor Robert A. Goldberg of the University of Utah, who guided this project when it was a dissertation. He offered me, as both a researcher and a teacher, an exemplar of good history, and I became a better writer and scholar while working with him. Dean May, who started as my graduate director and ended up my father-in-law, was also a great help. My husband Tim acted as proofreader (not always so successfully), sat through *Beach Party* movies, and never questioned the scholarly pursuit of watching *The Mickey Mouse Club*.

The editors and staff of the University of North Carolina Press were friendly and helpful at each stage of the publication process, particularly Sian Hunter and Kathy Malin. The reviewers of the manuscript, especially Michael Steiner of the University of California, Fullerton, offered helpful insights and comments.

My parents, Kent and Marilyn Granat, first taught me to love history. On family trips with their six children they drove miles out of the way to visit Pony Express trails and pulled over to read historic markers. I must also recognize my grandmother Elva Dewey, whose devotion to genealogy demonstrated the importance of fostering a connection with the past. And lastly to my son Ethan, who quietly sat in his swing and crib while I made final revisions and tracked down image permissions; I promise to take you to Disneyland someday.

Golden State, Golden Youth

Introduction

All good teenagers

go to California when they die.

—Brian Wilson, in Jurmain and Rawls, *California: A Place*

Americans in the postwar era often remember history according to the images of popular culture. Measuring time in decades, they conjure up the 1950s in personal terms and icons: Marlon Brando astride a motorcycle, James Dean, hula hoops, Elvis, rock and roll. When the lens is turned on the 1960s, revolution seems to be in the air: hippies of Haight-Ashbury, war in Vietnam, counterculture trends. Considering the power of radio, television, and film – then and now – to shape attitudes, values and beliefs this is hardly a surprise.

Historians, growing more tuned to popular culture's power, have grafted such symbols to their narratives. However, the inclusion of these images is problematic, since they are rarely the subject of serious analysis. Yet an investigation of popular culture offers insights that may hasten a new perspective, one that questions myths and creates a fuller understanding of past actors and events. Careful study of these images can challenge the view of the fifties as an age of conformity and stagnation, alter the picture of the revolutionary sixties, and reveal the critical links that bind the apparently different decades.[1]

In recent years there has been growing attention to this avenue of scholarship as an integral piece of the historical picture. The study of popular culture began as part of the late-1960s trend toward social history, a way of writing history beyond the focus on the elite and powerful. The *Journal of Popular Culture*, founded in 1967, countered misconceptions about the triviality and simplicity of mass culture. This move marked the "professionalization of the study." The debate changed from a discussion of the "vulgarity" of mass culture to the recognition of a tool that "could help reveal the mind of the masses."[2] Cultural studies, a multidisciplinary approach, has also brought attention to popular culture as a focus of study. It has expanded the definition of a society's "culture" and explored the ways in which culture encompasses ordinary and everyday experiences. The discipline examines how images produce meaning and shape perceptions, arguing that culture is the combination of these shared meanings. In addition, culture is viewed as a "process," one that produces interpretations in an unfixed way.[3] Although not monolithic, the goal of cultural studies is to increase understanding of "social transformation and cultural change."[4]

Popular culture is entertainment created for commercial purposes and designed to appeal to the masses; it differs from the elite culture. It can exist only when media technologies can push images beyond the locality of a folk culture, which is limited to a specific kin or ethnic group. This broad definition can include a wide variety of leisure pursuits, from television programs to sporting events, fast foods, music, and movies. Its images are inescapable, and its content is often imitative and derivative. The popularity of an activity or image offers insight into the values and beliefs of the mass audience. In subtle ways, popular culture may also shape those beliefs and values.[5] The questionable aesthetics or production qualities of a particular film, type of music, or television program do not lessen their cultural impact or importance.[6] Those who reject popular culture in their analyses often point to artistic failures or the material's avoidance of reality. To brand a piece of entertainment "escapist" raises many questions rather than dismisses the evidence. From what is the audience escaping? To where are they escaping? Why have they chosen this particular escape?[7]

Popular culture is generally limited in its presentation, due to either self-censorship or the drive for capitalistic profit. Yet, it is precisely this evidence in which scholars may "locate struggle, resistance, instability, and transformation," that is, as Joel Foreman notes, "in what is for many the least likely place: mass media popular culture." In Foreman's view, the eclectic components of popular culture "captured the needs, desires, and expectations of so many people as to provide significant indexes of the changing behavior and the internal tensions of that cultural body we call America."[8]

Historians study popular culture in relationship to its environment, production, and audience. Tuned to the times, historians must explore the interplay between the general and the specific, illuminating historical trends by examining the interaction between content and context. Their task is to paint the economic, political, and cultural backgrounds while focusing upon individual pieces of popular culture to create a pattern of understanding. A historian must discover what about the time helped determine popular choice. Perhaps more than any other discipline, the study of popular culture can best reveal the character of a society.[9]

Social and technological changes after World War II make that era's popular culture especially suited to historical study. It was an age when leisure time increased and entertainment choices multiplied. Technological transformation created the most powerful and far-reaching mass media in history. Before the war, film and radio were the two primary means of entertainment. These industries assumed a mass audience and tailored their product accordingly. After the war, however, the environment changed. The film industry, which enjoyed extraordinary profit and hegemony during the Depression and war years, faced many challenges. The Supreme Court's Paramount decree in 1948 outlawed Hollywood studio monopolies and forced a divestiture of theaters. New living and leisure patterns focused on the suburbs reduced weekly movie attendance. Television offered a new home version of screen entertainment that weakened the pull of the movies.[10] The radio industry also faced competition from the glowing box as well as from the emergence of a new musical form. Rock and roll threatened the exclusiveness of Tin Pan Alley, the traditional home of popular song writing, with an influx of new artists playing this new type of music. The baby boomers served as the "feedback loop" for all these changes in technology and lifestyles, intensifying and multiplying their effect with their numbers. Baby boomers heightened the fragmentation of audiences for all types of entertainment. The birth of the "biggest market in history" marked the beginning of popular culture becoming a synonym for youth culture, a trend that continues today.[11]

Initially, this study focused on the youth-oriented movies of the 1950s as a way of understanding the baby boom's impact on purveyors of mass culture. That investigation led to other creators of youth culture in television, music, fashions, and fads. Early youth-marketed films and popular media focused on aberrant juvenile delinquents and the dangers of rock and roll, capitalizing on the stereotypes of seemingly different and dangerous youth. These teenage archetypes reflected the postwar fears of a lost generation, the children born before World War II and scarred by the experience. Films like *Blackboard Jungle* (1955) portrayed inner-city youth, from a variety of ethnic and racial backgrounds, threatening the school system and society at large. Rock and roll emerged as a class and racial challenge to the status quo. The career of Elvis Presley represents this style, a white southern hillbilly copying the styles of African-American singers.

Yet, fans of early rock and roll and moviegoers attracted by tales of juvenile delinquency were not technically children of the baby boom. As the first true baby boomers entered grade school, a different mass-mediated model replaced the rebels on motorcycles, knife-wielding punks, and suggestiveness of rock and roll. There was less fear as the 1950s continued about the morals of this new generation and more concern about its purchasing power. Hollywood and its subsidiaries quickly recovered from demographic and societal changes to form multiple "transmedia" empires. A new definable teenage type was created, and it was an ideal of exclusion: white, middle-class, mobile, carefree, and conformist.[12] Aware of the possibilities of television, music, and film to create a model of the good society, popular culture focused on the commercial possibilities of the baby boomers.

One of the popular and dominant images by the end of the 1950s that fit this new cultural mood was that of California youth, a natural evolution considering the geographic location of mass media industries. The emergence of the California image was only part of the homogenization of youth and teenage culture. This study explores the appearances of California – both the place and the ideal – in movies, music, television, and magazines. I tie that movement into a larger cultural one, as the United States attempted to resolve by denial the problems that emerged in the sixties with a more satisfying and less threatening picture of its youth. The ascendancy of a new archetype and continued clinging to this California image reveals a cultural conundrum at the heart of postwar America.

The popularity of this strain of youth culture is not surprising, since both the concepts of the teenager and modern California were postwar creations. In particular, the wartime experience transformed Los Angeles, and it continued to be a destination of those looking for "the good life." Migration in the 1950s and 1960s turned California into a mecca for baby boom families, championed by magazines and lifestyle journals all across the country. The state became the postwar age personified – suburbanized, dependent on cars, and the home of the baby boomers. By 1962, the state claimed the largest population in the nation. Not since the discovery of gold had the state received so much press attention, and the majority of media coverage served to boost the dream. California was America's tomorrowland, in its population growth, suburbs, freeways, lifestyles, and focus on youth. Adding to its power as a magnet in the popular imagination was California's key role in the entertainment industry. This cultural reorientation went beyond the image making of show business. The modeling of the California family and California youth, a life of cars, fashionable clothing, the drive-in, and the beach, loomed large in the national consciousness.

Images of California as America's future were not unique to the postwar world. Kevin Starr argues in his series of books beginning with *Americans and the California Dream* that the state and its state of mind have had a unique influence on Americans.[13] Dreamers, however, have been continually torn between positive visions of the future and cautionary tales. These ideas persisted into the 1950s and 1960s and can be seen in youth culture and media representations of the California teen. The state served as a safety valve for generational fears, just as it had in earlier conceptions of the West's power to resolve America's problems. In a celebration of the beach culture and the media portrait of baby boom life in California, the United States was on the very edge of its frontier. In California one could find the last, best chance for postwar America and a model of modern possibilities.

This study begins with the year 1955 and the July opening of Disneyland in Anaheim, a suburb of Los Angeles. Walt Disney's dream of a new type of amusement park found its natural setting in California. It was a monument to middle-class values and the mythmaking of the Disney world, specifically designed to cater to baby boomers and their families. Disney was one of the first movie moguls to recognize the potential synergy of the entertainment industry, using television to finance his theme park, market films, and sell merchandise. The ABC television show *Disneyland* hyped the park a year before its unveiling, marking it as an event for children across the nation. Every newspaper and major magazine covered its grand opening. Another Disney project, the children's show *The Mickey Mouse Club*, premiered that fall, introducing California kids as role models and television stars.

After analyzing Disney's constructed world in California, I examine the state's youth in the various outlets they appeared. *Rebel Without a Cause* introduced a troubled middle-class protagonist and took place in a suburban environment. James Dean is the archetypal icon of mid-1950s juvenile delinquency, but the geographical and class setting of the film foreshadow the emergence of the California teen. With the success of youth-marketed films like *Gidget* (1959), movie studios moved away from the portrayal of kids in trouble to a more benign picture of sand and surf. The California sound emerged in the summer of 1961 out of the high school and garage band scene in Southern California. Groups like the Beach Boys communicated a worldview through their lyrics, offering California geography lessons and teenage lifestyle instructions. California's influence on fads and fashions made the Golden State the ultimate locale in which to be a teenager, inspiring copycat emulation across the country.

The American International Pictures (AIP) studio made its reputation and profits in the 1950s on exploitation films focused on teens in trouble: gangs, drugs, reform schools, drag races, and motorcycles. By 1963, however, AIP had changed its tune, releasing a series of *Beach Party* films. *Muscle Beach Party, Beach Blanket Bingo,* and *How to Stuff a Wild Bikini* were celebrations of the California youth culture. Advertised with suggestive posters and copy, these films were more sophomoric than scandalous. Other major studios attempted to imitate AIP's success, and a wave of beach mania characterized teenpics of the period.

This entertainment enabled American teenagers to experience the life of a California teen, and millions tried to buy into it. The California youth culture was important less for its ability to reflect reality and more for its successful creation of an image to which millions of teenagers could respond. Promoting the virtues of the California teenager suburbanized popular culture. These images left behind the urban problems of the rest of the country, avoided the growing discussion about civil rights, and domesticated temporarily the more dangerous elements of rock music. The trip briefly resolved the fears about rock and roll and juvenile delinquency that plagued the mid-1950s. This image of fun in the sun for white middle-class teenagers reigned, wielding its influence across the country into the mid-1960s.

As the baby boomers grew up, they grew out of the lifestyle created by popular culture. The influence of the baby boom was not monolithic, and its force changed with the times. As the 1960s progressed, the concept of the carefree California youth faced real-life threats from those left out of the mass-mediated picture. In particular, two events received nationwide attention: the campus revolt in Berkeley in 1964 and the uprising of pri-

6

marily teenagers and young adults in Watts in 1965. The racial eruption in Southern California, the source of the image packaged and marketed to the world, marked the end of California as the happy harbinger of things to come. The problematic issues surrounding the emergence of the baby boom first appeared in dramatic fashion in the Golden State.[14]

An emerging counterculture presented new alternatives to the all-American California teen. Instead of a middle-class, sun-tanned youth embracing the values of society, a new lifestyle that represented alienation from that society offered a more dangerous version of America's future. That picture was not one of reassurance and middle-class values but one of challenge to the status quo in fashion, ideology, and goals – the antithesis of the California teen image. Shock waves of the events in Watts and Berkeley caused a resurgence of 1950s concerns. In the election for governor in 1966, California voters chose Ronald Reagan, who promised to return California to greatness. Tapping into key attitudes, Reagan was able to transform the backlash against the youth of Berkeley and Watts into political victory. California's growing conservatism in 1966, which enveloped the nation by 1968, reflected the extreme antipathy toward this new image of California youth and the cultural power of baby boomers.

For this study I consulted secondary materials about the postwar era, the history of California, developments in the music, film, and television industries, and the impact of the baby boom. Many sources touch upon different aspects and images of California youth culture, but the subject lacks a synthetic treatment. Therefore, primary material was very important in exploring its creation, evolution, and power. Popular national magazines such as *Life, Look, Saturday Evening Post, Newsweek, Time, U.S. News & World Report, The Nation, McCall's, Ladies' Home Journal, American Mercury, New Yorker, Harper's Magazine,* and *Esquire* described these trends to a nationwide audience. The *New York Times* covered California, while the *Los Angles Times* offered an insider's perspective. *Seventeen* demonstrated the power of this image in teen-marketed magazines. *TV Guide, Variety,* and *Billboard* chronicled developments in their respective areas of television, movies, and music. Finally, I analyzed the popular culture artifacts themselves for evidence and insights into the phenomenon: the Disneyland programming, *The Mickey Mouse Club,* the songs of the Beach Boys and other surf music, the AIP *Beach Party* movies, advertising, and product packaging. The descriptions of the California lifestyle in these sources recaptured the mind-set of the era, helping to illuminate the reasons behind their popularity for teenagers and to explain the adult attitudes toward these images.

In examining this phenomenon there were many limitations. It is difficult to pinpoint why a certain song, movie, or fictional character elicit audience attention and consumer choice. The complex reasons behind the popularity of culture defy quantification or exactness. The image of California youth was just one of many competing images of the time. Despite these qualifications, several themes and issues are explored. How did Hollywood's conception of teenage California help shape the general view? What did contemporaries describe? How do the challenges of Berkeley and Watts play themselves out against this image? What were the political repercussions of image making? How might the ascendancy of this image be explained? What was this brand of California dreaming all about?

In the transition from the 1950s to 1960s, there existed in popular culture an icon: the California teen, a white, middle-class version of the American dream. It is the creation of this myth, and the brief strength and saliency of that image that my study examines. This California dream reveals a conflicted America facing the power of the baby boom. It reflects a cultural need and the tenor of the times beyond the borders of California. When the carefree middle-class world of suburbs, cars, and beaches failed to sustain itself through the challenges of the 1960s, the change of that image necessitated a reorientation of understandings about baby boom youth in general.

CHAPTER ONE

Suburban Eden

The idea of California was born when Spanish explorers christened their discovery after a mythical island full of wonders referred to in chivalric literature. With that name, California held the promise of potential treasure and first entered the realm of fantasy.[1] The discovery of gold in 1848 and the consequent influx of settlers enhanced California's identity, granting it a special place in American mythology and belief. The Gold Rush reinforced the vision of California as a place where dreams came true. From the beginning, the history of California was told from a white perspective, dismissive of the Native and Spanish past, using the gold discovery as the dawn of the California story. The boosters who followed, particularly those who settled in Los Angeles, continued to construct a mythology based on the dreams of white migrants.[2]

In 1850 California became a state, a region filled with promise for the future. When gold claims panned out, new dreams arose. To those who followed the rush to gold, California remained unique: a place to regain health, live on the frontier, build a railroad, exploit agricultural possibilities, discover oil, or make fortunes in real estate. For newcomers, it was still the land of the second chance, glowing with opportunity amidst sunshine. The dream was simple: "that because of a place called California, life might be better."[3] In the 1880s Southern California became the focus of a speculative real estate campaign, drawing tens of thousands to the paradise of a "family-size suburban lot amidst the orange groves."[4] This heralded opportunity for white settlers excluded those outside the booster portrait, creating the image of Los Angeles and California as "the sunny refuge of white Protestant America," in stark contrast to the immigrant experience of the rest of the nation.[5] Despite its exclusiveness, California's possibilities fostered a reputation for racial progressivism, offering a clarion call to black migrants as well. After a trip to California in 1913, W. E. B. Du Bois praised Los Angeles in his paper *The Crisis*: "Out here in this matchless Southern California there would seem to be no limit to your opportunities, your possibilities." Du Bois saw Los Angeles as "wonderful. Nowhere in the United States is the Negro so well and beautifully housed."[6]

Despite gold rush lore and the claims of boosters, California did not always inspire the stuff of dreams. Counter to the golden promise ran a current of negative imagery, a recognition that all was not sunny or bright. From its earliest days, California was not a dreamland but a battleground, often marked by exploitation and tragedy, plagued by racial conflict and social strife. Many of those who looked at California were continually torn between Edenic portrayals and corrupt visions, as the California dream came into harsh contact with challenging reality.[7] Often the reality of California, from the failures of gold seekers to the disappointments of would-be Hollywood starlets, was evoked by critics and naysayers to answer "each charming ingredient of the boosters' arcadia" with a "sinister equivalent."[8]

Yet, the early booster fantasies were overshadowed by the propagandists of the twentieth century, as California came to represent all that was promising about the nation's future. At the core of the image-making machine was Hollywood, growing as a motion picture colony in the 1910s. This new industry intensified earlier ideas of fantastic opportunities, adding a new kind of riches in stardom. World War I brought growth to California, and the Great Depression attracted Dust Bowl refugees with the promise of jobs.[9] In the darkest economic times, people continued to make the trek, strong proof of the belief in California as the special exception.[10] The migration after World War II, however, dwarfed all previous periods and helped push California to center stage. For new Californians trying to create a fresh start in the golden land, there was not a difficult past, only a bright future. As Carey McWilliams put it in *California: The Great Exception*, the state was now a "giant adolescent," filled with "new and shiny" suburban towns.[11]

The explosion of interest during the postwar period created salient images, new myths of California life building on the old. National attention sponsored in-depth coverage of lifestyles and cultural changes. Magazines, television, music, and film acted as conveyors of these ideas and, while reflecting the realities of the postwar environment, mythologized life in California. The state's growth, "the continuing inner migration to the legendary far-off land of El Dorado," stood out in an era of broad and significant transformations in the United States.[12]

The demographic and economic changes spurred by World War II accelerated development in California, which was a major part of the "New" West's emergence. In 1945, *Life* magazine predicted that the "California way of life . . . may in time radically influence the pattern of life in America as a whole," as it offered "the most glowing example" of postwar "modern living."[13] The United States experienced a "westward tilt," the result of "a nation so prosperous and so mobile that its people are free to go in search of a more luxurious way of life." Wallace Stegner described the space from Seattle to San Diego as "the national culture at its most energetic end . . . not a region, but the mainstream, America only more so."[14] Irving Stone wrote in late 1954 that California was a land "where life achieves a vibrancy man never knew before." The special nature of this golden land, while "not yet utopia" meant that humanity was on the cusp of "creating an anxiety free people."[15] "There is a general agreement that California . . . is a land apart" a 1955 article argued. As a "land of promise," the state had a "uniqueness" that provided a "melting pot where old ways and traditions are most easily discarded and where innovation and experimentation have their freest rein."[16] In his best-selling book on class behavior, *The Status Seekers*, Vance Packard wrote that California enjoyed a "yeasty social climate" in a "violently expanding economy"; as a result of the "free-and-easy frontier spirit," its residents were "the least status-conscious people . . . in the nation."[17]

World War II drastically altered the entire West with its influx of defense spending and people, but Los Angeles experienced a singular transformation. The war brought 340,000 blacks to Los Angeles for industrial work and armed forces service, enormously increasing Southern California's diversity.[18] City officials responded with the formation of a Human Relations Commission in 1943, one of the first cities in the nation to sponsor such a program. The African American population continued to grow after the war, from 97,000 in 1945 to 460,000 in 1960.[19] More blacks migrated to California than to any other state, mirroring the tremendous white flood during those same years.[20]

Los Angeles quickly surpassed San Francisco, the boomtown of the first gold rush in the previous century, as the state's new center. Glowing reports of opportunities replaced wartime stories of racial tensions, insufficient housing, and crowded streets. The *Los Angeles Times* reported in December 1945 that news of western job growth was spreading "like the story of the discovery of gold . . . luring hopeful men whose dreams are spun of golden opportunity."[21] Officials estimated in 1959 that 567 people arrived in Los Angeles County daily, and that a population of 6 million was within sight.[22] Fifteen years after predicting the boom in Los Angeles, the *Times* reported in 1960 that the city appeared "more fresh and full of promise today than she ever did in her boisterous youth."[23]

By 1965, the population growth of Los Angeles had "eclipsed every other metropole in the nation," with all of Southern California part of its nexus.[24] This journey ranked among the largest migrations in American history.[25] The lure of "sunshine and opportunities" continued to draw people westward, with the "station wagon" replacing the "covered wagon" of an earlier time.[26] National Van Lines, a moving company, tapped into this symbolism with its 1950s brochure. It showed a moving van heading across the desert. In the ghostlike shadows above, an ox-drawn covered wagon hovered, explicitly making the connection between the two great migrations.[27]

Most Americans made the trek by car. The Californian and the automobile were inseparable, despite the pollution the mobility habit created. The car was bred naturally for California, with its favorable climate, attractive scenery, and abundant good roads.[28] Before the war, Los Angeles began constructing urban expressways more ambitiously than anywhere else in the country. This system was essential, as residents favored private transportation for 86 percent of their travels in the 1950s.[29] The 1954–55 highway budget was the largest of the fifty states, yet planners could only say, "at the moment we are no longer losing ground."[30] Freeways supported the vision of Los Angeles as the "ultramodern metropolis," creating a fragmented suburban sprawl that appeared to make the good life universally accessible. In reality, criss-crossing freeways destroyed ethnic neighborhoods and obscured from view troubled neighborhoods like Watts. From the freeway, Los Angeles and other California communities could mask their appearance, truly looking to the mobile observer "like White City West."[31]

Los Angeles, due to its size and suburban sprawl, stood at the apex of car culture, offering vast freeways and the economic prosperity that guaranteed car ownership. Only six states had more cars than Los Angeles County.[32] By 1960, approximately two-thirds of the land in metropolitan Southern California supported car-related needs: highways, roads, driveways, freeways, parking lots, service stations, and car lots.[33] The urban freeways of California were objects of wonder as well as concern. *Life* presented a foldout cover of traffic in Los Angeles, describing it as "seemingly boundless in size and energy."[34] Others looked at the monstrous freeways of California and said, "I've seen the future and it doesn't work."[35]

Commentators agreed that trends in California were a forecast for the future of the United States. World War II had "integrated" the state into the nation, but California was now "the America to come."[36] Governor Edmund G. "Pat" Brown declared in 1963, "What we want the whole country to be, California already is."[37] For *Cosmopolitan*'s cover story "The Rush for Gold and Happiness," one author argued that in California "the enormous potential pleasures and problems of our machine-powered civilization have come into startling focus."[38] In 1962, *Look* magazine chronicled the growth of the state in an issue that was headlined, "Tomorrow's hopes and tomorrow's headaches are here today in our soon-to-be largest state."[39] To study California was to examine the "best place in the world for facing the problems of the future," since it was a place where "the future is happening every day."[40] These commentators hinted at the double-edged sword of the California phenomenon, suggesting that potential "headaches" and "problems" could accompany growth and change.

National opinion surveys heralded California as the "best" state in the union.[41] In the late 1950s and early 1960s, Gallup polls consistently ranked California number one as a vacation spot, an "ideal place to live," and the most beautiful state with the most beautiful cities. Americans in late 1956 mentioned California most frequently as the state where they would most like to relocate, citing job opportunities and climate as the main attractions.[42] In 1960, a *Look* poll revealed that 11 percent of Americans, if given the opportunity, would choose to move to California.[43]

California's boosterism filtered out the state's long history of racial conflicts, promoting the golden land as an ideal spot for minorities as well. National magazines and polls proclaimed the city and the state racially progressive. In 1957, *Look* called Los Angeles "a race relations success story," heralding its example to the rest of the nation. The city avoided urban conflict, moving "outward not upward," escaping the "massive slum areas that blight the centers" of eastern cities.[44] Los Angeles, on the surface, did not suffer from the recognizable urban dilemmas of housing projects and run-down apartment buildings.[45]

While California attracted both blacks and whites, minority new-comers found their choice of residence limited. The 1960 census revealed Los Angeles as more segregated than any city in the south, with fewer minorities living in suburban enclaves than all other northern cities with the exception of Chicago and Cleveland.[46] Poverty and widespread unemployment belied the image of golden postwar opportunity. These contradictions were largely ignored, leaving communities like Watts to simmer in discontent, allowing California to maintain its promise and its rosy suburban image.

Institutions and business ventures braved the westward journey as well. Television became a Hollywood studio staple after spending its early years as primarily a live, New York–based operation. The Brooklyn Dodgers baseball team joined the New York Giants in "their flight to the Pacific" in 1958, settling in Los Angeles and San Francisco, respectively.[47] In language reminiscent of the previous century, columnists wrote of the "gold rush west" and wondered if "the Dodger-Giant Gold Rush" would "pan out."[48] In the world of professional basketball, the Minneapolis Lakers traveled to Los Angeles, and the Philadelphia Warriors were reborn as the Golden State Warriors in 1961.[49]

With its growing population, the state became politically vibrant. The war in the Pacific and the founding of the United Nations in San Francisco increased awareness of the state's significance.[50] California politics were seen as a foreshadowing of national trends and a threat to "New York's century-old political leadership."[51] A 1955 *Los Angeles Times* editorial discussed the massive population growth and predicted a future harvest in congressional representation. The editors also pointed to the role that California had played "in the history of this nation" and to the idea that her "destiny" portended a "greater role in the future."[52] "Its politics will touch all of us," declared *Collier's* in 1956, recognizing that "the age of California independence has begun."[53] The *Saturday Evening Post* reported that the state provided "an almost ideal locale for studying the forces realigning both parties through the entire nation."[54]

The early 1960s brought a contentious controversy between New York and California, with the eastern state challenging the population claims of its western rival. The statewide egos tied to migration numbers acted as political and rhetorical weapons. In a 1962 advertisement the *Los Angeles Times* teased the story "California Population Now Exceeds New York," wondering what day that headline would appear.[55] Governor Edmund G. "Pat" Brown proclaimed December 31, 1962, as "Population Day," a special holiday to celebrate California's growth.[56] By 1963, census projections had the Golden State officially pulling ahead of the Empire State in population. New York City acted as the melting pot of European peoples in the nation's early history, but Los Angeles became the postwar gathering place, creating a society of new settlers.[57]

As newcomers without deep roots, many postwar Californians were pressed to create a sense of community and identity. They received guidance in that task from magazine writers, public relations experts, and boosters who downplayed the state's difficulties and stressed its advantages and attractions. This explosion of media coverage, the idealization of California as both model and magnet, was an exercise in regional mythmaking.[58] In 1959, *Look* profiled the state's tremendous growth in a special issue heralded as "sixty pages on vast, crowded, incredible California." In its back pages and print smaller than that of the banner headline, the articles inside described water shortages, high taxes, and the state's eccentricities.[59] *Life* called the population explosion "The Call of California" in a 1962 special issue devoted to the state's "splendor, its excitement, and why people go, go and go there." California hopefuls "have arrived, impelled by necessity or lured by a dream," it explained. "They have pursued the rainbow, as far as they can, to the rim of the United States."[60] "One thousand Americans head for the same ocean each day" reported a 1962 *Newsweek* cover story.[61] Even a *New York Times* author sarcastically wondered whether the massive move to California was "fulfilling the dream of all people through the ages."[62]

Yet, as one magazine declared, "The California way of life is something that people are usually violently for or violently against."[63] Another image, less than positive, disparaged promoters and questioned the glowing reports of settlers and columnists, occasionally rising above the din of postwar praise. Many were critical of the cultural sameness manifested in suburban culture. On the cultural defensive, New York and other eastern magazines attacked California's expanding influence, protective of their region's leadership in the arts, fashion, and politics. One writer entitled his piece, "I Hate Southern California," offering his critique on California's boosterism. Travelers to California, he wrote, were victims of "propaganda

LIFE

SPECIAL ISSUE

THE CALL OF

California

ITS SPLENDOR, ITS EXCITEMENT

WHY PEOPLE GO, GO AND GO THERE

A vivid biography of the state by IRVING STONE

CASCADE OF FIRE
LIGHTS YOSEMITE
AT DUSK

OCTOBER 19 · 1962 · 20¢

This 1962 *Life* magazine cover appeared
the same year that California became the
most populous state in the union. The
entire special issue was devoted to tales of
life in the Golden State, demonstrating
"why people go, go, and go there."

(Ralph Crane/TimePix)

initiated by the Southern Californians and carried to you by the published media, the movies and television" with little "semblance of the truth." Those migrants, "largely from the hillbilly sections of the country," swayed by the inundation of positive images, had seemingly ignored the problems of crime, smog, and strangeness that were paramount in the critical view of California life.[64] A columnist in *Esquire*, as part of a May 1963 cover story on "True and False Values in the State of California," offered cynical pointers to prospective Californians: "You are going from a city to a state," he wrote. "It does not matter where you plan to settle in California; it won't be a city." Bemused, he advised: "The first thing to buy is an eastbound return ticket. Keep it some place safe, like your hand."[65]

Critics vented particularly at Los Angeles, as its apparently helter-skelter growth was permanently altering what had been a quiet, unassuming town. "Sun-kissed vistas are smothered in smog, frenzied traffic makes driving an obstacle race, and the great subdividers disfigure the city's natural beauty" railed one native in *Look*.[66] In its December 1958 column on the nation's weather, *Newsweek* also recognized the problem of smog in the city of angels. It featured a picture of a woman breathing "pure crystal clear air" from a canister strapped to a man wearing a gas mask. "For want of fresh air, hair turned green" read the caption.[67] The growth of Los Angeles served as a cautionary tale to the rest of the nation, the "prototype" of an "auto-addicted" society.[68] The negativity of the critics questioned the shiny gloss of some magazine portrayals.

By and large, positive portraits of life in California overpowered pessimism. The constant California coverage in mass media publications meant that millions of Americans repeatedly read about life in the Golden State, attracting the interest of those who wanted to become part of the good life the magazines portrayed.[69] With seemingly little hesitation or doubt, thousands continued to come. For these newcomers, unburdened by and unaware of California's more complex and troubled past, the focus was on capturing a specific lifestyle, a California dream tuned to the desires of the postwar era.

In their journey west, prospective Californians strove for membership in a new middle class, with lifestyles created by postwar affluence. These Americans enjoyed the luxury of leisure time and money to burn. For a cover story in July 1956, *Look* examined "The Great American Week End," the $2 billion a year spent on leisure's growth industries. With "mass recreation on a staggering scale," postwar families created new activities.

For the young, backyards became "vest-pocket amusement parks" filled with "yard sized playthings" unmatched by those of previous generations of children.[70] *Life* also profiled this new consuming obsession in a December 1959 issue entitled "The Good Life." The cover featured "zestful Americans," white, middle-class suburbanites, enjoying ice skating, painting, relaxing poolside, dancing, celebrating a birthday, and gardening. The article focused on leisure as an integral part of American life and predicted its increased prominence in the 1960s. From the province of "a wealthy few," free time had become big business. With this freedom, an editorial proclaimed, Americans can "pursue true happiness . . . [and] raise standards of excellence higher than any in the world's past."[71]

Where better to celebrate this culture of leisure? This growing middle class was cradled and nurtured in California, a place tuned to the possibilities of the postwar economy. As part of its profile of "new frontiers in living . . . the life that lures the East," *Look* entitled its story on life in Los Angeles as "the art of living bumper to bumper." Yet the story focused on the life of a family of four, enjoying their barbecue, outdoor swimming pool, and jaunt to the Pacific beach, stressing "spaciousness and easy living" and not traffic problems.[72]

The suburban lifestyle came together to create a "new culture complex," most intrinsically dominant in California and aspired to by millions of Americans. As D. W. Meinig argued in his influential article "Symbolic Landscapes," the suburbs of California became part of the iconography of America, taking its place with the midwestern street and the New England town as the symbols for good family life. This symbol became particularly powerful in the postwar era. Its single-story homes, green lawns, and two-car garages marked the "landscape of California suburbia," with its easy access to burgeoning freeways. The diffusion of the landscape was made possible partly by the geographic location of Hollywood, which with its product presented an ideal "as if it were the best in American life, an obvious standard to strive for, a model for the future."[73]

As historians of American living patterns have demonstrated, the archetypal suburban landscape traveled across the country, bringing with it an attendant idealized lifestyle.[74] Developers across the United States used the "California fantasy" regardless of building locale. Subdivisions across the country could employ the images of "informal living, ideal weather and movie star glamour." One might find a "Hollywood closet" in a Cape Cod–style house in New Jersey.[75] Imitations of Californian architectural

SUBURBAN EDEN

styles like bungalows, Spanish stuccos, and ranch houses popped up in suburbs everywhere. In particular, the ranch house typified the outdoor leisure living most closely identified with California. This design represented the "new ideal of family" to homebuilders, advertisers, and buyers.[76] This diffusion of styles was possible because the popularized view of life in California was, as Meinig argued elsewhere, "more than locational and environmental, it was fundamentally cultural."[77] If Americans couldn't move to California, they could live a suburban lifestyle that closely approximated the experience and move someplace like it, striving to achieve the picture of blissful suburbia of magazine portrayals. As the United States became a suburban nation, a "metropolitan tilt" matched the western one.[78]

patio

Real estate developers advertised the "California living" concept to young baby boom families, a lifestyle focused on patios, barbecues, and swimming pools.[79] The outdoor private pool represented the essence of leisure and consumption. By 1959, Californians owned nearly 40 percent of the nation's home pools.[80] The celebration and appeal of informal living, in fashion and in discourse, corresponded to ideas about the universality of middle-class membership and aspirations.[81] A 1962 advertisement in the *Los Angeles Times* for a housing development in Simi Valley typified this kind of marketing. It depicts a father relaxing on his patio, overlooking rolling hills and sunshine. The mother, in heels and apron, is serving lemonade, while the son plays on the jungle gym with his cowboy gun hanging nearby and his dog playing happily. The ad nicknamed the area "Secure Valley," promising that prospective buyers "won't find a healthier, happier, more carefree environment in which to raise your family."[82] Not everyone celebrated the suburban ideal. An *Esquire* article in 1963 criticized the unbridled growth of suburbs in California and these marketing strategies. Historically, the state's images and the promise of opportunity acted as an "opiate of the people." In the 1960s, the author argued, Americans looked to "California as the quintessence of life in a capitalistic society."[83]

California had "a nation looking on," anxious for news of "the mystical 'Western way of life.' "[84] Millions shared the dream of a "palm-shaded 'pad'" with a patio, ten dollars down, 100 years to pay . . . lotus land on the installment plan."[85] Editors and writers appealed to popular interest in the "invigorating climate and independent spirit" of the state and included innumerable articles in their magazines. A popular feature showcased transplanted families in their new California homes. *Better Homes and*

The Larwin Development Company advertised its Simi Valley development in a June 1962 issue of the *Los Angeles Times*. The ad evokes the near-universal hope of postwar families, a "Secure Valley" where parents, children, and pets could enjoy the peace and quiet of the suburbs in the California sunshine.

(Courtesy Larwin Development Company)

Gardens profiled five families to show "what it's really like to move to California," highlighting the generally positive and happy new residents.[86] In 1960, *Changing Times* looked at the Stanleys, transplants from Chicago. For this family, it reported, "pleasure and comfort come first . . . and work is simply what pays for it." The article outlined household and recreation costs, contrasting those figures with life in the Midwest. Mr. Stanley, despite the increased expense, problems of smog, and traffic difficulties, felt positive about the family's move. He believed that "living is easier and informal and the kids eat up the outdoor life. We all do get more sheer pleasure out of being alive."[87]

California imagery was not only class-oriented, it was fixated on youth. In earlier waves of migration, California had attracted "older folks in search of retirement nirvanas." The postwar pattern was different, with "over 80 percent of these modern takers of Mr. Greeley's advice . . . young families in their twenties and thirties."[88] In 1940, the median age in California was the oldest among the forty-eight states and four years older than the country as a whole.[89] The postwar period changed that demographic, as California became the "promised land" for young parents, producing a bumper crop of kids. In a 1945 *Life* article, one father voiced what thousands of others believed: "My kids have a better chance to be healthy here than anywhere else."[90] The *New York Times* reported that these newcomers had "more children than the average American family."[91] By 1959, California ranked first in public school enrollment.[92] Schools found it difficult to keep up, with "twelve or thirteen new school rooms" needed every day.[93] One out of every ten school children in the nation attended school in California.[94]

The group most able to realize "the good life," the dreams of leisure and consumption, were the baby boomers. Many product trends and leisure time activities focused on their needs and desires. A *Life* cover story affirmed this by calling the baby boom children "a built-in recession cure." The explosion of families and economic growth meant that the United States had "a business bonanza in the needs of its kids," with a "new consumer every seven seconds."[95] Teenagers personified these trends, defining themselves by products consumed and leisure activities enjoyed. This youth culture, seen as separate and distinct from that of adults, was a "leisure class" in "a society so affluent that it [could] afford a large population of unemployed consumers."[96]

The average age in California steadily fell, a reflection of family migration and birthrates, and this nurtured a "child-centered" culture. The symbol of this world was "the California teen-ager, speeding with smug assurance down the freeway . . . as if the freeway and all it leads to were designed just for him."[97] The state itself was a teenager, "its rapid growth . . . attended by the bizarre qualities of adolescence."[98] Fashions and fads, the "provinces of the young," focused on California youth as part of the national fixation on the state.[99] Popularized lifestyles of California kids intertwined with symbols of the good life.

California's youth had not enjoyed such a positive spin in the years immediately following World War II. Instead, a negative characterization of the nation's youth reigned in mass media portrayals. Stories about juvenile delinquency captivated and concerned the nation, with explanations ranging from the threat of nuclear war, poor parenting during World War II, the impact of film and television, the new power of rock and roll, and class and racial tensions. This outbreak of concern about the nation's youth and the attention paid to troubling flash points was part of an overall anxiety about postwar changes.[100] The children coming of age in the early 1950s, born during the Depression and growing up in wartime, were what *Collier's* called the "most publicized, analyzed, speculated-upon, worried-about, frowned-upon generation of teen-agers in modern times."[101] In its 1957 cover story on teenagers, *Look* magazine explored the questions "why they go steady, why they go wild, why they don't listen" with evident concern. The article also pointed to the excesses of leisure time that might foster an environment for mischief.[102]

Discussions of California's youth mirrored national trends. The *Saturday Evening Post* chronicled the California Youth Authority's difficulties in dealing with a youthful wave of transients "geographically at the end of the line."[103] In early 1955, *Harper's* reported that California had a runaway juvenile delinquent problem, "40 percent worse than the national average," as youth poured into the state "by the thousands."[104] Sensational and popular stories detailing youth riots at reformatories had California settings.[105] The *Los Angeles Times* shared the obsession with juvenile delinquency. In June 1955 it began a series of seven articles detailing the activities of the juvenile courts and the city's delinquency problems. The paper profiled young murderers, thieves, and violent criminals and the various institutions that housed them. These state detention centers and jails, the articles explained, "will never wait for patients, not so long as there are delinquent children and delinquent parents, broken homes and demented young minds."[106] Front-page headlines in the *Times* spotlighted the activities of "frolicsome" graduating seniors who broke bottles and made noise, resulting in the arrest of thirty students.[107] As in the rest of the country, the use of the word "teenager" in a headline usually meant crime or trouble. By the mid-1950s the predominant image of California kids reflected the national fear of this generation's criminal behavior, spending power, and cultural influence.

At the height of these societal fears, the true baby boomers, those born after 1945, began to grow up. As the cohort aged, more positive models of baby boomer life replaced earlier images of delinquency. Stories of monstrous teens gave way to reports of well-behaved, well-meaning, middle-class teenagers, and California offered the perfect setting for a positive model. These earlier anxieties never disappeared, but the frequency of negative reports, attention by government, and concerns over media influence lessened. The problems that typified the mid-1950s seemed to vanish.[108]

Look's January 1956 cover named postwar youth the "most maligned generation in our history" while pointing out that despite media and news representations, "95 percent" were not delinquent.[109] *Newsweek* raised the percentage, with stories of "the healthy 97 percent that count" supplanting more "disquieting" stories of youths at the drag strip or rumble. "Our *Good Teen-Agers*," the magazine reported in November 1959, were the overwhelming majority and "perfectly normal." Not surprisingly, "speeding along the California freeways" was one of the places these "good kids" could be found.[110] The city council of Modesto, "sick and tired of hearing about" juvenile delinquency, sponsored a high school contest to nickname "non-delinquents." "Hi-fi citizens" received the top award, with "juvenile honorees, topteens, teamagers, and goal getters" named as honorable mentions.[111] In 1957, *Good Housekeeping* profiled a Los Angeles suburb where, it reported, "the problem of social behavior has been largely settled" with a plan of townwide rules for youth regulating bedtime, dress, and behavior.[112]

"Teen-ager" still appeared in *Los Angeles Times* headlines, and of course there was juvenile crime to report. However, the youths featured in its pages were more likely to be cover girl models and wholesome young people on their way to the prom.[113] Media focus on California supported this altered cultural perception and provided a place for new icons of middle-class youth to be created. Instead of looting and violence, stories described the "upstanding young" winners of the city's posture contest.[114] In national articles, the predominant picture was one of smiling youth enjoying the perks of the middle class. Leisure time was not an invitation for teenage trouble, rather it was a special ingredient contributing to the healthy development of youth. A 1957 *Cosmopolitan* issue described California as a "Teenagers' Paradise" where "mountains, beaches and play-conscious cities add up to a teen-age pleasure-land." The feature's pictures showed California teens playing in a band, cruising through a suburban neighborhood, innocently kissing in the park, picnicking, attending a rodeo, going to the movies, anxiously answering a teacher's questions in a high school classroom, serving in church as altar boys, strolling through an amusement park, and enjoying a formal dance. The myriad activities were necessary, the writer explained, because "California teenagers possess boundless energy and unlimited capacity for fun making."[115]

California was the home state and breeding ground for America's own superkids. As a result of outdoor activity and warm weather, young Californians bested their fellow Americans in health and energy. "In California," a 1959 issue of *Cosmopolitan* explained, "the boys and girls grow bigger and more beautiful. They are longer of leg, deeper of chest, better muscled than other American youngsters. Even their feet are bigger." What created such "tanned, healthy, exuberant, active" youth? The environment of California was part of it, providing "a packed suburban life that vies with expensive resort living" typified by healthy eating, year-round swimming, skiing, surfing, sailing, and sports. Such prolonged exposure to the sun created "anxiety-free youngsters." Outdoor leisure time did not preclude success in academics, as students also applied "their enthusiasm and exuberance to school work and [got] good grades."[116]

As part of its cover story on California in 1959, *Look* described the state's young people who "roar about in convertibles and sports cars." "Mountain climbing and skin diving" replaced "juvenile delinquency" as wholesome leisure time activity. These kids were "happy-go-lucky, big, bronzed and beautiful."[117] In that same issue, another article profiled the "co-eds" of Stanford and UCLA who had "[more than] only good looks in their favor." Despite the geographical space between the two campuses, the article argued, "these girls . . . share the same values and views," avoiding the "carousing of previous generations."[118] In the fall of 1962, *Life* reported that California's young women, just waiting to be immortalized in song, were the "prettiest, biggest, lithest, tannest, most luscious girls this side of the international date line."[119] In a 1963 book entitled *California: The New Society*, Remi Nadeau attempted to explain the sunny outlook and "ascendancy of teens," arguing that the state offered "too much life to be lived to sit around crying doom for long." For this reason, he believed, California youth were "more free, and more carefree, than their counterparts in other regions."[120]

The popular culture representation of Los Angeles youth was marked by its exclusion of minorities and nonsuburban youth. If minorities were featured in magazine profiles, it was to show that California's baby boomers were well equipped to carry out the democratic promise, using images that manufactured racial harmony. In 1957, *Look* examined Los Angeles, the city with "perhaps the greatest potential for racial trouble." Instead of conflict, the article noted, Los Angeles demonstrated "what people of different races can do to live side by side in harmony." The profile included pictures of this harmonious living, young Asians and African Americans laughing with white students on state campuses.[121]

Life offered another example of this tactic in August 1965. "The Young Americans," a Los Angeles–based choir group, boasted a membership of "wholesome, handsome teen-agers with conventional haircuts." Along with their melodic singing of patriotic songs, show tunes, and spirituals in their red, white, and blue costumes, the group represented Los Angeles's harmonious diversity, including black and Asian teenagers in their ranks.[122] California kids, representing the future in so many positive ways, were employed to highlight positive strides in racial understanding.

These articles offered reassuring models of California youth. Tuned to their adult readership, their content influenced the mythmaking. Young people also responded positively to these images, mirroring the adult dreams of California. *Look*'s 1960 poll asked teens: if income were un-limited, what would their plans for the future be? The majority expressed interest in a "sports car and a big house in California." A large percentage also believed that "the West is best for both fun and opportunity."[123] A 1963 poll taken of high school students nationwide posed the question, "Where would you like to live most of your life?" The largest percentage of those polled chose the West. In addition, of those teenagers who already lived in western states, 75.5 percent were satisfied to remain there.[124]

All eyes, if not all steering wheels, were turned in California's direction. Its growth, combined with the influence of the baby boom, fostered the image of the state as "perfect" for families and a home for beautiful and happy kids. The media blitz offered a golden promise, a reassuring vision of the family and the nation's future in its "good" young people. The model of youth represented California trends and middle-class America to the extreme: mobile, capitalistic, outdoorsy, consumer-oriented, involved in harmless, well-meaning fun. Here was the hopeful future of America unhampered by inclement weather or lack of opportunity. Such snapshots ignored other realities. The actual ethnic and racial make-up of California went unrepresented. The reality of California's history of conflict as well as the dark side of the dream remained in the blurry background. There were apparently no poor or troubled in the Golden State. With few exceptions, these exclusionary and positive images predominated.

From 1955 to 1966, the youth culture of California appeared in a variety of popular culture guises. Magazine subscribers read profiles of California teens, television viewers watched California images on the small screen, moviegoers enjoyed the antics of Gidget, radio listeners heard the celebratory music of the Beach Boys, and teens purchased fads and fashion with a California spin. The first step in the evolution of the California youth image came in the mid-1950s, when entertainment mogul Walt Disney capitalized on the mix of California dreaming and the lifestyle of baby boom families. Packaging this environment in new ways, Disney was the most culturally powerful entertainment figure of the age, wielding a wide influence in the lives of the baby boom generation. His playground encased the magic of California in concrete and steel, and his forays into the new medium of television achieved unprecedented popularity. The overwhelming success of his creations was due to masterful manipulation of California youth images.

CHAPTER TWO

California Disneying

Walt Disney created Disneyland, popularized Davy Crockett, and launched *The Mickey Mouse Club* – three powerful cultural archetypes of the mid-1950s. Disney, a transplanted Californian, had his "corporate finger in more sociocultural pies" than any other entertainment producer in the twentieth century.[1] The expansion of his company meshed with television's emergence and the cultural changes brought by suburbanization. This environment uniquely positioned Disney to flourish. His biggest dream, the Disneyland theme park, thrived due to its appeal to young suburban television viewers, a new postwar phenomenon.[2] The entertainment he produced tied its success to the growth of California, with national publications preaching the word. By creating a monument to dreams of youth, Disney offered a privileged model of life for mass consumption. He turned his corner of the California world into an international symbol of "the good life."

Disney traveled from Kansas City to California in 1923, a young man looking for gold in movie animation. He founded a movie studio that made landmark animated films and created an international star in Mickey Mouse. During the 1930s, he achieved critical acclaim, winning numerous Academy Awards and plaudits, with instant name recognition worldwide. However, financial troubles plagued the studio in the 1940s. The park project that carried his name was his last gamble in California, one for which he was willing to sell his life insurance policy to finance.[3] Disney recognized California as a tourist magnet, and wanted to channel its magic into his business venture.

California was a perennial vacation destination, with its beaches, forests, and deserts. Travelers to the Golden State might dream of seeing natural scenic beauty or perhaps a glimpse of a movie star. Before World War II, the most visited Southern California landmark was Forest Lawn cemetery, a monument to Hollywood's past with the gravesites of many movie legends.[4] In the postwar era, visiting a cemetery seemed at odds with more youthful tastes and trends. The country was ripe for what Walt Disney called "a new concept in family entertainment."[5] He wanted to break the mold, to move away from the working-class Coney Island concept and create a new type of family fun. Although the amusement park industry faced financial trouble in the 1930s and 1940s, the promise of the 1950s gave Disney high expectations for his middle-class dream world.[6] However, Disney needed more capital than either he or his studio could provide. His hopes dwarfed the original plan for a park adjacent to the studio. To attract crowds, the project required, as Disney quickly realized, "some kind of medium like television to let the people know about it."[7]

A few movie studios ventured tentatively into early television. A more vocal majority wondered about the threats of this home-based competitor. Yet, television was only one of the challenges faced by the postwar movie scene. As early as the late 1940s, national magazines asked, "What's Wrong with the Movies?" and wondered if the film industry had reached the "end of an era."[8] By all counts, the 1950s was a dark period for Hollywood. Average weekly attendance fell from an all-time high of 90 million in 1946 to 46 million in 1955, a drastic decline for which television was only partly to blame.[9]

The unknowable future impact of TV on audience numbers thus loomed large in the minds of many moguls. In 1952 the *Saturday Evening Post* wondered, "Will television turn three billion dollars' worth of movie theaters into empty, haunted halls? Or will Hollywood make TV just another outlet for its wares?"[10] The uniqueness of a "radio with eyes . . . the press without the travail of printing . . . the movies without the physical limitations of mechanical reproduction and projection" forced studios to adjust to the new reality or risk elimination.[11] With television transformed from a technological rarity to an everyday item, the resistance to audience research, self-examination, and business changes lessened. Moviemakers met the challenge of the small screen with Technicolor, 3-D spectacle, and controversial subject matter.

The industry explored the reasons for audience decline, as well as the possibilities of integration. Hollywood had ready-made facilities and personnel to produce for the small screen. As television historians have argued, the Paramount case of 1948 limited the big studios' monopolistic control of the film industry. The court decision acted as a hindrance to television involvement as well. Despite this roadblock, the major Hollywood studios paid close attention to developments in the television industry.[12] The movie studios did not ignore the growing influence of television or refuse to take part. Rather they hoped to take over production and looked for ways to increase their control and influence.[13]

As a consequence, New York's live television productions feared studio invasion and tried to avoid being "swallowed up by Hollywood."[14] With Hollywood's production base and talent advantage, television could not withstand the magnet of California for long. Nor could the movie studios remain uninvolved in the activities of their main competitor.[15] By 1955, eight of the nine major studios had entered the TV realm in some capacity. Hollywood was rapidly evolving into a "two-industry city" with a powerful interconnection between these entertainment worlds.[16]

Disney stood at the vanguard of this merger, recognizing early the commercial possibilities of television. As he told reporters in the early 1950s, he sensed the power of reaching "the audience without any middleman."[17] The Disney studio had some experience in television, having sponsored two successful Christmas shows in 1950 and 1951.[18] Both NBC and CBS expressed interest in doing business with Disney. Despite his financially precarious studio, he maintained a reputation as "cinema's maestro of family entertainment."[19] However, the speculative nature of the amusement park made the established networks wary of his package-deal requirement.[20]

Disney signed a contract with ABC, a weaker network that was looking to increase its viewership. The ABC/Disney alliance opened the door to collaboration between the two media, and it pushed television in the direction of California.[21] *Variety* called it "the first major step in the long-anticipated wedding between the major motion picture studios and the television networks."[22] The *New York Times* heralded the union as "the most important development to date in relations between the old and the new mass entertainment forms."[23] Disney's entry signaled a new direction in TV programming. As television matured, it moved away from the live anthology drama and ethnic urban comedies that had proved successful in its early years. Disney's shows blurred the lines between entertainment for children and adults and targeted middle-class suburban families. He offered television the first film studio production with a substantial budget aimed exclusively at an audience of baby boom families, the largest and fastest growing demographic group.[24]

Disney's decision to tie his risky theme park to a new medium had far-reaching implications. With outside investment secured, Disney set the timetable for Disneyland's construction. He ruled out locations near the beach, wanting to discourage the wearing of bathing suits. Engineers and urban planning experts looked at future freeway plans and predicted that the center of Southern California's population was moving south and east. This type of plotting led to an Anaheim orange grove being chosen as the future site of the park.[25]

The scouted location shared its name with the television show that would beam images of the park nationwide.[26] In a planning session for *Disneyland*, Disney revealed his high hopes and ambitious goals. He described the show's format in one word: "America."[27] In a cover story, *TV Guide* reported that he would lose money on the hour-long program. However, Disney was confident that the airing of the series would pay huge dividends: "There will be hardly a living soul in the United States who won't have heard about the Disneyland amusement park and who won't be dying to come see it. Yessir, television is a wonderful thing."[28] The television show was vital, not only because of his financial arrangements with ABC but because "the place that was also a TV show" needed to enchant families across the country.[29] Although its survival depended on California patronage, Disney's reach went beyond that state's limited audience.[30]

The series' first episode, "The Disneyland Story," aired on October 27, 1954, and featured a season preview, a studio tour, an inside look at Disneyland's plans, and a Mickey Mouse tribute. Disney handled hosting duties, playing the role of a "friendly relative eager to share yet another new surprise." The four planned park areas – Fantasyland, Adventureland, Frontierland, and Tomorrowland – found counterparts in the TV series, with its anthology format featuring corresponding segments.[31] To make the connection even more explicit, Disney said on that first program, "Disneyland the place and *Disneyland* the show are all the same."[32] *Time* reviewed the opening show, calling it "mostly an hour-long promise of good things to come" but with "the true touch of Disney enchantment."[33]

The show was an immediate hit, justifying ABC's gamble and Disney's confidence. The ratings victory revealed nationwide interest, coinciding with demographic trends, in all things Disney.[34] Partner ABC, traditionally the lowest rated network in most major cities, claimed victory after just one airing of *Disneyland*.[35] Within three months of its debut, *Disneyland* placed in the top ten. During some weeks it was "right on the heels of *I Love Lucy* for first place."[36] In a *TV Guide* poll at the end of the 1954–55 season, readers of the magazine chose *Disneyland* as their most watched program.[37]

That first year *Disneyland* featured three complete episodes revolving around the park's planning and construction. One episode, entitled "A Progress Report," aired on February 9, 1955.[38] It featured Disney taking a helicopter ride from his office to Anaheim, following and describing the highway route that visitors would travel. From this high perch the audience could see that Disneyland was located in "the most accessible spot in Southern California." On July 13, 1955, just days before its unveiling to the world, ABC aired "A Further Report on Disneyland." As host, Disney brought viewers "up to date on what's been happening," sharing "the joys and anxieties of our race against time."[39] The show operated on several levels, offering amusement while also urging TV watchers to plan a vacation trip to Southern California.[40] Created concurrently with the launching of the television show, Disneyland's geography became familiar to viewers even before the park came into existence.[41]

Disneyland was a landmark in the history of television, encouraging other movie studios to follow the same path. For the 1955–56 season, a year after Disney's entry into television, live prime-time programming fell from 50 to 30 percent. "Hollywood telefilms" gradually replaced New York–based anthology drama programs. A new era of salesmanship on television began as well. *Disneyland* set the standard for advertising on television, with more reruns per season, the largest number of commercial breaks per hour, and the highest number of minutes of each episode devoted to Disney product promotion.[42]

This commercial drive became more evident as *Disneyland* propelled one of the most popular fads of the decade. For the "Frontierland" segment of the show, Disney chose to highlight the story of Davy Crockett. The first season featured three episodes: "Davy Crockett, Indian Fighter" on December 15, 1954; "Davy Crockett Goes to Congress" on January 26, 1955;

and "Davy Crockett at the Alamo," designed to complete the series on February 23, 1955. The first episode aired on 163 television stations and reached an unprecedented 40 million viewers.[43] By the third episode and Crockett's death at the Alamo, the studio began to milk its hero's commercial potential.[44] Fans even hoped that the third episode would end happily, freeing Davy Crockett to return to the TV screen for more adventures, despite his historical death sentence.[45]

Manufacturers produced coonskin caps by the millions, and the show's theme song, written as network time filler, spent weeks at the top of the Hit Parade. The spending craze, fueled by television and family demographics, was the first fad of the era; $300 million spent on Crockett paraphernalia in seven months cemented Disney's entertainment power.[46] Disney was quick to capitalize on Crockett, licensing thousands of toy guns, grocery items, books, dolls, rings, records, guitars, games, wagons, and comics for eager young fans. Davy Crockett's status as a public figure so saturated the market that unlicensed toymakers profited as well.[47] In 1955, symbols of Davy Crockett emblazoned 10 percent of all consumer items purchased for children.[48] The Sears catalog in 1955 devoted an entire page to the craze, offering boy and girl versions of the Crockett hats, belts, shirts, coats, and pants with likenesses of the frontier hero.[49] The fad demonstrated the strength of the child market when combined with television's new powers of manipulation.

Newspapers and magazines featured the hoopla as a human interest piece, focusing on the buying power of children and the lengths to which some fans would go to wear a coonskin cap. The Los Angeles Times reported that a 7-year-old boy successfully defended his cap against a knife-wielding 10-year-old.[50] The New Yorker described a "tidal wave" of "flabbergasting" interest in one of the "hottest commercial properties in the country."[51] Life proclaimed the childhood frontier "subdued by Davy" all over the country, a development "unexpected even by the watchful Disney."[52] TV Guide's May 1955 cover featured Fess Parker, who played Crockett, and Buddy Ebsen, his frontier sidekick George Russell. The article called Parker "TV's first genuine overnight star . . . fingering real money for the first time in his life." Despite newfound wealth and fame, the profile emphasized his down-to-earth qualities and genuineness. Parker was the hero he portrayed.[53]

Disney shrewdly launched a 22-city promotional tour starring Parker in July 1955. The overwhelming response to his personal appearances demonstrated his appeal among "small-fry Americans," who were reduced to "squeals of delight or awestruck silence" in his presence.[54] Throngs of excited Crockett fans, similar to crowds attracted by Elvis Presley, congregated to see the buck-skinned Parker. These groups, however, were "entire families instead of teen-agers," drawn to a young television actor playing a Western hero.[55]

How might the show's impact be explained? Some have argued that the traditional mythology of the frontier and its heroes had simply found a new generation. The success of Davy Crockett was part of the general affinity for westerns in television's early years. The "fantasy of the West" combined with the storytelling of Disney was a "fulfillment of a shared subconscious need to identify with national history."[56] The "craze" fed into popularized cultural depictions of the frontier, manifested in advertising, design, and political rhetoric. The "cap," therefore, was the "perfect symbol of American democracy."[57] Other scholars have pointed to the Cold War environment, which supported patriotism and the decisive actions of strong military men. The Disney Crockett was a hero of the frontier, who operated by the motto "Be sure you're right, and then go ahead."[58] This popularized version of a "patriotic ancestor" offered "the most concentrated lesson in Cold War Americanism" seen on television. In Crockett, viewers learned Disney's lesson for contemporary America, watching a historical figure become a "hero for the Cold War."[59]

Frontier and western icons like Crockett were particularly appealing in Cold War America. The Disney Crockett affirmed America's self image and brought past and present into harmony. As a peace-loving frontiersman, Crockett resorts to violence only as a last resort. His selflessness and sense of duty lead to the sacrifice of his family, political career, and eventually his life. The consistent motive behind his actions is a striving to do the right thing. He is an Indian fighter and an Indian's friend, one who lives the commandment "Thou shalt not kill"; a family man and a rough frontiersman; a politician with an honest streak; a white settler who honored the land claims of Indians with the belief that "they're folks same as anybody else"; and a superhero of the frontier who treated war like a game but met his death at the Alamo.[60] Television viewers responded to Disney's conjuring, for it embodied in its tales both a western mystique and modern-day rhetoric.

Disney released the three Davy Crockett episodes in June 1955 as a repackaged feature film.[61] The 1955–56 season of *Disneyland* debuted two more Crockett adventures that also delivered high ratings. By the fall of 1955, however, Davy had become an examplar of what *Collier's* described as "half-real, half-fabled heroes who have marched into the bright sunlight of young America's fancy and then passed into the shadows beyond."[62] By this time every child owned his or her Crockett merchandise, and the craze subsided.[63] The commercial surprise of the Crockett boom and the swiftness of its fall offered a model for merchandisers and a design for profit making. What had been an "unplanned" phenomenon became the rule, as "total merchandising" of a product through its various entertainment venues was adopted as the Disney standard.[64]

While Crockett faded, the new western icon of Disneyland was born. Millions of American families, by viewing the program, became vested in the success of the park, partners in its construction, with shared, privileged knowledge of its secrets.[65] Magazine writers helped create its mystique as a baby boom child's utopia, reinforcing the TV picture. The opening of a children's amusement park in California was one of the biggest news stories of the year.[66] Disneyland would be a place offering "pleasure for children and adults," gushed *Look* nearly a year before the park's completion.[67] An early 1955 story in *McCall's* chronicled construction progress on the "160 acre playground in California." Disneyland would animate "Walt Disney's cartoon world . . . bigger than life and twice as real."[68] As contractors added the finishing touches and opening day approached, the *New York Times* offered glimpses into a "juvenile world's fair" where "the appellation amusement park is inadequate."[69] *Popular Science* described a "steel and concrete Never-Never Land for youngsters."[70] *Life* expressed concern that the "most lavish amusement park on earth . . . may be more than kids can bear."[71] Before the park's completion, *Woman's Home Companion* predicted that Disneyland would be "probably the closest yet to life-as-we-wish-it-were combined with life-as-it-is."[72]

The anticipation surrounding the unveiling of a "17 million dollar wonderland of past, present, future and fable" demonstrated the growing connections that television fostered between different areas of the country. The park was Disney's dream to "share with America," but its location was California, adding to the state's allure as a travel destination and a magic land in the minds of children.[73] As *Travel* promised, the park was "an entirely new concept in family entertainment" in "California's new fairyland."[74] The *Los Angeles Times* noted that "practically everyone in the world already knows" its dimensions. Disneyland's high profile made it destined to become one of "Southern California's greatest attractions."[75] *Time* quoted one East Coast parent who lamented the extensive media build-up: "Every kid in this country will be hounding his father for a trip to California!"[76] *Look* described the park in a cover story the month of its opening, confirming in the public mind the image of California as a magic land. Disneyland had "sprung from the California earth a fantastic monument to the imagination and genius of one man" with "an honest-to-goodness castle towering seventy feet in the California air."[77]

Disneyland's dedication show, a very special episode of the *Disneyland* program, aired on July 17, 1955. The day of the broadcast, a *Los Angeles Times* headline proclaimed, "Fans Await Debut of Disneyland Via TV Screens Today." It was "the only show on television" in the minds of Californians, and the columnist wondered whether "the same interest evidenced locally" existed beyond Southern California's borders. "Set the channel selector at 4:30 this afternoon," the story advised. "You won't be able to get the kids out of the house anyway."[78]

"Dateline: Disneyland" ran for ninety minutes, live from coast to coast. It began with a chaotic newsroom abuzz with reporters rushing to chronicle the story of the park's opening.[79] These actors playing news reporters mirrored the real-life coverage in the previous eleven months of the park's construction. Sensing the nationwide excitement, the network orchestrated "the greatest concentration of TV equipment and operating personnel ever assembled in one place."[80] The show employed sixty-three engineers and twenty-four cameras, more than any broadcast to date. The confusion caused by the number of cameras and other technical problems made the show less than stellar. Disneyland's debut was filled with gaffes, miscues between hosts, costume problems, and poor camera communication. Despite these difficulties, hosts Bob Cummings, Ronald Reagan, and Art Linkletter proclaimed numerous times that viewers were witnessing history in the making.[81] Cummings compared the opening to that of the Eiffel Tower, proclaiming, "Standing here has been one of the most exciting moments of my life. I'm very proud to say I was at the opening of Disneyland."

Calling the park the "eighth wonder of the world" and "a family affair," Linkletter quizzed his own family on what attraction they looked most forward to experiencing. This ploy briefly introduced each section of the park and highlighted the "tremendous parking lot." Cummings also brought his family along to accompany his hosting duties. The program introduced Walt Disney riding the Disneyland Railroad, piloting dignitaries and the children of all foreign consuls of Los Angeles to Main Street for the dedication ceremony, the most reverential segment of the program.

Three military chaplains, representing the Protestant, Catholic, and Jewish faiths presided over the ceremony. Another minister, coincidentally Disney's nephew, spoke of the "spiritual motivation . . . in the heart of this man who has dreamed Disneyland into being." He continued, stating the ideals of the park as a dedication "to understanding, to goodwill among men, laughter for children, memories for the mature, and aspirations for young people everywhere," and concluded, "Let us unite in a silent prayer that this and every worthy endeavor may prosper at God's hand."[82]

Politicians in attendance included California's governor Goodwin Knight, who gave an official state welcome and salute to the park.[83] In his speech, Knight honored the park as a place where all Americans could be proud, "built by American labor and American capital, under the belief that this is a God-fearing country and a God-loving country." Disneyland represented every city in America, a replica that was "just like your hometown." He also reminded the gathered crowds and home viewers of their favored status: "the fortunate ones to be Americans." Knight might also have been thinking of a slightly smaller group of Americans, the truly lucky Californians living the good life in close proximity to the park. The park stood as a monument, the governor proclaimed, communicating "to everyone everywhere the great ideals of Americanism and peace on earth, good will towards men."[84] Disneyland functioned as a portrayal of all America, its past and future. California, the park's home, represented to the nation the fastest growing present and the promise of the postwar future.

Disney added his accolades with the introduction of a commemorative plaque describing his goals. It read: "Here age relives fond memories of the past, and here youth may savor the challenge and promise of the future. Disneyland is dedicated to the ideals, the dreams, and hard facts that have created America . . . with the hope that it will be a source of joy and inspiration to all the world."[85] As a final part of the ceremony, military personnel stood by for the raising of the flag and the singing of the national anthem, while a squadron from the California Air National Guard flew over the park.

Each of the four lands was introduced separately, with the three hosts highlighting each area's wonders. Disney dedicated every section with plaques, granting historical and ceremonial importance to new structures.

The *Disneyland* television show on ABC was used to promote the theme park of the same name. Here Walt Disney, as host, is seen posing in front of the camera with Sleeping Beauty's castle in Fantasyland rising enticingly in the background. (© Bettman/CORBIS)

Ronnie Reagan, as the telecast introduced him, invited viewers into Frontierland for the first time, "to enter the gates of time into our very historic past."[86] A flock of doves released into Tomorrowland opened that area of the Magic Kingdom. A band of Eagle Scouts from the forty-eight states played, representing the "citizens of the future . . . the world of tomorrow belongs to them." Children were at the center of much of the program. Disney invited 500 children from Orange Country schools to join in the celebration as special guests of the "$17,500,000 world of fantasy dedicated to children and hope." These children were the first to cross the drawbridge to Sleeping Beauty's castle, escorted by Disney characters.[87] Disney dedicated the Fantasyland castle "in the name of the children of the world."

In addition to spotlighting the attractions and the pomp of the dedication service, the show focused on the many celebrities gathered to honor Disney's achievement. Sammy Davis Jr. and Frank Sinatra appeared riding Tomorrowland's Autopia. Irene Dunne christened the Mark Twain Steamboat with waters from every major river in America. Danny Thomas and his family popped up several times during the program. Fess Parker and Buddy Ebsen of Davy Crockett fame rode in the opening parade and performed a special musical number in Frontierland. Disney closed the program by expressing gratitude to those who helped build the park and walking with Art Linkletter to Fantasyland.[88]

The dedication of Disneyland revealed much of Disney's worldview, granting the site religious and cultural import and inviting television watchers everywhere to feel a part of the proceedings. Disney utilized every conceivable American institution to join the celebration of his achievement. The presence of church figures underscored the moral bent of the commercial enterprise, reinforcing the "goodness" of Disney's venture. Political authorities lent their legitimacy to the scene, while the military presence strengthened the connection between the wholesomeness and rightness necessary to fight the Cold War in defense of the theme park's values of Americanism and nostalgia. Another institution, Hollywood, democratically offered its celebrities to the proceedings both as stars and park visitors. In its attractions, Disney evoked the power of the west in the frontier past. The park also featured a "Tomorrowland" with technological hopes for the future, geographically and culturally set in California, the land of America's destiny. All these ideological pieces came together to form a consensus vision, a homogenized and safe world with no conflict or outside influences to disturb the theme park's picture of reality. Disneyland's ceremonial dedication codified the popular version of life in California enjoyed by the white middle class.

Despite the overt exclusiveness of his vision, Disney called his park "the essence of America as we know it" and hoped it would "focus a new interest upon Southern California." Disney believed that the park would be "a place for California to be at home, to bring its guests, to demonstrate its faith in the future."[89] Disneyland was a celebration of the American dream, with a geographical location uniquely suited to foster those hopes. In a state portrayed as the fulfillment of that dream, California mirrored its new theme park.

Approximately 90 million viewers witnessed the unveiling.[90] The *New York Times* commented critically that "the ceremonies took on the aspect of the dedication of a national shrine" and had the "gloss of a commercial travel brochure."[91] *Newsweek* saw the premiere as an unusual extravaganza even by California standards. A state accustomed to movie premieres and Hollywood excitement "had never seen anything like" the hoopla surrounding the event.[92]

What attracted the first visitors to Disneyland? The barrage of media coverage before the unveiling, the dedication broadcast, and the novelty of a family-focused, Disney-designed amusement park attracted huge crowds. Adding to this magnetic allure, *Los Angeles Times* readers found in their June 15 Friday newspaper a special 22-page insert. "Disneyland has been designed for the enjoyment of all," it read, "a magic place where every family can find and share happy hours and experiences together" on their "first and future visits."[93] The insert also included a map with the best routes from various cities in Southern California. Regardless of the impetus, those first anxious park visitors descended by the thousands on the official opening day, July 18, 1955. The crowds created the largest "traffic jam in Southern California history," changing the Santa Ana freeway to a slow-moving ride to the park.[94] As the *New York Times* reported, the "play park on Coast" had 15,000 people in line by 10:00 in the morning. Some had waited all night for the park to open.[95]

Visitors entered through a turn-of-the-century small town's "Main Street U.S.A.," an idealized version of a midwestern past.[96] The 1959 guide to Disneyland described the Main Street entrance as a "friendly way of life . . . [and] an important part of our heritage." Frontierland was a tribute to "the pioneering spirit of our forefathers . . . whether 10th generation or naturalized Americans" where "youngsters thrill to safe adventures." Tomorrowland offered a vision of the decades to come, "adventures which are a living blueprint of our future." The guide described attractions in Adventureland as "true to life," taking visitors to "mysterious far-off places . . . far from civilization." The goal of Fantasyland was to create a "land where dreams could actually come true . . . for everyone who is young in heart." The last page of the guide entitled "Dreaming" offered sketches of future attractions.[97] Disney took pride in the idea of a continuously unfinished project forever being redesigned and rethought.[98]

National viewing audiences and those first visitors encountered a singular entertainment phenomenon with ambitious aims. Disney's goal was to "sell happiness" in a place made conducive to that end by offering a "pleasant experience in the company of happy, smiling, friendly people." Success of the park would not be "because we keep it clean and don't sell gum or because we provide great fun and games, it will be because our personnel sincerely sells happiness. . . . That's what we all want, isn't it? A little bit of happiness?"[99] Disney hoped that visitors, or "guests" in the Disney lexicon, would feel happiness and "find . . . knowledge" in his "show place of magic and living facts."[100] Happiness was what postwar America was geared up to sell, especially in the dreamland of California. Disneyland, in microcosm, represented that larger trend.

Like scenes from a Disney movie, Disneyland rides, attractions, landscapes, and personnel were tidy and clean. In fact, "imagineers" fashioned the park experience as a movie-like outing, with carefully written scenes and recognizable characters. By opening day Disney had twenty-two attractions in operation, with dozens more on the drawing board.[101] The Jungle Cruise, Disneyland Railroad, horse-drawn wagons and cars, Indian Village, Mark Twain Steamboat, Rocket to the Moon, Hall of Chemistry, Space Station X-1, and the King Arthur Carousel were some of the first attractions. Their appeal lay in their familiarity, as part of American history, fairy tales and legends, or Disney characters. The "imagineers" designed the proportions, spatial arrangements, and tone of the attractions and rides to "make people feel taller and confirm their belief in progress."[102]

Strict dress and grooming codes governed those working in the park as ride operators, concession sellers, and attraction guides. Rules required the wearing of themed outfits suited to their park area. Young adults from the Los Angeles area primarily comprised the staff. Their carefully constructed appearance complemented Disneyland's overall design.[103] Just as Disneyland represented a vision of America, those employed at the park suggested an ideal image of smiles and politeness, systematically designed to offer reassurance to park visitors. This picture did not reflect Southern California reality. The park did not employ African Americans in any job until 1963, and that change was due to pressure from the civil rights movement.[104] Disney wanted to create, as he described it, "a small world in itself – it would encompass the essence of the things that were good and true in American life."[105] In Disneyland, the meanings of "good and true" were at their core exclusionary, evasive of reality in their construction of an image.

Walt Disney, prospering in film and television and with an amusement park had pulled off the "greatest triple play in show business."[106] In an era that celebrated middle-class leisure, his success should not have been surprising. Disneyland, designed for consumption and heralded as a place to recapture the past and celebrate the possibilities of the future, was bound to thrive.[107] The emergence of the Disney empire, both in Anaheim and on television, coincided with the years of the baby boom and highlighted the nation's children and their entertainment choices.[108] The park's success gave Disney and his company the financial stability that had eluded him in previous decades. The *Wall Street Journal* saluted Disney's success in February 1958, calling his company the "kings of the kid frontier." The business journal admired the myriad moneymaking operations, "angles," diversification, and integration that tied Disneyland into the product mix.[109] Disney's proven success in film animation inspired television's financial support. A weekly show and a live television event promoted his various productions. Print journalists from all over the country hyped the building of Disneyland and spotlighted its unveiling. This "constant promotion" created an unprecedented "national impact."[110] Five days after its opening, the *New York Times* predicted that the park would attract such crowds that "Mr. Disney will be petitioned to construct a similar wonderland in the East for the benefit of youngsters who are unable to make the trek to California."[111] In its first seven weeks of operation, Disneyland played host to 1 million visitors.[112]

The park utilized television and film promotion long after its ballyhooed opening, both in the anthology series that bore the park's name and in specials designed to highlight certain attractions and events. Disguised as part of its "People and Places" series, Disney released *Disneyland, U.S.A.*, a repackaged Cinemascope feature to national and international theaters in 1956. *Gala Day at Disneyland*, produced in 1960, hoped to attract moviegoers to see its wonders.[113] The most constant exposure continued to be on the small screen. "An Adventure in the Magic Kingdom," which aired twice in the spring of 1958, featured Tinker Bell taking the audience on a pixie-dust flight over the park. "Kodak Presents Disneyland '59" repeated the 90-minute live show format of the park's premiere. In the spring of 1962, "Disneyland After Dark" showcased not only Disney stars but the newest attractions. "Holiday Time at Disneyland," which aired December 23, 1962, featured such varied celebrities as Santa Claus, Tinker Bell, Prime Minister Nehru of India, President Eisenhower, the shah and empress of Iran, and Annette Funicello. In the summer of 1962, a limited series called "Meet Me at Disneyland" attempted to boost summer evening attendance. The 13-episode run featured musical guests like the Four Preps, Annette Funicello, the Osmond Brothers, and Harry James performing around the park.[114]

In less than three years Disneyland became the "biggest tourist attraction in California and the West," increasing the Golden State's allure.[115] Its exponential growth was a testament to the power of media to both produce and promote new types of entertainment. The language of the Disney world entered advertising as a symbol beyond its mere existence as a theme park. A 1957 *Life* ad featured an archetypal family of four in front of Sleeping Beauty's castle. The copy compared Disneyland, where no family could "resist the magic of happiness" and all could "leave their troubles behind," to the peace of mind offered by Insurance of North America.[116] Disney enjoyed a "pixilating power to strike the youthful nerve in Americans," *Time* wrote in 1957, in the "magic realm of California." One parent complained, "After years of sitting in front of a TV set, the youngsters are sure it's a fairyland before they ever get here."[117] A 1957 Ohio newspaper recognized the drawing power of the park and its statewide identification. "A trip to Disneyland," the paper concluded, "seems almost synonymous with a visit to the west coast."[118]

By 1958, 4 million made the pilgrimage to the "paradise for kids" every year, and over 40 percent of that total came from outside California.[119] Television spectaculars and magazine features clearly communicated the message: Disneyland was an unforgettable place with attractions unique to Anaheim. Its inescapable television presence made "young viewers feel 'left out' if they've never been there."[120] Familiarity meant that Disneyland was "one of the best-known vernacular landscapes in the world." As a consequence, a "whole generation of American grew up believing that they'd almost rather go there than go to heaven."[121] Perhaps the best measure of Disneyland's success was the number of imitators that sprung up across the country: Magic Mountain in Denver, a park near Dallas, and Pleasure Island outside Boston.[122]

Disneyland was a favorite spot for celebrities and politicians. Vice president Richard Nixon was a frequent visitor, bringing his family for a photo-op in December of 1955 and dedicating the monorail as part of the park's fourth anniversary in June 1959.[123] Visits from Nixon were commonplace, but 1959 was the year that a Southern California theme park entered international politics as a Cold War icon. That fall, Soviet premier Nikita Khrushchev requested a visit to Disneyland as part of his national tour. For security reasons, the United States denied his request, and the resulting publicity surrounding the nonvisit traveled around the world. Reports had Khrushchev responding angrily: "I would very much like to go and see Disneyland . . . why not? What is it, do you have rocket-launching pads there?"[124] As an editorial in the *New York Times* sympathetically stated, Khrushchev's wish to see the park had "echoed through millions of households and lent shape to vacation plans, tour itineraries and budgets of countless families." In less than four years, Disneyland had achieved the status of "international institution, less an amusement park than a state of mind."[125]

By its seventh year of operation, Disneyland was part of the "Call to California." As the number-one tourist destination in the entire country, it was "as far as the nation's kids are concerned, the most important reason for California's existence."[126] A visit to the park came to symbolize a special rite of passage, particularly for California's youth, as Disneyland introduced graduation night parties for Los Angeles area high schools in 1961.[127] The celebrations involved more than 100,000 area students by the mid-1960s. These gatherings hoped to turn "ordinarily difficult nights into safe and sober occasions" as part of efforts at "domesticating the teenager."[128]

In 1965, Disneyland's tenth anniversary, overall park attendance equaled one-fourth of the total population of the United States. In those ten years, the park debuted over forty-five attractions and engineered expansions to the originals. Revenues from Disneyland amounted to over $35 million and accounted for over 32 percent of Walt Disney Productions income. These numbers continued to climb.[129]

One customer argued in April 1965 that the park had subsumed the city's image: "To our children, Los Angeles is merely a suburb of Disney-

CALIFORNIA DISNEYING

43

land."[130] A 1965 article in a Twin Falls, Idaho, newspaper defined the park's place in the American psyche, moving beyond identification with only Los Angeles. Most visitors to California, the article explained, were invariably asked, "Did you visit Disneyland?" revealing a narrow conception of what California represented. The mental maps of most Americans in the East would show the park as taking up "most of the territory west of the Mississippi."[131] To broaden his geographical appeal, Disney began to consider a second location, this time with complete environmental control of the surrounding restaurants and hotels. The company announced in late 1965 the plans for a Florida site, nicknamed "Disneyland East."[132]

Despite its overwhelming success, or perhaps because of it, Disneyland was criticized for its artifice and inherent commercialism. As they did with much middle-class mass culture, intellectual critics ignored the hype of its many champions and challenged its image-making.[133] One writer called the park "the heartland of the depthless."[134] A *New Yorker* columnist who finally made the "pilgrimage" argued that visitors to the park experienced "uncritical euphoria" based upon a "carefully controlled atmosphere." Even the "attractiveness" of personnel was the "product of calculated effort."[135] Julian Halevy, one of the most noted critics of the park, compared the slickness of Las Vegas to the crass capitalism of Disneyland. The park was "clean, cute, . . . safe, mediocre, inoffensive to the lowest common denominator, and somehow poignantly inhuman." He argued that it poisoned and reflected the whole of Southern California. Los Angeles was simply a "suburb of Disneyland," a place where "all men's striving for dominion over self and nature" became a lesser "sickening blend of cheap formulas packaged to sell."[136]

Author Ray Bradbury responded to Halevy's criticism in a letter to the editors of *The Nation*. Halevy, he suspected, "truly loved Disneyland but is not man enough, or child enough to admit it. I feel sorry for him." Bradbury labeled him an example of "people who, for intellectual reasons, steadfastly refuse to let go and enjoy themselves."[137] He continued his championing of the park, responding to similar criticism for a 1965 *Holiday* magazine. Disneyland offered a place where one could be "truly happy," Bradbury wrote, causing "you to care all over again."[138]

Intellectual critics were not alone in challenging Disney's hegemonic success in the child imagination market. A controversy in late 1965 questioned the value of all Disney productions. In the spring of that year, Max Rafferty, California's superintendent of public instruction, called Walt Disney "the greatest educator of this century" in a *Los Angeles Times* article. He praised Disney for providing "square" entertainment, "lone sanctuaries of decency and health" in Hollywood. Frances Sayers, a lecturer at UCLA, responded to this acclaim in a letter to the *Times*, calling Disney's output a "debasement of the traditional literature of childhood." Many Los Angeles parents, believing that Disney provided "good literature and culture to the young people of the twentieth century," found Sayers's characterization of Disney products offensive.[139]

Even those who recognized Disneyland as an "automated, cotton-candy world" called it a place that "warms everybody save those who demand their own kind of realism, even in a place dedicated to kiddish fantasies."[140] More Americans seemed thrilled by artifice than offended by it, disagreeing with the intellectuals by their continued attendance and allegiance to the park. *Holiday* called the park "better than real" in 1963.[141] By 1965, despite a real-life world that continually challenged the philosophy presented by the park, *Newsweek* still described it as a "cultural institution . . . a charming . . . happy place to be."[142]

Almost from the beginning, and enhanced by TV and media treatment, Disneyland represented more than an "amusement area" and quickly became an "abstract concept" representing larger postwar developments.[143] Observers situate the park in 1950s American culture, a mirror and product of that world in its attractions and design. Disneyland celebrated the American past, gloried in innocent fantasy, and looked positively toward the future.[144] It represented Disney's version of the world and came to be the most emulated landscape in modern America. At its heart, Disneyland was a nostalgic celebration of a Hollywood western frontier located in California, America's newest place of dreams and adventure.[145] The park's architectural design reflected its Southern California setting. Contemporaries saw Disneyland's location as an extension of the "man made . . . gigantic, magical improvisation" that made up the Los Angeles area.[146] The use of "fantasy" and the creation of "environments . . . intended to be experienced in motion" were elements of California living.[147] For visitors, the many transportation systems regressed adults to childhood, making them passengers rather than drivers."[148] Perhaps this is one reason that grown-ups outnumbered children in the park by four to one, this ability to enjoy the fantasies of children by experiencing childhood mobility patterns.[149]

The park was a product of its California location and the 1950s cultural environment, but it also served as a critique of the difficulties of modern Los Angeles. Unlike the growing city, Disneyland was designed as a close-range pedestrian experience.[150] As cultural critics have recognized, the park contains the past and the future but no present within its boundaries.[151] The park took advantage of California sunshine, the state's growth, and the newly built system of freeways to Anaheim, but it presented a world without traffic jams, urban blight, or litter for middle-class baby boom families to enjoy. In contrast to Los Angeles, which was suburban and modern, lacking a city center, Disneyland was "old-fashioned and urban . . . a tacit protest against modern America."[152] The high walls surrounding it served an important design function. For the illusion to work, the walls shielded the public from the outside world for the duration of their stay. Disney explained, "I don't want the public to see the world they live in while they're at the park. I want them to feel they are in another world."[153] The park was part of Los Angeles, an "important public space" in a city without a center, "an emblem of a whole way of life built around suburbanization and the automobile."[154] It was also a repudiation of the postwar world, an escape to a simpler time, a theme-park representation of the community Americans wished they had.[155] In short, Disneyland shared the confusion of postwar America.

Park visitors experienced homogeneity and shared key attributes with their fellow guests. The choice of Anaheim, a community beyond public transportation and the more heterogeneous populations of Los Angeles County, had direct consequences on the demography of Disneyland's "guests." It limited those traveling to the "happiest place on earth" to the automobile-owning middle class. High entry and attraction fees also influenced the look of Disneyland customers, limiting it along class and racial lines.[156] In his reconstruction of a midwestern past, Disney contributed to the myth of Los Angeles as a bastion of a "new suburban whiteness" despite the increasingly racially diverse reality of California's largest city.[157] From California, the park took its locale, employees, customer base, and its setting.[158] What it gave back to the world was a specific model of white, middle-class leisure.

Both the Golden State and the park were icons unsurpassed in their reach, both through first-hand visits and television coverage. Like California's propaganda, Disneyland's theme park presentation of yesterday and tomorrow was exclusionist, avoiding racial and class issues in exchange for a celebration of baby boomers and American opportunities. That barrier informed California's entire image-making machine. The park represented the epitome of the popularized California worldview, sharing the blinders that avoided a more complex picture of America.

Disney's dream was uniquely suited to thrive in the California environment. The state represented America's future, and for millions Disneyland and California were synonymous. Disneyland, through a midwestern past and a futuristic tomorrow, presented to the world a golden vision matched only by the boosterism that characterized California's publicity. Millions responded to both the state's reputation and the park's magical renown. Park guests and television watchers paid homage to Disney's exclusionary vision through their continued pilgrimages to Disneyland and their allegiance to Disney television programs.

The year of the park's debut, Disney produced another such privileged ideal, a show created for children, offering models for behavior and using California kids as stars. With benign T-shirts and eared hats the Mouseketeers captured the imagination of millions of children across the nation. Utilizing now perfected cross-promotion techniques, Disney continued with the daily children's show what he began with *Disneyland*, capturing the child market, pocketbook and soul, and popularizing his view of a Californized America.

CHAPTER THREE

Come Along
and Sing Our Song

Not content with just shaping the travel plans for millions of baby boomers, Disney designed a children's show that prescribed a youth lifestyle in the California setting. *The Mickey Mouse Club* offered California kids as TV stars, the Mouseketeers, and its content reflected the worldview promulgated in other Disney productions, a postwar confidence combined with an attachment to fixed ideals and values. As a daily after-school experience, the importance of joining the "club" reached into millions of homes all across the country. The Mouseketeers represented an ideal, costumed and packaged like Disneyland Park. These mouse-eared children codified the hope for the future that baby boomers represented and demonstrated the consumer possibilities of appealing to that market. As a peer experience tied to a new medium, *The Mickey Mouse Club* gave the postwar generation their first group identity, broadcast directly from the Golden State.

Disneyland's dedicatory program introduced this group of hand-picked young performers, the "Mouseketeers."[1] They were part of Disney's next project, a children's show that was the natural offspring of *Disneyland*.[2] To produce a show for children made prudent business sense. Television viewership had increased most dramatically in homes with youngsters.[3] The new medium offered the unprecedented opportunity to influence the nation's children as consumers and as young Americans. Reflecting Disney's outlook, the show moralized its content, teaching patriotism, safety, and right behavior for all its viewing Mouseketeers.[4] The public relations de-

partment described it as a show for the "leaders of the twenty-first century,"
who, with the help of the program, would "help fashion a better world for
tomorrow."[5] Disney trusted "that watching the Mouseketeers and their
guests in action, boys and girls in homes throughout the land will feel
impelled to discover and develop their own talents."[6]

Hesitant about its limiting label, Disney told sponsoring advertisers
that the idea of a children's show was "disturbing," as it implied inferiority
and lack of creativity. He said: "At our studio, we regard the child as
a highly intelligent human being. He is characteristically sensitive, hu-
morous, open-minded, eager to learn, and has a strong sense of excitement,
energy, and a healthy curiosity about the world in which he lives. Essen-
tially the real difference between a child and an adult is experience. We
conceive it to be our job on *The Mickey Mouse Club* to provide some of that
experience, happy, factual, constructive experience whenever possible."[7]
Disney maintained that the show would most importantly not "talk down
to the kids."[8] He wanted a show "good enough" to appeal to a wide
spectrum of viewers. By aiming for the 12-year-old audience, he believed,
"the younger ones will watch . . . the teen-ager will be interested, and
adults, too."[9] Bill Walsh, the show's producer, wanted variety in the program, believing "a child's mind is such an open thing that it gives us the
whole world to play with."[10]

The network ABC, with the proven success of *Disneyland*, was bullish on
the new program. Its president proclaimed this "tremendous family show"
would "revolutionize daytime television."[11] Before *The Mickey Mouse Club*,
ABC affiliates exercised their station option in the five o'clock hour, usually
playing local shows. Confident in the Disney name, ABC promised 90 percent coverage by its affiliates to prospective advertisers and a potential reach
to almost every American child each weekday.[12] Twenty advertisers, paying
$500,000 each, signed up as show sponsors.[13] As a result of that high price
tag, the network demanded twenty-two advertisements per episode, more
than any other show and breaking the record set by *Disneyland*.[14]

Television commentators also predicted high ratings for *The Mickey
Mouse Club* and gave it a high profile for the new season. A few days before
the debut, *TV Guide* featured Mickey Mouse on its cover and described the
show as the next step in Disney's successful, and expensive, production for
television.[15] *Look* anticipated the show's victory over competitors for children's attention. It remarked, "Heaven help the homework on *Mickey
Mouse Club* nights. Heaven, for that matter, better help *Howdy Doody*."[16]

The Mickey Mouse Club premiered on October 3, 1955. The program's review in *Variety* praised the show's unique format, anticipating that it would "keep the kiddies in every household glued to their sets most every afternoon." Another critic applauded the "junior jukebox of pint-size delights with some suitably charming Walt Disney daffiness and ingenious diversion." A syndicated columnist cheered the "good clean fun" of "tidbits designed to improve little minds or improve little characters." *Billboard* called it "the type of show that will appeal to adults, not those with a juvenile mind, but those who enjoy children."[17] *TV Guide* heralded Disney's continuing ability to "educate, inform, or point a moral for youngsters without cramming dry pedantry down their throats."[18] One critic, however, disagreed with those who enjoyed the program. The *New York Times* reviewer, evidently out of the cultural loop, failed to understand the growing power of Disney. He called it "familiar nonsense . . . bordering on the disastrous" that would "not woo the tots away from *Howdy Doody* nor the young adults from the afternoon westerns and mystery movies."[19]

The show was another instant success for Disney, and the debut of a children's show based in Southern California was a forward step in the western takeover of television. *The Mickey Mouse Club* aired from 5:00 to 6:00 P.M., competing head-to-head with the New York-based *Howdy Doody Show* at 5:30. Within the year, after nearly a decade of success, *Howdy* retreated to a weekly Saturday spot.[20] By the end of the first season, *The Mickey Mouse Club* drew more than 10 million viewers every day, more than any competing afternoon program.[21] At its peak, the show had a larger audience of children than any other program except *Disneyland*. It captured three out of four televisions in use, reaching more total viewers than any other daytime program.[22]

The Mouseketeers, along with the Disney name and product, provided much of the show's appeal. Unlike *Howdy Doody*, *Kukla, Fran and Ollie*, and other contemporary children's shows, *The Mickey Mouse Club* showcased children as entertainers rather than using adults to amuse children.[23] The child performers were the center of the show, evidenced by a March 1955 planning memo that read; "Call kids Mouseketeers – get costumes, sweaters, little hats."[24]

For his Mouseketeers, Disney selected average kids without the precocious nature of child stars. Their role, according to the show's architects, was to "bridge the gap from Disney cartoons to live people in a manner that is believable and entertaining."[25] The children of greater Los Angeles provided the talent pool, enlisting to represent and entertain children all over the country. These kids from Disney's backyard enjoyed a golden life, the epitome of the baby boom experience and the California brand of happiness. These youth had escaped the "hunger and fear" of previous generations, replacing those experiences with dance lessons. Except for Bobby Burgess, who hailed from Long Beach, all the first team Mouseketeers came from the San Fernando Valley.[26]

In tryouts, Disney explained to producers, "I don't want those kids that tap dance or blow trumpets while they're tap dancing or skip rope or have curly hair like Shirley Temple or nutty mothers. . . . I just want ordinary kids."[27] Disney also encouraged producers to scout local schools for natural-looking kids with star quality.[28] Another Mouseketeer requirement was family togetherness. Only children from "normal, stable, wholesome" family lives made the final cut.[29] The stars of *The Mickey Mouse Club* needed to reflect Disney's outlook concerning the baby boomers. He believed that "despite all the publicity about delinquency, America's youngsters are a pretty good lot."[30]

The show uniformed the Mouseketeers with Mickey Mouse ear caps, shirts with names in clear letters, and slacks for the boys, skirts for the girls. This allowed the show to avoid the controversial adolescent styles and dress of the mid-1950s.[31] Later seasons outfitted the Mouseketeers in suits, ties, and jumpers. In this simplified Disney world, these kids represented an entire generation.[32] By the second season, *Variety* reported, the show's "big attraction" was the "attractive, talented kids . . . in mouse ears and white sweaters."[33]

Much was made of Mouseketeer normalcy, their school attendance, and closeness with family. *Motion Picture Daily* saw the Mouseketeers as the key to the show's appeal, their "lack of self-consciousness born of the knowledge that before their audience they are equals."[34] In *TV Guide*, one of the show's directors insisted, "The Mouseketeers are just normal kids. Most of them happened to take dancing or singing lessons when they were younger, without any thought of getting into show business." One reason for their good behavior and healthy perspective about television stardom, the article explained, was the banning of mothers from the set. Although "undoubtedly talented," they were characterized as "not particularly ambitious," content instead to enjoy their time as Mouseketeers without big dreams of future entertainment success.[35]

Television critics heralded the reassuring image presented by the show and its child stars. The *Boston Post* in April 1956 called the Mouseketeers "a symbol of all American youth" who "epitomize all that's healthy, normal, and happy." With such role models, parents had "no reason to worry about our own teenagers."[36] Throughout the show's run, Disney sponsored public auditions for new Mouseketeers, trying to "foster the impression that the stock company members were just like the well-scrubbed youngsters on any block."[37] During the show's second season, *TV Guide* covered the Burbank studio auditions, showing hopeful youngsters and their family and friends performing for the Disney judges.[38] A children's book, *Walt Disney's The Mouseketeers Tryout Time*, allowed readers to imagine becoming one of the elite young Californians appearing on the show.[39]

Between 1955 and 1958, Mouseketeer admirers wrote more than 350,000 fan letters.[40] Personal appearances inspired the same sort of frenzy that greeted Fess Parker during the Davy Crockett craze.[41] For the show's viewers there was an easy way to feel a part of the club: consumption. The Mickey Mouse ear caps worn by the Mouseketeers spawned the second Disney-inspired hat fad in two years. The hat was the best-selling Disney item to date, surpassing the coonskin cap .worn by Davy Crockett.[42] Within twelve broadcast weeks, fans of the show purchased 2 million hats.[43] At the show's zenith, 24,000 a day disappeared from store shelves nationwide.[44]

Other items with tie-ins to the show enjoyed popularity as well. Five months after the show's debut, thirty-eight companies were actively producing and promoting *Mickey Mouse Club* merchandise. *Walt Disney's Mickey Mouse Club Magazine* had a circulation of 400,000 during the first two years of the show.[45] The Spring 1956 Sears catalog advertised "anklets for all Mickey Mouseketeers" along with a "manufacturer's entry card" for a contest to win a week's vacation at Disneyland.[46] The young baby boomers' favorite TV show sold comic books, T-shirts, puzzles, nightlights, roller skates, sleepwear, wagons, scooters, and toothbrushes. Recordings of the show's featured musical numbers sold well, as did performances by Mouseketeers. Disney marketed Mouseketeer paper dolls and coloring books by the dozens.[47]

The show represented a new era in advertising, setting the standard for what would follow.[48] In 1954, advertisers spent $1 million on child-focused advertising. These ads were mostly for breakfast food and snacks, encouraging youngsters to influence their parents' choices.[49] Other markets, like toys, experienced an advertising push only around Christmas time and did not attempt to foster brand loyalty. The opportunity to build name recognition of toys through direct advertising to children proved lucrative, and those who took the earliest gambles were richly rewarded. Mattel, the only toy company in the original group of sponsoring advertisers, introduced the "Burp Gun," in November 1955, one of the first new toys advertised on the show. An unprecedented sales jump resulted, directly corresponding to its television appearance.[50] With that lesson, Mattel introduced its teenage fashion model doll, "Barbie," on the show in 1959.[51] Advertisers quickly recognized the profit potential of featuring toys amidst a shared viewing experience. Associating their products with the Mouseketeers was an effective ploy and an advertiser's dream. By 1956, companies spent $25 million a year on direct advertising to children.[52]

The millions of children watching the antics, lessons, morals and fun of the *Club* were the target of these commercials. Fans joined in singing the theme song, eager to be a part of "the club that's made for you and me . . . marching coast to coast and far across the sea." The opening invited children everywhere to "come along and sing a song and join our family." Before introductions, the Mouseketeers danced and sang a welcoming, reassuring promise: "We're the Mouseketeers, we want to say hello, and give three cheers, for all of you who see us everyday – you're okay!" The end of every program featured a song tinged with sadness; "Now it's time to say good-bye to all our family. M-I-C – See you real soon. K-E-Y – Why? Because we like you, M-O-U-S-E."[53]

In addition to offering models of "normal" kids, Disney wanted to present, as he put it, "certain educational things." "But," he added, "that's a bad word to use. Basically, let's say there will be entertainment dealing with factual subjects."[54] To stress the show's educational goals, he published a 12-page *Disney on Television Classroom Guide* and distributed 300,000 to the nation's teachers. The guide emphasized the educational possibilities of both *Disneyland* and *The Mickey Mouse Club*, encouraging teachers to promote and integrate those programs into their lesson plans.[55] Overwhelmingly, the educational focus of the program was "morality . . . nothing less than a philosophy of life [and] a picture of the ideal world."[56] The show constantly reminded young viewers of their status as "leaders of the 21st century," with important responsibilities.[57]

These objectives were evident in the show's structure. Beginning with a rousing, trumpeting theme song, each show introduced by "roll call" the Mouseketeers. This repetitious format helped viewers identify and recognize the major players and learn the show's songs.[58] Segments included newsreels, live-action musical numbers by the Mouseketeers, and serialized stories featuring the cast in acting roles. The show gave the vast vaults of Disney cartoons their first television exposure, giving new life to the mouse that had started Disney on the road to success.[59]

The show devoted a great deal of airtime to moralistic segments but managed to interweave those lessons with advertisements for Disney products. *Disneyland* served as the cross-promotion model for the modern children's show. "You can't help but learn something from a fellow as smart as Mickey," viewers learned, turning Disney characters into role models. The show featured Mouseketeers taking trips to Disneyland and introduced educational topics while plugging Disney publications: "You'll be able to read about that in your *Mickey Mouse Club* Magazine."[60] Even newsreel segments publicized Disney productions. In its trip around the world, the newsreel crew included stories of children in Disneyland, California, realizing their dreams. A feature of the show, "Mousekapreview," always highlighted an upcoming Disney production. During the third season, the Mouseketeers met model Carol Lynley, the star of the newest Walt Disney picture. Annette narrated scenes from the film, stressing its exciting characters and drama. She also took a field trip to Walt Disney studios, explaining the value of storyboards to viewers by spotlighting the newest True-Life Adventure film release.[61]

Each day of the week had a theme: Fun with Music, Guest Star, Anything Can Happen, Circus, and Talent Round-Up. On Friday, Talent Round-Up day, the Mouseketeers were costumed in matching Western gear.[62] Disney marketed similar clothing as "A Mouseketeer's Western Outfit," a box that contained a hat, tie, badge, belt, two guns, and two holsters.[63] Winners of the talent contest were usually from Southern California. Jerry Brown, future governor of the state, appeared in a 1957 talent contest, as did dozens of other local children.[64] National contests were held, usually sponsored by department stores in conjunction with the sale of *Mickey Mouse Club* merchandise.[65]

Featured talent winners took advantage of Disney-themed entertainment in their performances. The Mobley trio from Whittier, California, appeared during the third season, singing a Disney tune, "Be Sure You're Right, and Then Go Ahead." The lyrics advised, "It's up to you to do what Davy Crockett said."[66] A teenage boy and girl played the bass and accordion, while a cheeky little boy sang lead vocals. The Mobleys, as was the custom, became honorary Mouseketeers after their appearance. Another pair of winners, Linda and Jenny Ballis from San Diego, featured the younger girl serenading a Goofy toy with "Oh You Beautiful Doll." The pair then entertained with a dancing, singing rendition of the Disney song, "Zip-E-Dee-Doo-Dah."[67] Another winner, Becky Dailey from Santa Clara, performed a gymnastic tumbling routine to Disney music.[68]

The show focused on the Mouseketeers and other child guest stars, but maintained a strong adult presence. Jimmie Dodd, the friendly uncle fig-ure, guided the Mouseketeers with his guitar and folksy manner. In the sec-ond season, Dodd began offering a daily "Doddism" of advice, a "mouse-kafable," or an interesting educational tip.[69] TV *Guide* called him a "Pied Piper" who "entrances young America with a Guitar and a Mouse-Eared Hat." Dodd led "12 million children a week away from competing pro-grams into the ABC pasture." The Mouseketeer "chief" was "amazed" at his power over children, who, he said, "memorized everything about the show." A highly religious man and a prolific Disney songwriter, he seemed the perfect Mouseketeer leader.[70] Songs he wrote and performed made the connection between religious and moral teachings explicit:

> God gave you a conscience to know what's right from wrong
> By doing things the honest way your character grows strong
> If you're always honest in everything you do
> You'll fill your life with honor and then life will honor you.[71]

A song from the first season, entitled "Do What the Good Book Says," encouraged Mouseketeers to "love one another."[72]

Admirable, middle-class character traits, reinforced in song, skit, and cartoons, were a strong component of the show. Another Dodd segment, "Words to Grow By," offered practical advice to young viewers. A popular song featured on the show had these lyrics:

> The race is won by running, there is no other way
> And if you keep on running, you will win someday
> It's fun to study grammar, to learn what it can teach
> When you're elected President, and have to write a speech
> So dig right in and do it now, whatever should be done
> You're a dope to sit and mope when everything is fun.[73]

A Mouseketeer production number admonished viewers to "Get Busy . . . on Saturday morning when there is no school, you can apply the golden rule."[74] "Smile and the world smiles with you, that's the way to live, Mouseketeers," Dodd advised. In a singing duet, Dodd and Mouseketeer Darlene taught, "Beauty is as beauty does. . . . If you would be lovely, just lend a helping hand, and everyone who needs your care will say that you are grand."[75]

The baby boom's social, economic, and political potential impressed the show's creators. Seeing their opportunity, they sought to shape and mold the future with calls to greatness and forecasts of world leadership. First-season slogans for the newsreel segment reinforced this theme: "Dedicated to *You* – the Leaders of the Twenty-First Century" and "The News of Today for the Leaders of Tomorrow." Mouseketeers sang songs with lyrics such as, "We've got a lot about our ears, the talent given to you and me, we must develop faithfully."[76] Dodd, as the adult figure on the show, frequently offered words of advice. "A lot of you listening to me right now will become visionaries of the future, dreamers whose dreams will leave their mark on the world," Dodd explained with typical enthusiasm. In a "Words to Grow By" segment, he compared the baby boom children to earlier pioneers: "Someday, your generation will be the one to carry on the study and pioneering of the advances that must be made. So Mouseketeers, it's important to start preparing yourselves to start studying for this pioneering work to be done."[77]

The Mickey Mouse Club focus on the future was a limited one, as the exclusiveness of the California-based Mouseketeers reflected only a white middle-class version of childhood. The curtain raised on every show featured a depiction of two Mouseketeers, a white girl and boy. During the show's run, there were rare exceptions to this pointed exclusion. Mary Espinosa was a Mouseketeer for part of the first season, although she never became a featured player on the first team. Talent Round-Up Day infrequently featured African American artists as winners of the weekly contest.[78]

The show's content mirrored the strict gender separation of American culture. For its segment, "What I Want to Be," the show featured airline job opportunities. The boy shadowed a pilot, while the girl acted as hostess, bringing the captain and his apprentice their meals. In a segment called "Time to Cook with Minnie Mouse," Jimmie Dodd and his wife Ruth sang gender-appropriate lyrics to accompany the making of mouse-shaped cookies. Ruth sang to girl viewers "You'll find out that pots and pans can be a lot of fun," while Jimmie sang "And for you boys there'll be a lot to eat before we're done."[79] In the song "When I Grow Up Someday," Mouse-keteer Darlene lists her future options in the lyrics "a nurse, a hostess, a bank cashier . . . a teacher and teach the kids in school." The boy's version of the song contained different future options; "a doctor, a lawyer, or financier."[80] The show continually presented traditional male and female role models. Through skit, story, song, and activity, *The Mickey Mouse Club* depicted the proper venues for boys and girls, offering exemplars of each gender.

Similarly, the most popular serial featured on the show took place in an exclusively male domain. Fifties television galloped with adult westerns, and *The Mickey Mouse Club* offered a child's version. *The Adventures of Spin and Marty* was based on *Marty Markham*, a children's book published in 1942.[81] The series connected with historical western images and contemporary thinking by using California as its setting, the new frontier where baby boomers thrive. The setting of California and the rural West provided safe haven from more difficult locales and subject matter.

Spin and Marty began as the continuing saga of Martin Markham, who spends the summer at the Triple-R Ranch, and his fellow camper Spin Evans, the most popular boy at camp and an aspiring doctor. According to the series narrator, the camp for young boys is "the best in the whole fan-dangling West."[82] Filmed at Walt Disney's ranch, the series contained timeless themes about the power of the West, the frontier as builder of a boy's character, the democratized loss of formality (Martin becoming the more familiar Marty), and the awesomeness of nature.[83] *Spin and Marty* featured riding, roping, and the running of a ranch, offering situations "the kids can identify themselves with." This modern-day western repeated many of the lessons and ideas taught by the Davy Crockett series, illustrating "how a group of boys live and work together on a vacation ranch."[84] Fans of Spin and Marty wrote over 30,000 fan letters over the course of the show, more than Davy Crockett received at the height of his fame.[85]

The first episodes of the series introduced Martin Markham, who arrives at the Triple-R Ranch in a chauffeured black car with a manservant. He immediately antagonizes his fellow campers. With an obvious "chip on his shoulder," he calls the ranch a "dirty old farm." He lies about playing polo and boxes with Spin Evans. The other boys respond by mocking him with a campfire song, short-sheeting his bed, scaring him with a frog, and holding a snipe hunt. In consequent episodes, however, Marty learns to ride a horse, Skyrocket, and discovers the excitement and adventure that the ranch offers. He trades his cotton slacks and loafers for jeans and cowboy boots. His courage riding bareback alone and bravery after breaking his arm impresses the other boys. Marty's homesickness disappears, and the frontier spirit wins over his servant as well. The finale, a rodeo showdown, ends happily, with the Triple-R winning thanks to the Westernized Marty.

The serial's first season developed the Marty character in much the same way the Mouseketeers represented normalcy. For young viewers not living in California, following Marty's adventures and growth offered a model of right behavior. In addition, the transformation of Martin to Marty, from a class-conscious elitist to an egalitarian team player, hearkened to earlier myths of the frontier and contemporary beliefs about California. In the West, class distinctions disappear and democracy reigns, free from the encumbrances of Eastern-based snobbery. The new pioneers of postwar California could succeed in the Golden State of opportunity, creating a classless society. Disney was especially focused on making this the goal of the baby boomers. He combined the reputation of western virtues with the possibilities of the postwar era to celebrate his vision of the rising generation.

As the camp leader of the Triple-R explains, "watching cowboy movies and hollering and yelling while you gallop is no way to learn." These boys, and by extension the home viewers, watched and learned as campers rode horses, roped calves, tied knots, hiked and camped on the trail, and participated in a rodeo. The camper's adventures often took a back seat to shots of animal life, long segments of horse riding, and scenic western vistas. Despite its rural setting, the show didn't completely divorce itself from its status as a Disney production. As campers share comic books in an early episode, one of the boys asks, "Who has the Mickey Mouse book?"[86]

The Further Adventures of Spin and Marty aired in 1956–57 and continued these themes. Marty returns to the Triple-R for a second year, and pretends to have reverted to his pre-Westernized behavior as a practical joke on his fellow campers. The second season added a nearby girls' ranch. *The New Adventures of Spin and Marty* followed in 1957–58. The pair arrive at the ranch in a souped-up roadster, a popular California pastime that Spin and Marty, now best friends, worked on together. The car catches fire and then damages the ranch house when it is accidentally started.[87]

The three seasons of the serial made the young acting pair who played Spin and Marty popular among viewers. *TV Guide* profiled the two actors in June 1957, highlighting their interests and youthful pastimes. The main interest of Tim Considine (Spin) was foreign sports cars, while David Stollery (Marty) was a "polite, serious, thoughtful lad" fascinated by horses, fishing, and motorcycles.[88] Both young men were prime examples of the new California life.

Spin and Marty was the favorite serial of *Mickey Mouse Club* viewers and role modeled for boys. However, the show's most popular Mouseketeer was Annette Funicello, an example for girls both on television and off the set. Like millions of other newcomers, the Funicellos had moved to California in the postwar period. Annette became one of the original twenty-four Mouseketeers after Walt Disney discovered her at a dance studio recital. She wanted to change her Italian surname to the more show business–sounding "Turner," but Disney insisted, "Once people learn how to pronounce it, they'll never forget it." Despite the lackluster predictions of producers, she received the most fan mail, over 6,000 letters a month, and became the most important member of the young cast.[89] Annette led the way in Mouseketeer merchandise, with her own coloring book series, paper doll set, and music recordings.[90]

Funicello's dramatic serial in the show's third season, *Annette*, chronicled the travails of a young girl from a Nebraska farm sent to live with her aunt and uncle.[91] Her relatives were initially wary about taking her in. Uncle McLoud wondered about "youngsters nowadays – what do we know about them?"[92] *Annette* also starred Tim Considine and David Stollery from *Spin and Marty*. It was another "fish out of water" teen drama, equivalent to Marty's first experiences at the Triple-R Ranch. Having lived on a farm, Annette was similarly out of touch with her new suburban environment. Evidently she never watched television.

The serial traced her development from a country cousin, dressed like Heidi with long hair, to a modern teenager, in contemporary dress and sporting a short hairstyle. Annette maintains her wholesomeness, quickly making friends but refusing porch good-night kisses, and drinking a lot of milk. The teenagers she meets plan hayrides and frequent malt shops and are often breaking into musical numbers. Spoiling the fun is a jealous girl who accuses her of stealing a necklace. In true sitcom fashion it is discovered inside a piano. The serial's final scene featured reconciliation with friends and relatives and the celebratory drinking of some warm milk.[93]

In magazine features, Annette put forward a public persona based on innocence and middle-class morality, a "normal teenager" who just hap-

A 1955 studio portrait of Mouseketeer Annette Funicello, sporting a white turtleneck emblazoned with her first name but without the mouse-eared hat.

(Hulton Getty/Archive Photos)

pened to work on television. Paramount to Annette's identity was her attachment to family, her role as big sister, and the importance of school studies. Annette was both beautiful and smart, a hard worker who exuded femininity.[94] A 1957 profile in *Walt Disney's Magazine* chronicled Annette's typical day on the set, future dreams, reading material (the *Girl Scout Handbook* and *Mother's Encyclopedia*), and outdoor hobbies of swimming, diving, and horseback riding.[95]

TV Guide spotlighted Annette in May 1958, proclaiming "Fair Weather Ahead" for "one of the most popular actresses in America today." Although her show business career seemed secure, Annette's real problem was the car that, "like most 15-year-olds," she wanted for her sixteenth birthday. "Despite her busy schedule and her fame," she still had parental rules to obey. Disagreements between mother and daughter threatened her "wish" of a car from coming true. The "normalcy" that characterized Annette's life, the article explained, made her "the envy of a legion of mothers who compare her to their own aspiring offspring."[96]

Coronet proclaimed Annette "stardom bound" while still enjoying the regular teenage perks: watching television, collecting stuffed animals, and "having her own telephone, which buzzes constantly with boys asking for dates." "Her own Thunderbird," the result of her mother's relenting, completed her happiness. Both Annette and her fans wondered contentedly, "Who could ask for anything more?' "[97] *Photoplay* asked "What is an Annette?" and offered a simple answer: like "any girl sixteen years old," she enjoyed hot fudge sundaes, football games, beach parties, and eye makeup.[98]

Magazines profiled Annette's dating of other teen stars, especially her relationship with singer Paul Anka. These teen idol stories stressed the similarities the stars shared with their normal teenage fans, describing the concerns of meeting parents; issues about going steady and teenage jealousy; calling a boy or remaining "old fashioned"; feeling moody, insecure, confused about the future; and talking about marriage.[99] In 1960, at the age of eighteen, she was honored with a biography that interested young fans could purchase.[100]

Annette was the only original Mouseketeer still under contract to Walt Disney when *The Mickey Mouse Club* ended. She found success in other branches of the entertainment industry as well, launching a recording career, with the help of Disney-produced records, and being named the "*American Bandstand . . .* most promising female vocalist" for 1959.[101] The

Annette and the Afterbeats recording of "Tall Paul," released on the Disneyland label, was a Top Ten hit that year. Disney productions published a series of mystery/adventure books featuring Annette that continued into the 1960s.[102]

Despite her show business success, profiles of Annette highlighted her desires for a home and family away from the spotlight. In *Photoplay*, she expressed a desire to "try combining marriage with a career, though I'd give it up if my husband wanted me to. I'd give it up to raise a big family." Despite her celebrated dating of other young people in the public eye, Annette maintained that she wanted "to marry a businessman. A lawyer maybe. Because I think it's seldom that two people in show business get along as man and wife."[103] From her stuffed animal collection to plans for the future, Annette represented an example to fans of safe success, reinforcing her gender identity and fulfilling her defined role.

Annette's idol status was perplexing to contemporary observers. She evidently enjoyed a "star quality," the kind Disney had sent his producers to find on California playgrounds. The overwhelming audience reaction to "the not-too-beautiful teen-ager whose singing is just adequate and whose dancing is only fair" confounded *TV Guide*. It wondered if fans of the show, "in passing up the slicker Mouseketeer personalities for Annette [were] making a psychological beeline for Big Sister . . . and the heck with glamour."[104] More physical interpretations of her popularity directed attention to her adolescent development over the show's run and its appeal to her male fans.[105]

The reasons behind Annette's popularity remain difficult to pin down, and interpretations vary. One cultural critic argued that as the only ethnic star she held a special attraction, standing out in a sea of "white suburban pre-teens."[106] An analyst of the show concluded that Annette succeeded as the era's representation of moral aspirations. That "her on screen and off screen personalities were the same" strengthened this power.[107] Funicello believed that her status as the only "ethnic Mouseketeer" partly explained her show business success.[108]

Despite her ethnicity, Annette stood firmly in the middle class. Her celebrity position offered a perfect example of the gold rush story, the rags-to-riches tale of a cute Italian kid achieving fame and fortune. Her identity as a young Californian, beyond her everyday appearances on television, made her intrinsically attractive to young TV watchers, evidenced by her continued fame throughout the period. Her profiles in Disney and teen-marketed magazines highlighted the California lifestyle of cars, dating, and clean-cut fun that she enjoyed. Along with the image of California generally, Annette posed no threat to traditional sex roles, remaining throughout her career a shining example and celebration of the status quo.

During *The Mickey Mouse Club* heyday, the transition from local to national programming, a live format to a filmed Hollywood production was complete, guided by the path that Disney had marked. For the 1957 TV season, Hollywood studios or their subsidiaries produced over 71 percent of all network shows, with a number of the remaining live shows moving their broadcast to Southern California. With Disney-produced television, the ABC network built its success by focusing on "youthful shows" and young stars.[109] Despite its evident popularity, ABC claimed it had difficulty in attracting sponsors who wanted to appeal to juveniles.[110] *Variety* noted that the child performers were rapidly aging, and lack of sponsorship might be due to the loss of "novelty."[111]

In the 1957–58 season, ABC cut *The Mickey Mouse Club* to a half hour. This decision by ABC met with widespread protest. One parent wrote that the show reached "just the right balance, helping the youngster to interpret the world around him." Another adult viewer called the show "refreshing, from the talented Mouseketeers to the moral-giving serial to the innocent cartoons or to the educational little messages."[112]

The network's motivation for cancellation was cost, as it was less expensive to produce its own shows than pay Disney. The 1958–59 season was a compilation of reused and unused material, without any newly produced segments. The show's popularity continued, however, despite its lack of freshness. *The Mickey Mouse Club* ended its ABC run in September 1959. The show experienced a second life in syndication from 1962 to 1965, reaching 12 million viewers in its first year back on the air.[113] The show continued to be a merchandising magnet, with seventy-five manufacturers licensed during syndication to produce *Mickey Mouse Club* paraphernalia.[114]

Disney ended his relationship with ABC in 1961, bringing his talents and a new program, *Walt Disney's Wonderful World of Color*, to NBC.[115] The influence of Disney-produced television was astonishing. Disney had carved out a role for his corporation in the life of American families.[116] The popularity of his shows, products, and characters defined the baby boom's childhood experience. Through television, Disney myths and images entered millions of homes beyond the previous reach of Disney films.[117]

Government witnesses and education experts established the power and

influence of television on children before *The Mickey Mouse Clu*
the airwaves. Organized to investigate the role of the entertainmen
on juvenile delinquency, a Senate Subcommittee announced its findin
the fall of 1955. The committee found that television had a greater imp
on the behavior of youth than movies or radio and that crime program
might inspire copycats and violent behavior. It suggested that both the
government and parents should exercise more control over the broadcasts
that enter homes "to protect children against this danger."[118] An investigation in California reached the same conclusion, charging television with
making children "callous by showing them too much violence."[119]

What these studies failed to suggest was a similar connection between
television and the effects of moralistic programming. If television had the
capacity to influence delinquency, could it also foster moral behavior and
middle-class ideals? Might it teach and model "a certain monolithic view of
America"?[120] The picture of life on television obscured differences and
diversity and distorted the vision of America. Images created in California
studios permeated the medium, with attendant ideas about middle-class
life, childhood, success, and America. These programs offered a "TV version
of moral life."[121] As an early 1960s study on television argued, "The chief
effects of television are likely to be the long, slow effects on values . . . and
on culture and individual behavior."[122]

As the new medium traveled west to Hollywood, the setting of television became California. While many programs shared this California milieu, only a few shows used the Golden State as an overt locale in the 1950s
and 1960s; *77 Sunset Strip*, *The Real McCoys*, *The Beverly Hillbillies*, and *The
Mickey Mouse Club* were exceptions. Yet the television world was Californized in a sense – largely white, middle class, and suburban. "Anywhere,
U.S.A.," invariably evoked California both in its obvious geographical
place of production but also in its use of California's youth and its presentation of a fictional suburb. Dozens of programs used "1950s Southern California sitcomland" as their setting, a suburbia that celebrated ideal family
life and childhood experiences in white, middle-class neighborhoods.[123]
What television watchers could see in their homes was a laugh-tracked
version of the American dream, using the California suburb to represent
postwar America. Places like Mayfield, the fictional setting for *Leave It to
Beaver*, and the Andersons' town of Springfield on *Father Knows Best*
evoked a "sunny, easy and perfect" ideal, personified by the "West Coast
way of life."[124]

The Mickey Mouse Club was among the earliest and most successful television shows to shape baby boomer values and ideals, sharing with many of the era's sitcoms a California setting and presenting its youth as icons. Its power initially and then in continuous reruns created "the" peer group that invited boys and girls to accept its embrace. While offering laudable moral sentiments, the show also proscribed reality to exclude those outside the white middle class. Like most Disney-produced television, it beckoned all to "join our family," yet tailored content to reinforce exclusionary images. Disney discovered a ready audience for his messages of good and right. He influenced the character of children's television along with presenting visions of California's young people as wholesome suburban icons. The Mouseketeers' popularity and the following enjoyed by Annette indicated a widespread acceptance of these youth images and a desire to emulate them.

California and the mythic qualities of the West were integral parts of Disney entertainment. These themes can be traced most overtly in the magical attributes of a Mecca-like Disneyland and the moral lessons of *The Mickey Mouse Club*. Disney's world was patterned on the California mold of middle-class leisure, consumption, and suburbia, with each success fostering an exclusionist view but one that seemed to resonate with millions. Having learned how to behave as children, baby boomers moved into their teenage years requiring new icons, new models of life. Not to be outdone, other studios created archetypal expressions of California lifestyles and focused on this audience. These were California tales specifically tuned to the advancing age of the baby boom, moving beyond the ranch life of *Spin and Marty*, offering more modern a story than Davy Crockett, and creating a more mature idol than the typical Mouseketeer. Two of the most noted examples, Jim Stark of *Rebel Without a Cause* and Frances Lawrence of *Gidget*, offered two distinct but eerily similar "reel" life pictures of California teenagers. In these two film representations, the evolution from juvenile delinquent to an idealized version of California youth can be traced, a transition from concern to celebration, matching that of the culture at large. Hollywood films helped create an adolescent world that, like Disneyland, was "better than real."

CHAPTER FOUR

Gidget
Without a Cause

As Disney discovered the power of the California stage, the film world focused its attention on the baby boom market. The teen film was a postwar phenomenon, born of the desperation of filmmakers and distributors to fill movie houses, the business practices of minor studios, and demographic realities. Major studios produced entertainment for the teen market, with higher budgets and production values, but along similar lines. Two key 1950s characters in youth films, Jim Stark from *Rebel Without a Cause* and Frances Lawrence of *Gidget* represent this type of moviemaking. While seemingly dissimilar personalities, their common class and geographical location offer theme and continuity for tracing the development of youthful screen idols. Focusing on California imagery is a departure from traditional postmodern or feminist critiques and offers a social and historical perspective on these two iconic products. The analysis demonstrates an evolutionary connection between the two images as well as key differences that reveal a changing postwar culture. The films illustrate emerging ideas about California's youth as well as attributes and beliefs of the audiences that made them popular.

James Dean and his archetypal *Rebel Without a Cause* created a mystique in the California setting that would outlive him and the film. His brooding amidst the affluent suburbs pioneered an archetype that inspired copycat films and charmed young moviegoers. The *Gidget* character enjoyed the longer life span, spawning sequels and a television series, offering an idealized portrayal of teenage life in California and an equally salient, though comic, image. *Gidget* put California's youth on the teenage cultural map, dramatizing for the first time the state's unique pastime, surfing, to a national audience and highlighting the wholesomeness of its young. The connections between these film images illuminate developments in Hollywood and reflect the changing mores of American culture. Viewed together, the films suggest a cultural transition, a shift from concerns over the wartime generation's delinquency to a celebration of baby boomer lifestyles, especially those found in California.

Evolution of the postwar environment created such popular characters. In 1955, juvenile delinquency was a national obsession; it was a period of intense national worry about troubled youth and their effect on society.[1] FBI director J. Edgar Hoover called the threat from the "juvenile jungle" equal to or surpassing the communist menace.[2] This uneasiness permeated mass entertainment and even became a source of black humor. In November 1955, *Collier's* featured a cartoon showing a man held at gunpoint by a baby carriage. Onlookers questioned: "You wonder where it's all going to end!"[3]

Hollywood capitalized on this fear, targeting younger audiences and producing films with teens as dangerous protagonists. Studios tried to have it both ways, exploiting and condemning youth delinquency. While trumpeting the seriousness of the juvenile crime problem, Hollywood dramatized the subculture in ways that fascinated impressionable moviegoers.[4] Filmmakers claimed solidarity with those combating juvenile crime, but critics argued that by catering to sensationalism these films were creating destructive and harmful role models.[5] Three familiar screen personalities represented this trend: Marlon Brando on a motorcycle in *The Wild One* (1953), the wayward high school youth of *Blackboard Jungle* (1955), and the ultimate archetype, the misunderstood teenager James Dean in *Rebel Without a Cause* (1955).

Warner Brothers studio took *Rebel*'s title from a 1944 psychologist's study of urban youth. His research focused on teenage troublemaking amidst poverty and broken homes.[6] The subject matter reflected the general trend of 1930s and 1940s screen delinquency tales. These types of films were set mainly in eastern cities and appealed to an audience anxious about the consequences of the Great Depression and World War II on the nation's families. The mid-1950s concern about the nation's young people was a continuation of the perceived social strain caused by absent fathers and overworked mothers during the war. The studio adopted the catchy phrase,

"Rebel Without a Cause" and completely transformed the story. Three troubled middle-class teenagers living in a Los Angeles, California, suburb replaced the characteristic East Coast urban youth as the film's protagonists. This was a natural migration, as moviegoers by this time were trained to see the city of angels as an archetypal setting for postwar America.[7]

Rebel Without a Cause opens with a shot overlooking Los Angeles, suggesting another urban story of delinquent behavior. However, the setting quickly changes to a suburban street where a drunk Jim Stark (James Dean) falls to the sidewalk. The police take him to a rather clean station filled with troubled youth. Judy (Natalie Wood) is another teen caught wandering the streets at night, an activity immediately suspect in the suburban environment.[8] She left the family Easter celebration because her father called her "a dirty tramp" for wearing lipstick. A third youth, Plato (Sal Mineo), killed some puppies and has been called in for questioning. His parents, through divorce and lack of love, have abandoned him to the care of a family servant.

What are these teenagers rebelling against? They have their own rooms, cars, stylish clothing, servants, and ample leisure time. Yet, the three suffer from familial dysfunction; parental absence in the case of Plato, lack of love and understanding for Judy, and the sexual imbalance of Jim Stark's family that is "tearing him apart."[9] It is the failure of adult society that brings three teenagers to a police station on Easter Sunday.

The Starks' experience is typical of postwar western mobility. As Jim explains in the police station, his family believed that in a California suburb, "everything'll be roses and sunshine." Despite changing hometowns, the problems remain. Jim's parents fail to understand the source of Jim's discontent. Their reaction to his continuing misbehavior is one of incredulity. His father questions; "Don't I buy you everything you want? A bicycle? A car?" Jim asks the police officer, "How can anyone grow up in this circus?"

The next day begins at Dawson High, a school with palm trees and students sporting the typical West Coast casualness of T-shirts and jeans. Jim joins the junior class field trip to the Griffith Observatory, but at the planetarium Judy's group meets his friendly overtures with hostility. Buzz, the group's leader and Judy's boyfriend, challenges Jim to a knife fight. Their confrontation offers vistas of the Los Angeles Valley in the blinding sunshine, an atypical setting for teenage violence. Buzz calls Jim a "chicken," and challenges him to a "Chicky run" that evening. The contest involves racing two cars toward a steep cliff; the first to jump before the car pitches over to the ocean below is the loser. The fun and games turn tragic as Buzz is unable to escape his car in time, and with a fiery crash both cars fall into the sea.

The accident's aftermath brings Jim, Judy, and Plato together. However, it causes the final break between Jim and his parents. Jim's father discourages his decision to confess his role to the police, telling him, "You can't be idealistic all your life." Jim rushes to the police station but finds no one willing to listen. With Buzz's gang in pursuit, Jim takes Judy to a deserted mansion in the Hollywood hills, a hideout of Plato's. The three troubled youth play house, each assuming a familial role and filling a vacancy in their lives.

The arrival of Buzz's gang ends this playful pretending, terrorizing Plato while Jim and Judy are upstairs. Plato shoots one of his attackers, escaping to the Griffith Observatory. With police in pursuit, Jim and Judy follow, trying to save Plato from a violent end. Jim removes the bullets from Plato's gun, but a trigger-happy policeman shoots him as he flees. Jim's concerned parents appear, and over Plato's body his father quiets the mother and insists he can be the strong role model that Jim needs.[10]

Studio executives, sensitive to criticism of its exploitation of juvenile delinquency, closely monitored the film's content. The Production Code governing sexual and violent content still operated, and the subject matter made censors all the more skittish. The finished film excised innuendo about Judy and Jim's sexual relationship, downplayed hints of incestual feelings in Judy's family, and subdued violent confrontations. Despite these limitations, director Nicholas Ray tried to create a realistic film.[11] Ray researched juvenile delinquency cases at the Los Angeles Police Department, incorporating "rituals" of the lifestyle into the screenplay.[12] The more realism, it was assumed, the better the movie would perform at the box office. James Dean, in an interview before the film's release, argued that young moviegoers didn't want "some far-off idyllic conception of behavior." For the film to resonate, Dean believed, it had to "show what it's really like."[13]

Warner Brothers promoted the film as a tale of suburban delinquency, with advertisements displaying sensitivity to the troubled teens' plight. A magazine poster promised the "challenging drama of today's juvenile violence," calling Dean a "teenager – from a good family . . . their families gave them everything – but a good example."[14] An ad in *Variety* provocatively suggested, "Maybe the police should have picked up the parents instead!"[15] Another ad ominously asked, "Jim Stark – a kid in the year 1955 – what makes him tick . . . like a bomb?"[16] The hype prepared moviegoers for the film's themes and unique setting.

Rebel was a controversial box-office hit. The "child-parent hostility theme" alarmed some moviegoers, while youth educators and officials praised *Rebel* for bringing to light the pervasive delinquency the country faced beyond class and racial boundaries. The director of clinical services for the California Youth Authority commended the film for challenging the "defensive and often condescending smugness" of those who "refuse to believe that delinquency is not just a matter of 'unfortunate circumstances.' "[17]

Unlike teen movies before it, the film's setting was a "split-level upper-middle-class Los Angeles milieu," away from the seedy big-city underworld typically portrayed.[18] Reviews of *Rebel* keenly recognized the transposition of the traditional juvenile delinquent setting. *Films in Review* described the "social distortion" where "teenagers from decent but inharmonious homes are made to behave as though they came from crime-infested slums."[19] *Time* believed the film sought "to show that juvenile delinquency is not just a local outbreak of tenement terror but a general infection of modern U.S. society."[20] *Variety* attributed the "shock value" of the film to the "pleasant middle class community" in which the story unfolds. The "boys and girls attend a modern high school . . . are well fed and dressed and drive their own automobiles."[21] The *New York Times* critic called *Rebel* a "violent, brutal and disturbing picture of modern teen-agers . . . children of well-to-do parents, living in comfortable homes and attending a well-appointed high school in the vicinity of Los Angeles."[22]

The film used the Los Angeles area as a visual stand-in for the postwar American suburb. This location gave the film more power and hinted that California, despite its "land of sunshine" image, was not immune to problems of delinquency. The setting made the film more disturbing than previous film treatments of delinquency. If it could happen in a California suburb, the film suggested, it could happen anywhere.

Rebel placed among the year's top grossing films and inspired a generation of critical writing on its meaning. Despite the controversy surrounding the film when it was first released, cultural critics and film historians have come to notice the intrinsic conventionalism of the film. As Peter Biskind notes, these sentimentalized delinquents are "more moral, upstanding, and law-abiding than anyone else."[23] Another commentator points out that the trio's troubles stem from their parents' deficiencies, as people and role models. Fathers are weak, or lack the ability to give their children the love they need. Mothers are smothering, absent, or inconsequential.[24] It is the children who represent tradition and propriety, asking their parents to fulfill traditional roles and return to the status quo.[25] Although it contains a powerful "expression of middle-class alienation," critics Peter Roffman and Jim Purdy characterize the film as a "personal drama of identity crisis," not a critique that questions larger societal issues.[26]

The film's finale offers a profoundly conservative solution. Plato, the most severely troubled youth, does not survive. This conclusion makes rebelliousness truly without cause, as the reasons behind Jim's dissatisfaction disappear with Plato's violent death.[27] The Starks' reconciliation and the possibilities of a new family beginning with Judy and Jim end the film on a hopeful note.[28] The film does not reject the mainstream values of the era; in fact, it celebrates them. Jim Stark rebels to join society, to be accepted into the dominant culture.[29] Economic need does not drive these teenagers to commit crimes or adopt delinquent behavior, nor is their environment deficient in material comfort. James Dean played a rebel only in the white, middle-class sense of the word, protesting his parents' materialism and lack of real love and support.[30]

Rebel appeared at an important moment in developing images of baby boom youth, and California's role was critical. Palm trees, ocean bluffs, and mansions in the Hollywood Hills provided recognizable landmarks, placing the film specifically in California. In the minds of many moviegoers, the young people from the Golden State typically enjoyed the mobility, leisure time, and affluence of the teenagers portrayed. Some analyses recognize the connections between the film and its setting. Critic David Thompson, remembering his first reaction, felt a kinship to California teens, even though, he admits, "this California adolescence was unlike my own in many ways."[31] Film historian Nora Sayre, a self-proclaimed "easterner and cultural snob," recalls being impressed by "the lavishness of technology in education and the loutishness of the students and the fact that all of them had cars." For Sayre, the "eroticism of California only highlighted the passions portrayed – if only more New Englanders and New Yorkers had been able to yell like that."[32]

Using the setting of suburban California, a place rapidly becoming the ultimate destination of postwar families, made the film disturbing for many moviegoers. Yet, despite the juvenile delinquency perspective, middle-class rewards shower the characters in *Rebel*. Viewers of the film could take away a cautionary message, but they might also recall the attractive locale and the privilege and comfort enjoyed by characters in the film. The conservative slant of *Rebel*, the hope for understanding and reconciliation within the nuclear family, suggests a connection with emerging cultural beliefs about California's promise for the future.

Driving his "channeled" 1949 Mercury, Jim Stark represented postwar California youth.[33] James Dean's untimely end also reified images of California: a turnpike car crash in his hot rod, en route to weekend road races in Salinas.[34] His death, three days before the opening of *Rebel Without a Cause*, heightened his mystique. The "posthumous worship" of the star puzzled many who failed to understand why "thousands of teenagers have made a religion of his memory."[35] The extraordinary reaction to Dean was demographic, cinematic, and mythic. As the numbers of teenagers grew, baby boomers comprised larger percentages of the moviegoing public. His screen persona resonated with those who dreamed of life in California.

For the rest of the 1950s, films designed to appeal to teenagers bore some resemblance to the environment of *Rebel* and often featured a Dean-like character.[36] Major and minor studios released dozens of teen-marketed films with middle-class settings depicting juvenile delinquency in all its exploitable forms. These teen films exhaustively mined the subject matter brought to the fore by *Rebel*'s success. Smaller studios such as American International Pictures (AIP) appealed to younger audiences with tales of troubled teens. Dozens of titles, such as *Juvenile Jungle* (1958) and *Dangerous Youth* (1958), reveal studio preoccupation with middle-class teenagers gone wrong.[37]

These imitative films shared *Rebel*'s conservatism and did not delve deeply into the social psychology of teenage rebellion. The most provocative features were their advertisements, titles, and posters, often conceived before production began, and designed for the growing drive-in crowd. Hot-rodding, high school violence, sexual rebellion, teenage reform schools, crime stories, drug abuse, motorcycle gangs – all were popular plot contrivances.[38] In 1957, two years after *Rebel*'s release, *Variety* bemoaned "the seemingly endless spate of tales about teenagers and parents who don't dig them."[39] The schism between adult and youth movies had grown, ending the universal appeal of the Hollywood product. A Motion Picture

Association study in 1958 revealed that 58 percent of moviegoers were under the age of twenty-five.[40]

Rebel and films inspired by its example targeted moviegoing youth, but as the 1950s progressed, the make-up of that focus audience shifted. Concerns about juvenile delinquency lessened as the generation scarred by the Depression and war aged. Baby boomers, those just beginning to enter their teenage years in the late 1950s, were the future of film. *Variety* predicted that these youth, schooled in mass media and hungry for their own icons, offered moviemakers the "potential for a great attendance revival."[41] These young people were ripe for new heroes.

This generational shift in moviegoers was reflected in the theme and content of Hollywood films. As the movie capital began to value its youth audience for survival, the focus of teen-marketed movies changed. A new protagonist emerged, again out of suburban California. In the same setting as Jim Stark and facing similar problems, but with a tone more in tune with changing cultural beliefs and societal needs, Hollywood introduced a new California kid. *Gidget* ushered in the "clean teenpic" era, with its draw to young female moviegoers while offering bikinis, surf, and sand to its male constituency.[42] Hollywood's portrayal of "tomboy and teenybopper heroines" toward the end of the decade turned teenagers into paragons of innocence, a picture miles away from mid-1950s youth portrayals.[43]

This turn away from juvenile delinquency was partly cyclical, as Hollywood major and minor studios had exhausted the genre and their patrons with tales of teenage crime. The change was cultural as well. Walt Disney pioneered the wholesome image of baby boomers, casting California kids as stars. The timing of Disney-produced entertainment mirrored and moved the transition of screen icons, as film teens became less rebellious and more committed to the status quo as espoused on *The Mickey Mouse Club*. From where but California could the new character emerge? Gidget, the teenager with the surfer nickname, would ride a wave of popularity that reached almost every media outlet from the late 1950s to mid-1960s. Her success and longevity hinted at the altered cultural environment that nurtured dreams of California living.

Gidget's road to stardom began with Southern California fifteen-year-old Kathy Kohner, the daughter of Frederick Kohner, a Hollywood screenwriter. One mid-1950s summer, Kathy joined the surfing crowd on Malibu Beach, adopting the "bizarre slang" and learning how to brave the waves. In 1957, Kohner turned his daughter's summer experiences into a novel.

Columbia Pictures recognized the screen potential of such a California-based tale and purchased the rights for $50,000 and 5 percent of the gross. *Life* profiled father, daughter, and their literary collaboration in October 1957. The story's photos focused on the "real-life Gidget," with Kathy frolicking in sun and sand. The images showed the girl surfer flanked by "muscular, deeply tanned surfboarding pals," "shooting the curl," sitting near her surfboard in the "California sun," and putting her board in a convertible car. Gidget represented baby boom consumerism, enjoying all the "gadgets" – a car, surfboard, swimsuits, and leisure time – that surfing required. The article was sure to point out, however, that Kathy's surfboarding was just a harmlessly fun hobby. While "surfing talk on the phone fills many hours," this California girl was also starting to think "a little less of surfing and more about school work and getting into college." *Gidget* sold best on the West Coast, but found readers far away from surfing territory.[44]

Some critics praised the book, comparing it to *Catcher in the Rye*.[45] In the popular paperback version, Kohner included references to *Playboy* and smoking marijuana, and sprinkled his story with colorful phrases such as "bitchin'."[46] The film adaptation offered a milder version of the beach, toning down the strong language and putting a sanitized Hollywood glow on Gidget's summer activities. The script excised overt references to sex and swearing and involved Gidget's parents in a larger role as well-meaning guardians. The object of her affection, Moondoggie, became on the big screen a well-off Princeton man masquerading as a surf bum, fulfilling both the teenage and adult ideals. This Ivy League surfer also satisfied the democratic requirements of the California ideology. Moondoggie represented a "regular guy" enjoying the beach, just as Marty in *Spin and Marty* had become westernized on the ranch.

The film focused on what had made the book popular, offering an inside look at a California youth subculture on the brink of becoming a national obsession. As a "reel" depiction of the teenage Southern California world, *Gidget* provided international exposure to the state's surfing scene for the first time. The film helped define a marketable and attractive West Coast teenage lifestyle, an avenue that surprisingly had escaped commercialization.[47]

In contrast to the film cycle that *Rebel* inspired, *Gidget* represented a new type of film youth, a more comforting version of the American teenager. Using the novel as its text and responding to changing notions of

America's young people, adult filmmakers and screenwriters crafted a story with a heroine marked by conformity, despite her membership in a mildly rebellious surfing clique. *Gidget*'s story takes place in a homogenous world, filled with wholesome, well-meaning young people who simply love the beach. Despite this focus on carefree amusement, the film ends with a reassumption of adult responsibility and acceptance of society's roles. With the California beach as the locus of action, *Gidget*'s audience entered a story defined by place, just as *Rebel*'s audiences experienced the California suburb. The film helped influence the developing images of teen life in the Golden State.

Gidget's opening credits and theme song set the stage for a breezy coming-of-age look at teenage life, far removed from the harsh tone of earlier films. Frances Lawrence (Sandra Dee) begins the film with voice-over narration: "This summer was the turning point in my life. For sixteen years I'd gone blindly along, enjoying life." Her friends drag her from childhood, forcing a trip to the beach for her "first manhunt." Her disinterest annoys her seemingly more mature friends, who wonder if Frances needs "a few hormone shots." Unable to snag the attention of surfers, the friends leave Frances to her snorkeling. While swimming, she is caught in some kelp. A surfboard rescue by Moondoggie (James Darren) results in a crush on both rescuer and board.

Frances begs her parents for surfboard money, exuding excitement for her newfound passion. Her father, with his wallet, holds the key "to sheer heaven or months and months of stark solitude." As part of her plea, Frances exuberantly exclaims that surfing is "outta this world. You just can't imagine the thrill of shooting the curl. It positively surpasses every living emotion I've ever had!" With the money from her father, Frances believes she has a "gilt-edged guarantee for a summer of pure happiness."

The surfer clan allows Frances to become part of the group, dubbing her Gidget, a nickname derived from girl and midget. To ingratiate herself, Gidget happily serves, running food errands for the surfers and responding good-naturedly to the group's initiation rites. Kahuna is the group's leader and the most accomplished wave rider, as he is able to complete a surfing run with a still lit cigar. Gidget becomes a mother figure to Kahuna, offering to make his coffee on their first meeting, since she's a "wizard in the kitchen," and asking pointed questions about his life decisions. The other surfers are part-time surf bums, beach-bound in summer but in college by September. The object of Gidget's chief affection, Moondoggie, is the true rebel of the film. He rejects his allowance checks, determined to join Kahuna in the life of a surfer bum and forgo college despite his father's wishes.

After another unfortunate run-in with kelp, Gidget is grounded by illness for two weeks. As she convalesces, she determines to accomplish two things: first, to "be the best female surfer in California," and second, to capture Moondoggie's heart. Despite her mother's admonition that "it's not up to you, it's up to the young man," she maps out "a plan of attack."

The "bang-up finish to the whole summer" is a luau on the beach. Paying one of the surfers to take her, Gidget hopes to inspire jealousy in Moondoggie. The luau date provides the climactic clash between Gidget and her previously supportive parents. Disappointed that his daughter's escort is not a "gentleman" who will pick her up, Mr. Lawrence is even more aghast as his daughter reveals she had to pay for the date and is stealing food from the family fridge as an additional bribe. The father bellows, "What kind of insanity has taken over this family? . . . Is this what the boy of today wants?" Gidget's reply is the boldest expression of rebellion, both to her parents and society's rules, contained in the film. She responds, "The man I'm after sure does want something, and I'll see he gets it!"

Defying her parents, Gidget drives to meet her date for the luau. As luck would have it, the surfer she hired has given the job to Moondoggie, fouling up her master plan. At the beach they find Hollywood's version of a beach party, featuring intoxicated surfers without scenes of actual drinking.[48] A singing group, played by the wholesome Four Preps, provides the entertainment. Their singing promotes the group and the film's "with-it" rock and roll appeal. Meanwhile, as Moondoggie pretends to adore Gidget, he enjoys his own soundtrack opportunity to perform.

Gidget misleads Moondoggie, telling him that Kahuna was the target of her jealousy scheme and lies about her plans to attend one of his "little private parties" at a beach shack. Kahuna unknowingly obliges Gidget and, once her intentions are clear, plays along, offering her beer and creating mood lighting. Despite her earlier bravado, Gidget is unable and unwilling to overcome her inhibitions and challenge traditional sexual mores. Moondoggie crashes the party, and as Gidget runs away, Kahuna sees this as the opportunity to dissuade his would-be surf bum partner from joining the profession. Upset by Kahuna's apparent mistreatment of Gidget, they scuffle, and a nosy neighbor calls the police. A flat tire strands Gidget on the road, where the police pick her up and take her to the station.

Her parents, having learned of her jaunt at the beach shack, have also gone to the police station to report their daughter missing. A heartfelt reunion occurs, despite the police officer intoning, "We found her on the road, she'd obviously been at a shack where they'd been drinking beer, had a fist fight." With the threat of grounding and a traumatic evening behind her, Gidget gladly returns home.

The next morning her erstwhile friends from the beginning of the summer return, expressing pity for her lack of beach conquest. Gidget is also despondent. She informs her mother, "After all those hours of concentrated effort, I come home as pure as the driven snow." Her mother simply explains that she has misunderstood the definition of womanhood and points to her grandmother's cross-stitch sampler that reads, "To be a real woman is to bring out the best in a man." Her rebellious attitude of the previous evening has vanished with maturity and a better understanding of the true feminine role replacing it.

Gidget's father arranges a date with Jeffrey Matthews, the son of a business acquaintance in town for the summer. Jeffrey and Moondoggie, it is revealed, are the same person. Gidget begrudgingly joins him for a farewell to the beach, where they meet Kahuna, who has decided to rejoin the working world. This change is due to Gidget's influence, who as Kahuna remarks "might be pint size, but she's quite a woman." Jeff/Moondoggie finally expresses his love, offering her his fraternity pin. The final scene is one more panoramic view of the California beach, with happy kids in love strolling down the sand.[49] As the couple walks, with casual clothes replaced by more formal attire, the beach is transformed from a surfing haven of teenage fun to an affirmation of traditional values. Kahuna recognizes the value of work over leisure, while Jeff returns to Princeton to get an education and, it is assumed, to later marry Gidget. The film offers a confirmation of American values and ideas about work, leisure, sex, family, and marriage, set in the reassuring beach culture of the California coast.

Gidget was a perfect vehicle for Sandra Dee. She starred in both *A Summer Place*, a melodramatic tale of summer romance at the beach, and *Gidget* in 1959. Both films helped cement her place in the teenage pantheon of stars, with her primary appeal among female moviegoers.[50] By playing a "regular kid on the beach," Dee found a loyal following.[51] In a *Newsweek* interview, Dee explained that her "fan mail jumped" after *Gidget*'s release and attributed her continued success to the fact that "[studios are] making a lot of movies for the teen-age audience and I can play a girl of twelve or nineteen."[52]

Dee was one of the top ten box office stars from 1960 to 1963.[53] As "queen of the screaming teenies," she shared that rank with popular adult actresses Elizabeth Taylor and Doris Day.[54] Magazine profiles highlighted Dee's "pals" relationship with her mother and her California youth fantasy lifestyle. When work on the movie set ended at 4:00 in the afternoon, fans learned, "She removes her makeup and jumps behind the wheel of her Thunderbird, bought on her sixteenth birthday with her $1,000 weekly salary."[55] Dee stood in for baby boomers of all ages in her movie adventures, and then lived the dream life of a California star.

The songs in *Gidget* brought surf culture into popular music for the first time.[56] The Four Preps provided the rock and roll appeal, "clean cut college boys" suited to the film's tone. The foursome first won fans with their number-two hit "26 Miles (Santa Catalina)" in 1958, a tune romanticizing the idyllic island not far from the California shore.[57] In the film, the group sang the title song and another one of their hits from 1958, "Cinderella." James Darren's version of "Gidget" reached number forty-one on the Billboard charts. Its lyrics reinforced the film's traditional values, the joys of adolescent activities, and the eventuality of marriage and happiness. According to music historian Richard Aquila, the song was one of "the worst hit records ever palmed off to the public as rock and roll," but it revealed a market for soft pop tied into a successful film.[58]

Columbia was a major studio, and consequently numerous newspapers and magazines reviewed *Gidget*. What stood out in the majority of these critiques was the film's California location and its focus on largely innocuous, fun-loving, middle-class kids. For teenagers, the most authoritative statement came from Dick Clark, the popular host of *American Bandstand* and adult representative of the late 1950s "clean teen" movement in music and movies. A *Seventeen* advertisement headlined "Dick Clark Goes for *Gidget*" read: "Hey Gang, I just saw something that's the greatest! It's a new movie . . . all about a cute teen and her fabulous Summer with the surfboarders at Malibu Beach. It's the first movie I've ever endorsed this way – and I'm sure you'll go for "Gidget," too!" The pictures in the ad featured Sandra Dee curled up on the telephone, with inset photos of the film's principal actors and The Four Preps. Showing Gidget on the shoulders of Moondoggie and Kahuna, the ad proclaimed, "She's the Sweetheart of the Beach Generation."[59] The advertisement reinforced the film's wholesome image and content, clearly marking the differences between *Gidget* and earlier teen films. There are no dangerous words in the film's title, no images of cars, weapons, or delinquency. The heralding of a "beach generation" indicated that rebellion had crested and receded, while California's surfers were riding high.

Reviews in adult periodicals also highlighted the sharp contrast between *Gidget* and earlier teen films in the *Rebel* mold. *Variety* offered a possible subtitle for *Gidget*: "I Was a Normal Teen-Age American." As a "classic teen-age comedy in which the kids are, for once, healthy and attractive young people instead of in some phase of juvenile depravity," the reviewer commended the break with the teenage film tradition. He made special note of the appealing setting, "mostly out of doors on the ocean front west of Los Angeles that constitutes the play grounds and mating grounds for the young of the area." Despite its spring debut, he wrote, the film "effectively captures the summer spirit."[60] This review, in calling *Gidget* a "normal teen-age American," revealed a cultural belief about California kids. Sun and surf could be utilized as symbols of wholesome conformity, offering a reassuring setting for tales of nondelinquents.

Library Journal also endorsed this vision of the nation's youth, describing *Gidget* as a "wholesome teen-age film which shows that adolescence is not necessarily synonymous with delinquency." As a bonus, the film also captured "the full excitement" of the beach and surfing for its viewers.[61] The *New York Times* praised the film for its enchanting beach scenes and its pleasant "surf portrait of adolescent America" with a "relaxed air befitting its nice young people." The film was "enough to make anybody leave one of the neighborhood theaters . . . and light out for Long Island sound." With the story focusing on "the balmy California shore," it was the perfect way "to usher in the beach season."[62]

Films and Filming, a British film journal, argued that *Gidget* was "little more than the basis for a mass of exhilarating surfing shots, and some amusing dialogue of the 'real cool' American teenage variety." However, the reviewer welcomed the "relief from the cheap sensationalism" of teen exploitation films and hoped that the youth portrayed were "more typical of the American way of life."[63] Typical or not, viewed as a foreign film, *Gidget*'s depiction of California teenagers was seen as representative of young life in the United States. A British reviewer in *Sight and Sound* was not as sympathetic, challenging in his estimation the falseness of its por-

Columbia Pictures advertised the original *Gidget* movie in the March 1959 *Seventeen* with Dick Clark as its cheerful advocate. Along with Clark's endorsement, this "cute teen and her fabulous Summer" in California stood as the main draw to teenage moviegoers.

(Columbia Pictures)

trayal. He criticized the teenagers in *Gidget* as "characters dutifully quaint but never funny" with an "emotional pitch wavering from timid satire to sentimentality." This "teenage musical set at Malibu Beach" was a disservice to real teenagers, who have "more spontaneous gaiety than this and surely deserve something a little more up-to-date."[64]

Historians and cultural critics have shared the opinions of contemporary reviewers. Film histories dismiss *Gidget*, disregarding its commercial success and the longevity of its title character. Those analyses fail to see the value of a closer examination, preferring to explore more artistically or thematically powerful films. Feminist film historians have devoted some attention to *Gidget*, describing Sandra Dee as part of Hollywood's "transition between the fifties' naiveté and the sixties' nymphet." Marjorie Rosen argues that *Gidget* represented an ideal, who by the end of the film "emerges with a boyfriend, an ability to surf, a new femininity, and the knowledge that she helped redirect the life-style of a perennial bum."[65] Julie Burchill writes that *Gidget* signified "America's pat on the back," demonstrating that the country "must be doing something right to produce a teen-ager as cute, high spirited, decent, and just all-around wonderful as Gidget."[66] Others point to the insurgent rebellion beyond the film's suburban veneer. In some ways, surfing did contain hints of subversion against "middle-class objectives."[67] However, the surfers in *Gidget* are part-time bums and full-time members of society. The film gave surfing a middle-class spin, portraying surfers on vacation from more mainstream pursuits.

What critics failed to see was any connection between *Rebel* and *Gidget*, the two most notable suburban California teen films of the period. Rosen points to the "surface romantic gloss" that the two films share but fails to delve deeper in her comparison.[68] Warner Brothers marketed *Rebel* as a dramatic melodrama of family conflict, and Columbia Pictures advertised *Gidget* as an "amusing comedy."[69] An examination of both films reveals the power of their shared setting and helps chronicle the evolution of California youth images.

Despite differences in tone and subject matter, the films are linked by time and place. The middle-class suburban home is the locus of conflict. Most notably, both films feature dramatic staircase parent-child confrontations, representing the central and superior place of the child in the family configuration. The California and nonfamily activities of the two teens – drag racing, surfing, luaus, and joyriding – drive the plot. Gidget and Jim both are high school juniors and only children, spoiled by convertibles and allowances. Their cars provide escape from the house and from parents in similarly staged climactic scenes. Both teens are enmeshed in middle-class consumerism and absorb their identities from material goods. The two films demonstrate the inherent flaws of a family that lacks the support of church, school, or extended relatives.

Jim and Gidget could have been neighbors, but there are some key disparities. Unlike the mother in *Rebel*, Gidget's mother is close to her teenage daughter, playing a key role and guiding the moral tone of the film. It is she who teaches Gidget the power that "good girls" wield.[70] The characters express their rebelliousness in very different ways. Gidget couches her challenges to parental control with "I don't mean to be edgy or rude to you, but oh gee, I've got a real serious problem." When expressing disagreement, she insists, "I don't mean to yell, or be fresh."

Gidget, like Jim, asks advice of her elders. However, she questions her mother, who is confident of her answers, unlike Jim's father, who vacillates and frustrates Jim with his lack of surety and parental knowledge. The two films both feature emasculated fathers, with voices that lack authority. Mr. Stark wears an apron, while Mr. Lawrence's voice cracks when angered. Yet the Lawrence home does not share the turmoil of the Stark household; the proper role of mother and father are well defined. Gidget's parents express concern but lack the controlling confusion that plagues the Stark family.

Both films include key scenes at a police station, with authorities offering guidance to the troubled teens and their families. In *Rebel*, these scenes introduce the main characters and the seriousness of their family problems. *Gidget* uses the situation for laughs, with officers volunteering unneeded advice to both wayward parents and child. While Jim's parents coddle him, the Lawrences establish limits for Gidget. However, their discipline consists mainly of brief voice raising, such as, "Francie, shut off that infernal racket."

On a deeper level, the films have more similarities than differences of theme, both offering a spectrum of teen experience, different in tone if not in kind. The films are about the trials of adolescence, the masks worn and the techniques employed to win friends and conform. The main characters express such statements directly, dramatizing the pitfalls of growing up. Jim Stark explains his wish to the cop at the station: "Boy, if I had one day when I didn't have to be all confused and ashamed of everything – or I felt I belonged some place." Judy's mother dismisses her daughter's problems:

"She'll outgrow it, dear. It's just the age. . . . It's the age when nothing fits." Gidget expresses a similar sentiment when she feels out of place among her friends: "I guess I just don't belong anymore." She has trouble fitting into the boy-crazy world of her friends. Her mother recognizes her daughter's difficulties by saying, "Growing up is a very slow and painful process for a girl."

The issue of "sincerity" in adolescence appears in both films. In *Rebel*, Judy fails to behave true to herself. She tells Jim, "You shouldn't believe what I said," explaining that her identity remains hidden when she's with "the kids." Gidget's girlfriends put on an act at the beach to attract attention and then abandon her. The surfers are incapable of revealing their true feelings or motivation in front of the group. Moondoggie hides his interest in the tomboy. Gidget resorts to trickery to win her surfer. Kahuna is "Burt Vail," a veteran pilot, and Moondoggie is Jeffrey Matthews, a Princeton boy, disguised.

The films' conclusions offer a final parallel. *Rebel* ends with a reaffirmation of the middle-class family, the implied future union of Jim and Judy, and the traditional role reassumed by Jim's father. *Gidget* also endorses the status quo. Gidget turns rebellious Kahuna into an upstanding employed citizen and helps Jeff decide to return to Princeton. The male characters end the movie rejoining the mainstream, and the coupling of Jeff and Gidget fulfills the dreams of both parents and teenagers. While *Rebel* is a melodramatic film about delinquency and *Gidget* is a lighthearted comedy about teen romance, the two films offer key insights into popular ideas surrounding California's youth.

How to explain the lingering popularity of the smiling Gidget, only a few years after the iconic appearance of brooding Jim Stark? The California youth image, personified by Gidget and heralded in dozens of popular culture venues, overpowered earlier portrayals of suburban youth in trouble. *Gidget* marked the big-screen arrival of teen heroes and heroines more in keeping with changed beliefs about the nation's youth. She emerged out of the nation's celebration of life in California, a party where Jim Stark was not welcome and seemed out of place. In four short years, the image of California teen traveled from suburban delinquency to the beach. Significantly, Jim Stark did not experience the popular culture longevity that Gidget enjoyed. With a change of gender, filmmakers hit upon a formula suited to magazine profiles touting California as a "teenager's paradise."

In purchasing the *Gidget* novel, Columbia Pictures undoubtedly perceived the box office possibilities of the surfing story. Perhaps those behind the scenes understood the connection between their film and the growing mythology surrounding California's youth. The best evidence for Gidget's cultural resonance was her continued presence on America's movie screens. Judging from ticket receipts, filmmakers found a heroine who appealed to millions of moviegoers, primarily young people but also adults who found her teenage adventures entertaining and reassuring.

The success of the first *Gidget* film inspired two sequels. *Gidget Goes Hawaiian* appeared in 1961, with Deborah Walley replacing Sandra Dee in a film more concerned with teenage appeal than a family audience. James Darren reprised his role, and several other characters from the first film made the trip to Hawaii. The film's plot involved romantic misunderstandings and dramatic break-ups while on vacation, with parents in tow.[71]

Critics were in disagreement over the film's quality. *Variety* declared that "those who may have been surf-bored with the Sandra Dee starrer of a few years back will find even less to cheer about in the follow-up." The entertainment industry paper, confused about the target audience for the film, explained, "It is not quite sophisticated enough in its depiction of the modern young person to win the favor of the older teenager and yet, in tangling uneasily with several ticklish adult issues, it won't make too satisfactory an attraction in sports for the younger teener." *Variety* did salute the casting of the young California vacationers, calling them "fresh and promising young people whose looks make them likely targets for a barrage of fan mail and juvenile adulation."[72] The *New York Times* review characterized Gidget as the "briskly virtuous teenager who magnetizes beach boys," praising the "bouncy pretty Hawaiian scenery" as the film's sole drawing point.[73] The *Los Angeles Times*, on the other hand, called the film a "worthy sequel" showing a "coterie of precocious, but not delinquent, juveniles" who "frolic on the beach and engage in the affairs of the heart."[74]

The successful box office of the Hawaiian adventure led to the production of a second sequel, *Gidget Goes to Rome*, released in the summer of 1963. In this film Gidget escapes the confines of her California teen identity and becomes a world traveler, representing teenage America on a goodwill tour. The second sequel featured Italian scenery in place of ocean waves, with Cindy Carol in the leading role. *Teen* heralded Carol, chosen to play the ideal California girl, as having won "the most enviable role in cinema history."[75] *Seventeen* featured an interview with Carol in July 1963, highlighting her California background. The actress explained that her casting in the role was natural, because, she said, unlike Sandra Dee, "[I am] practically . . . a Gidget myself. I surf and spend loads of time at the beach, and the story of the first movie was almost my own. . . . I'm about ninety-two percent like Gidget."[76]

Seventeen chose *Gidget Goes to Rome* as its picture of the month for August 1963, calling the film, "the latest, and in many ways, the best of the trio of films about the popular teen heroine."[77] The film even inspired a special fashion line spotlighted in the teen magazine. The collection featured: wool sweaters for "young intellectuals on a Roman Holiday"; girdles "for young Gidgets in air-borne Lycra"; and dresses inspired by the film "in a rich Roman plaid."[78] *Seventeen*, the teenage Bible of fashion, acted as Gidget's patron, revealing a powerful fan base for the California girl.

Some adult reviewers enjoyed Gidget's continuing adventures. The *New York Times* review described her as that "wholesome American Girl with the wide-eyed appeal."[79] Other publications were not as kind. *Variety* was the least charitable to the "losing cause" with a "limp screenplay," charging, "If this is the best that can be done with Gidget, then the time has come to discontinue the series." The reviewer questioned whether the audience of "young people for whom this third and skimpiest installment presumably [was designed]" would discover anything "of even remote interest or stimulation."[80] *Time* headlined its review "Surf Boredom," giving low marks for the newest adventure of the "wholesome as a popsicle . . . chirpily brazen and healthily sneakershod" heroine.[81] *Gidget Goes to Rome* received Harvard Lampoon's award for 1963's worst movie of the year.[82]

Despite critical drubbing on the big screen, the Gidget character still enjoyed popularity among teens, and Kohner penned several more novels chronicling her adventures.[83] His books appeared in ten different languages and sold a million copies worldwide.[84] These world adventures in novels and films took Gidget away from the source of her appeal. In California, the home of movies and television, studio production for the big and small screens was interconnected. This meant that a character from a novel brought to the big screen could become a television subject. In 1965, Gidget conquered yet another medium, returning her to California and the beach.

The situation comedy *Gidget* followed a television programming tradition of using the California setting. Television producers employed familiar images of California suburbia, replacing nuclear family plots with tales of surf-loving teens on the beach. The *Gidget* TV show aired on ABC from

September 15, 1965, to September 1, 1966, and chronicled the teenage travails of the famous California teen.[85] Screen Gems, the television subsidiary of Columbia Pictures, produced the series. The network's interest in teenage girl protagonists was largely the result of falling ratings and an attempt to win the baby boom audience. *The Patty Duke Show* about identical cousins was another example of such programming.[86] That same fall, ABC premiered *Tammy*, based on the film series about a hillbilly girl's adventures.[87]

The idea for a television series developed in tandem with the movie sequels, with producers recognizing the weekly sitcom's potential. The first film's structure provided the early outlines for the series, similarly focused on the interaction between Gidget and the surfers.[88] In subsequent planning drafts, everyday high school life became a stronger component, taking some of the emphasis away from surfing.[89]

Television producer Harry Ackerman met with Gidget creator Frederick Kohner in 1961 to discuss series possibilities. Kohner preferred his original novel story to the movie version. The result was a decision to minimize the role of the mother, and instead focus on the father-daughter relationship, making the father a "professor of English in a Los Angeles college." The "beach background" remained important as "part of the special quality and feel" of the project. Ackerman had high expectations for the program. He hoped, he said, to create a "human comedy of extra proportions" and to "do our bit to decry the frightening rush toward conformity in this country and put in our word for the importance of the role of the individual."[90] Ackerman's goal seems curious for a sitcom about a good-natured and well-behaved California teen.

The producers conducted extensive screen and audience reaction tests to find just the right actress to play the television Gidget. After dozens of auditions, casting narrowed the field of prospective girl surfers to two actresses. Studio officials distributed questionnaires asking for comparative reactions and preferences to an audience ages twelve to fifteen.[91] A majority of respondents chose Sally Field, an eighteen-year-old California native. Field had enrolled in a Columbia Pictures actors' workshop the summer between high school and college, which led to her audition and casting for the series.[92] TV *Guide* reported that Field saw "the first *Gidget* movie six times," more than enough preparation for the part.[93] *Seventeen* spotlighted the actress in September 1965. Field described the show as "real," saying, "You can identify with them. That's the thing I like about *Gidget* — it makes

Sally Field poses as Gidget in a promotional shot for the television show of the same name. Field beams toward the camera, holding her surfboard and waiting for the next wave.

(Courtesy Harry Ackerman Collection, American Heritage Center, University of Wyoming)

much more sense to me than any of the other teen-age shows that I've seen."[94]

Paramount to the show's success was this "teen-aged authenticity," and while producers recognized the program's "primary appeal to teenagers," they hoped that the "father and daughter" angle would create "an all-family program."[95] The goal was to "appeal to both young and adult audiences who will readily identify with their counterparts on the screen."[96] Audience screen tests of the pilot revealed an "interesting discrepancy." Older viewers, while indicating that the show would be appealing to teenagers, "responded more favorably than younger viewers" to the program.[97] A divide existed between what young people enjoyed and what their elders believed they would appreciate. Adults admired the wholesome portrayals and positive relationships, but the show's success would depend on the identification teens felt toward the image.

Test audiences described the pilot program as "Good and wholesome entertainment . . . good for all the family." The father-daughter relationship received high marks, with the father described by one test viewer as "the way most parents should be." Viewers "especially enjoyed" the beach setting and surfing scenes.[98] Male audience members in particular expressed a desire for "more action, more surfing, and more of the beach setting." A different actress playing the role of Gidget posed no problem for viewers, who had few difficulties with the concept of "having seen a different Gidget in previous *Gidget* movies."[99] Respondents described Gidget as a "fun going American girl" representative of her generation as a "realistically" portrayed "typical California teenager."[100] Her California youth identity was the heart of the sitcom's marketed appeal.

This sitcom turned the novel and film character into a television one, charting in thirty-two episodes the "heartwarming adventures of Southern California teenager Frances Lawrence."[101] Promotional material described Gidget as "a winsome surf-bunny who is going through the same stages any kid her age is going through – and viewers both young and old are certain to love her and to empathize with her growing pains."[102] Her father became a widower in the series, making the focus of the show the relationship between the two. Another change from the film's cast of characters was the reinstatement of a meddling sister and her husband from the original novel. The show also introduced Larue, a misfit best friend. Moondoggie (Jeff), central to the film treatments, made only two appearances on the show, although references to him were pervasive. The show opened and closed with a monologue spoken directly to the camera, a voice-over narration technique used to "appear more authentic to girl viewers."[103] The sitcom's theme song highlighted the cuteness of the main character and utilized the setting of a safe California world.

TV Guide's fall season preview described the show as recounting "in moving detail the love affair between a girl and her surfboard," highlighting the innocence of its plots. The picture accompanying the series description showed father and daughter, stressing their relationship as the show's core.[104] The *Los Angeles Times* called the show and its star "delightful."[105] Partly a carryover of criticism that the *Gidget* film sequels received, other TV critics designated the show as "one of the ten programs television critics liked least" during the fall of its debut.[106] *Look*'s television critic savaged the show, calling it a "blank in my memory [except for the] surfboard."[107]

Despite its lack of critical acclaim, *TV Guide* profiled the sitcom on three separate occasions during the show's run. The first detailed Sally Field's attempt to learn Gidget's famous pastime, since the actress had never surfed. As the story explained, for the "new series about the surf set, the newest Gidget incarnation had to learn the ropes."[108] The next *TV Guide* feature, a story written by Gidget's original creator, retold the story of Kathy Kohner and the evolution of the book, film, and television character. The article's accompanying photo showed Frederick Kohner and Field looking over a copy of the book that had started it all.[109] The final *TV Guide* spotlight featured Field on the May 1966 cover of the magazine striking a Gidget-like pose. The title proclaimed, "Sally Field's Actually a Lot Like Gidget," with the article highlighting the similarities between the actress and the character she played. It emphasized Field's connections with family, friends, down-to-earth pursuits, and her future wishes of "getting married and having a family."[110] Field shared the qualities of other famous California teens. Like Annette, she remained a fine example of the state's youth despite her foray into the Hollywood world.

The show shared the characteristics of the *TV Guide* profiles: lighthearted comedy with dashes of surfing and teenage appeal. Episodes featured formulaic situation comedy plots: family misunderstandings, conflicts with friends, and high school minidramas in keeping with the show's boundaries and the carefree middle-class teenage life it portrayed. Much of the action took place on the California beach, and surfing footage played as opening and closing credits rolled. The pilot episode introduced Gidget and her "world of sun and fun" with beach and surfing scenes.[111] The show's second episode found Gidget "dateless for the class luau."[112] Her biggest dilemmas were falling in love, lacking a car of her own, working at a part-time job, and meeting prospective in-laws.[113]

The close relationship between father and daughter provided several episodes' worth of sitcom fodder. In "Is It Love or Symbiosis?" Professor Lawrence, worried he is too dependent, decides that a school in Paris for Gidget is the right thing for both of them. Rather than disappoint her father and what she believes is his desire for "la dolce vita," Gidget agrees to go. Before her departure, they realize the importance of their relationship and cancel the trip.[114] Other episodes explored Gidget's jealousy and concern surrounding her father's social life.[115]

There were attempts to keep current, to include in the show some part of a changing California. These episodes portrayed Gidget's well-meaning efforts to better the world and her propensity toward activism. "Operation Shaggy Dog," involved conflict between father and daughter over the bulldozing of a teenage hamburger hangout for a new art museum. With disagreements between adults and youth solved in sitcom time, easy compromises breached the generation gap. Despite the simple answers provided by the script, some have argued that the show occasionally went beyond surf tales to express a contemporary sensibility in its plots.[116]

For example, *Gidget* hinted at growing tensions between men and women, the idea of a boycott, and the weapon of protest, serious social problems and issues of the mid-1960s. In an episode entitled "The War between Men, Women and Gidget," Gidget "uses strategic tactics when a rival group invades her stretch of the beach."[117] In "Chivalry Isn't Dead, It's Just Hiding," the girls stage a boyfriend boycott to try to force their boyfriends to behave better.[118]

In employing these themes, however, *Gidget* was using them, as did most television of the era, as rhetoric, without the danger of their political content.[119] For example, folk music appeared in two episodes, both in comedic treatments. In "All the Best Diseases Are Taken," Gidget enlists "the aid of a folk singer to help stage a protest against 'unfair movie prices.'"[120] In the episode "Gidget's Career," Larue and Gidget are members of a folk singing group that "switches to rock and roll" to enter a television contest.[121] *Gidget* featured some references to a turbulent world. However, these issues appeared in sitcom fashion, draining them of any larger contextual meaning. The show asked audiences to enjoy the light-hearted adventures of a surfer girl, a performance of teenage life increasingly out of step with California realities.

As the 1960s progressed, teen shows proved less successful. Marked by conservatism, television presented teenagers as "universally inoffensive." As a result, TV networks retreated into a fantasy vision of youth, of which *Gidget* was a part.[122] These bland and safe images failed to attract the necessary viewers, leading to the network's decision to cancel the show in 1966, temporarily closing the door on the icon's adventures. The show's end after only one season met with some protest. A petition signed by 150 young women called it "one of the best teen-age shows ever put on the air" and begged that the program be renewed.[123]

Despite these small efforts, low ratings pointed to a show unable to connect with its targeted viewers. *Seventeen* included the program as evidence of TV's attempt to brainwash the nation's teenagers. The magazine criticized the *Gidget* world as "limited by parents, friends, little brother, dates and dances, apparel shops and soda fountains," complaining, "Civil Rights, college boards, difficult family problems simply don't exist." As a "living Barbie Doll," the writer jeered, Gidget and other TV characters demonstrated how "teens should really be," adding, "And if you're not, maybe you will absorb the lesson to the tinkling sound of sound-track laughter."[124] *Seventeen*'s dismissal of the program and charge of indoctrination marks a shift in the magazine and a cultural evolution. The light-hearted adventures of a surfer girl failed to connect with teen viewers, indicating a loss of identification with the series' version of young life in California.

Gidget's adventures held an evident lack of salience for the young television audience in 1966. New visions of California youth, angrily protesting instead of happily surfing, appeared. Yet, the surfer girl's influence on popular culture throughout the 1960s points to the power of the image. The safe suburban view of California teen life found producer, studio, and network interest, and its profitability indicated an eager audience. In contrast, network executives never pitched a television series called *Rebel Without a Cause*, the continuing adventures of Jim and Judy. The image of youth on screen evolved from well-meaning rebelliousness to cheeky surfing fun. The beach party mantle would later be picked up by AIP, as that studio attempted to recapture the Gidget magic at the box office.

As the cinematic Gidget traveled out of California in the early 1960s, more young people were journeying to the state through their consumption and viewing habits than ever before. As the sixties opened, the action was in California, with fads, fashions, and lifestyles influencing young people all across the country. These images were not limited or confined to one medium. Surfing provided one such commodified example, its explosive popularity helping to export exclusive images of California. Magazine articles and television profiles brought surfing to the nation, while a new brand of popular music domesticated the sport's more dangerous elements. As moviegoers swallowed a sugary package of "fun in the sun," young radio listeners tuned in the California sound. The music promoted images of white middle-class youth cruising to the beach in fashionable leisure clothes. The harmonies celebrated the predominant images of the state's youth, finding fans far away from the coast who dreamed of life in California.

CHAPTER FIVE

Wish They All Could Be California

The baby boom generation grew up in a mass media environment pervaded by California images. The state provided one of the main sources of cultural authority, an exploitable resource to advertisers and promoters eager to capture the teenage market. As *Variety* explained, "What's popular with them in the West is usually popular with them in the East."[1] The impression of young California, fostered by opinion- and image-makers, reflected an exclusive ideal, one of wholesome prosperity in the golden suburbs. The interconnections of California's media industries allowed this model to expand its reach into baby boomer pocketbooks while reassuring adults. For example, *Gidget* introduced surfing to the world, providing a glimpse into a slightly strange and hedonistic lifestyle. Subsequent media coverage helped reform surfing's image, selling California while it manufactured icons. This rehabilitation was tied to developments in popular music, as these images inspired the creation and popularity of teen anthems based on the cult of the automobile and the surfing craze. Record companies promoted musicians, most notably the Beach Boys, who sang of an endless summer filled with surfing, cruising, and beachcombing.

Landlocked teens could turn on the radio and vicariously enjoy the beach or a joyride. Dozens of artists exploited the musical fad in the early 1960s, topping the charts and inspiring fan devotion. The cultural environment that molded California teens into leisure-minded consumers guaranteed the success of the music singing their praises. The automobile craze could easily travel from its home in California, while surfing provided a test case, demonstrating the power of California youth images to move beyond geographical limitations. The craze's musical complement helped the sport overcome its negative reputation and become another shining example of California's youth.

Surfing came to the West Coast from Hawaii in the early 1900s. Between the two World Wars, the number of surfers grew, with the automobile allowing a small band to travel farther afield in search of the perfect wave. Pictures from the period document bronzed aficionados dedicated to the physical nature of the sport, enjoying records and parties on the beach. From a core group of about 5,000, the surfing population boomed after World War II.[2] In 1955, *Westways* reported, "Good California athletes by the hundreds are today turning their coordination surfward." With the invention of lighter boards and the allure of California's beaches, the magazine promised "lots of fun and excitement in the years to come."[3] As a 1958 *Saturday Evening Post* described, "Surfing is dangerous, but the thrill of sizzling down a mountainous wave at breakneck speed is drawing hordes of new addicts to the boards." The article argued that the sport's growth tied into perennial western myths. Surfers represented the "last frontier. Civilization drops behind them when they leave the shore, and the beauty and challenge of the great oceans is all around them." As the article's accompanying pictures made clear, the sport was more than just time on the board. Beach parties, rich tans, loose clothing, and surf-ready cars were all part of the image, as there was "more to surfing than the sea."[4]

The appearance of the novel *Gidget* expanded surfing's fashionable influence in Los Angeles high schools, while the 1959 film version brought international exposure to the growing craze.[5] Despite Gidget's wholesomeness, rumors about the "noisy, wild, late-night party" aspect of the sport dominated accounts of the late 1950s. As *Senior Scholastic* indicated, *Gidget* "gave surfing a boost in California, [but] it also helped give it a bad name." Some viewers remembered only the film's partying, drinking, and lazy carousing, identifying these with the sport itself.[6] Such images lingered, supported by newspaper reports of coastal disturbances.

The *Los Angeles Times* spotted the trend in 1960, profiling the "young businessmen" made wealthy by the growing sport. Technological changes in boards and increased focus on leisure among California's youth spurred its expansion. The article touted surfing as fashionable: "If you've a surf board this year, you're in style." It mentioned the sport's dangers but emphasized the civic responsibility of most wave riders. Surfers were, according to the *Times*, "as happy as the swimmers to see the beach a safe place to play."[7]

In a 1961 profile on surfing, *Life* featured a picture essay heralding a "new way of life on the wavetops." The article indicated that surfing's "addicts are mostly teenagers for whom the sport, besides being healthy and immensely exhilarating, has become a cult." The article quoted one Los Angeles high schooler's definition of cool: "If you're not a surfer, you're not in." Photographs offered examples of California's "established craze": a tuxedoed surfer, a 16-year-old Malibu native lifting a surfboard, a line of surfers enjoying the crest of a wave at Doheny Beach, a group of boys and girls on the beach "hoping for heavies," and a "vintage vehicle" piled high with boards and boys. Despite Gidget's cinematic example, *Life* reported that "most girls lack strength" to lift the boards and served to simply "decorate the shallows."[8] Surfing's marked gender exclusion matched its economic, demographic, and geographical boundaries.

The *Saturday Evening Post* investigated California's surfing scene in the summer of 1962 and reported that "California's 40,000 surfers" were "a young, clannish bunch" characterized by baggy outfits and private language. In over 200 locations along the "southern coast," surfers gathered. Although plagued by the occasional outbreak of trouble from "roughnecks," teenage surfing clans imposed strict rules and standards on their fellow wave runners. "Surfers are calming down ashore," the article reported, but "they are as wild as ever on the water."[9]

Seventeen's surfing feature in July 1962 noted its evolving image. Although physical harm was one concern of parents, the majority cited the bad reputation of "the surfing crowd" as the reason for their opposition to the sport. One teen surfer said his mother "couldn't have been more upset if I had announced that I had become a beatnik."[10] The September issue of *Seventeen* featured letters to the editor praising the surfing article for challenging parents' negative impressions. One subscriber from Ventura, California, wrote, "All the surfers I know are wonderful kids!" Another letter indicated that the article "[helped] more people understand the thrills of surfing and realize the true surfers want no part of 'hodaddies.'" The last letter expressed gratitude for the article's reinforcement of the sport's positive attributes: "When the surfing bug caught on in my crowd, my mother changed her opinion of my friends. . . . But after reading your article, she now sympathizes with us. Thank you! I may learn to surf after all!"[11] In a few short years, thanks to a more positive media spin, images of surfers evolved from a source of concern to a celebration of civic-minded youth. In 1963, *Time* called surfing "good clean kamikaze." As the article explained, the sport had matured from "the private passion of a few bronzed dare-devils"; now attracting a "better ilk," it represented a "clean-limbed skill" that families at the beach could all enjoy.[12]

California's brand of rock and roll was a key player in both the expansion of the craze and the remaking of surfing's image. The surfing lifestyle, most notably in southern California, spawned a music that schooled land-locked teens across the country in the sport's appeal, offering a teenage element of the California dream. The music whitened rock and roll, creating a mythic place of carefree consumption and endless summer. Through a facade of universality, it served as an exclusive theme music for white, middle-class baby boomers, a soundtrack for "good kids." Performed by California natives who acted as message and messengers, it communicated an ideal teenage existence through lyrics and harmonies. The Beach Boys and other recording artists, wrote one journalist, made "teen life in the California landscape almost heroic."[13] The music was innovative stylistically but carried a familiar message: a glorified evocation of life in the state that represented "an everyday Disneyland."[14]

Never before in the short history of rock and roll was the focus so exclusively on particular lifestyles, marked by mobility and the beach, in such a specific location. First inspired by the surf, the sound expanded to include themes of the good life. California's recording industry fostered young artists who charted hits throughout the early 1960s. The genre took advantage of existing beliefs about California living, issuing a siren call to those living far away from the inspirational source. The music also rehabilitated the dangerous elements of surfing and cars, giving California teen lifestyles a makeover and influencing the general view.

California's magical virtues had been the subject of popular song before. In the 1920s, songwriters penned "California, Here I Come" with lyrics that heralded the rediscovery of a second Eden.[15] As music geographers document, songs about Southern California dominated popular music in the early 1960s.[16] The music echoed images a hundred years old but gave them new meaning, creating a "musical identity" based on youth.[17] Los Angeles overtook eastern centers of rock and roll production to become a recording industry powerhouse.[18] Aspiring artists first latched onto the surfing subculture as inspiration, playing this new type of music at small venues – civic auditoriums, high schools, and meeting halls – slowly building a Southern California fan base.[19] The key ingredient of early surf music was the instrumental guitar, stylistically played to recreate the feeling of riding the waves.[20]

A prime example of this pattern was Dick Dale, a trendsetter who contributed to surfing's positive spin. Born Richard Monsour in Beirut, Lebanon, he grew up in Quincy, Massachusetts, before moving to El Segundo, California, in 1954 for his senior year of high school.[21] Monsour, taking the stage name Dick Dale, learned to combine his guitar talent with surfing's appeal. He played to surfer crowds, frequenting the Rendezvous Ballroom in Balboa. Guitar manufacturer Leo Fender gave Dale an electronic reverb that echoed his guitar, creating a "wet" sound like the pounding of the waves.[22] His first album, released on his father's label, *Surfer's Choice*, sold 88,000 copies in 1961.[23]

Local airplay pushed Dick Dale and his group, the Del-Tones, onto the *Billboard* charts in September 1961; "Let's Go Trippin'" reached number sixty, the first surf hit to reach a nationwide audience.[24] In December 1961, he performed the song on *American Bandstand*.[25] With strong sales in Southern California and record companies' faith in the craze's possibilities, Dale found himself the target of "hot bidding." After one of the toughest "battles for talent in recent disk history," Capitol Records signed Dale in February 1963.[26] Dale's first album for Capitol, *King of the Surf Guitar*, featured him in the ocean up to his shoulders, smiling and waiting to catch the next wave.[27]

While Dale was attracting national attention to the surf craze, five young Californians geared up for their takeover of the charts. The three Wilson brothers, Brian, Carl, and Dennis, were second-generation Californians whose parents had traveled to the state in search of a better life. Their birthplace of Hawthorne was a typical Southern California town, only five miles from the ocean and part of the suburban sprawl of Los Angeles.[28] Typical area residents, the Wilson parents took their children to Disneyland twice a year.[29] With the Los Angeles recording industry booming, hundreds of groups aspired to have a local hit propel them to national stardom. Brian, Carl, and Dennis teamed up with their cousin, Mike Love, and a neighbor, Alan Jardine, to form the Pendletons, taking the name of the surfer's favorite shirt brand. Fortuitously, their first record company decided to change the name, setting them apart from the competition. The choice of the Beach Boys as a band name allowed a versatility of subject matter connected to themes beyond the surf.[30]

Although the California coastline was familiar to the group, their adolescent leisure time was spent away from the beach.[31] Despite their lack of first-hand surfing knowledge, Love later recalled: "We grew up in that Southern California environment. It was a very specialized jargon and way of not only talking but looking and dressing and acting and there were different groups and one was the surfers and the other was the hoods or the greasers or whatever you call them. We identified more with the athletic, you know surfers, good time cruisers rather than the real heavy type of other thing."[32] From the beginning, the Beach Boys identified with an image, one that they were not truly a part of themselves. This would give their music an added power, as they appealed to listeners who were also not part of the surfing scene or who lived outside California.

Dennis Wilson, the group's only true surfer, suggested the topic of their first record. Mike Love and Brian Wilson wrote the lyrics using terms picked up from surfing reports on Los Angeles radio stations.[33] "Surfin'" was the result, a song that invited listeners to join a privileged world of youths and their surfing obsession.[34] Rather than trying to recreate the feel of surfing through rolling guitar lines and reverberation, the group captured the surfing lifestyle for their listeners through their lyrics. "Surfin'" enjoyed extensive local airplay throughout early 1962, reaching number seventy-five on the *Billboard* charts in June.[35] After strong lobbying and an impressive demo recording, the Beach Boys signed with Capitol Records.[36]

"Surfin' Safari," the first single recorded for Capitol, reached number fourteen in June 1962, right on the heels of "Surfin'."[37] It held that position for two weeks. Tellingly, New York City area stores ordered the largest number of records.[38] This song made the invitation to join the surfing clique more explicit, suggesting that everyone was rushing to the coast. The lyrics taught a geography lesson to those unschooled in California's surfing hot spots and introduced the sport's slang to the uninitiated.[39]

Record company promotion of the Beach Boys took a back seat to the hype that Dale received. Capitol's promotional material compared Dale to Frank Sinatra and Elvis Presley, as he attracted similar numbers of "highly enthusiastic young people" to his concerts. His audiences were "actually well behaved. . . . There are no fights, no rowdiness, nobody getting out of line." In speeches from the bandstand, Dale extolled "the Golden Rule in current jargon." Parents, the ad insisted, "instead of objecting to their kids attending the dances where Dick Dale appears," were "urging their youngsters to go!" With Dale's success around Los Angeles, Capitol anticipated "he'll hit like a tidal wave in every town in the country" and become "one of the giant attractions of the music business."[40] The record company predicted Dale would become "Teen America's New Favorite."[41] To make rock and roll less threatening and promote acceptance, the record company depicted Dale as a safe musician, a fine representative of California youth.

Capitol's pro-Dale propaganda interested national magazines, who helped characterize and popularize the surf music craze. *Life* called him a "thumping teen-age idol who is part evangelist, part Pied Piper and all success," describing his music as "wet rock and roll [which] presumably echoes the sound of the big California surf." Dale enjoyed a leisured existence, a star who "roars about in sports cars and lives it up in a bachelor house at Costa Mesa." Despite these questionable pastimes, the article insisted that Dale maintained an environment for "civilized behavior" among his fans. For example, his ballroom venues banned "liquor, short pants, fights and Capri slacks." Concert rules prohibited audience members from leaving the music for possible boy-girl activity, and between songs Dale offered his young fans valuable advice. He humbly discouraged applause after performances, ending nearly every concert with a spiritual.[42] Dale often performed in a suit and tie.[43]

Newsweek knighted Dale "The King at 24" in August 1963. Despite his success, Dale maintained a humility; "I don't have a swelled head or nothin.'" This "tanned, blue-eyed, and sincere" teen idol worked hard at maintaining the "sturdy, outdoors image of the surfer."[44] An unassuming rock star, he tempered the wildness of his surf guitar with an image and persona orchestrated to inspire good behavior in his fans. While his music communicated a boisterousness, his image and performance balanced the rock and roll. His album covers portrayed a swinging young Californian, who surfed, raced cars, and enjoyed time by the pool, a fun-loving bachelor who personified a safe level of rebellion. Unlike rock and roll artists surrounded by moralistic controversy, Dale preferred to cultivate his image as a wholesome surfer, influencing the way in which surfing and its lifestyle were perceived.

The surf music craze gained momentum, yet Dale never achieved a national following to match his local appeal.[45] An East Coast tour in the summer of 1963 failed to attract the attention the record company had hoped, despite television appearances, profiles in *Life* and *Newsweek*, and persistent advertising by Capitol.[46] Dale sang in rhythm and blues baritone, a sound that clashed with the youthful California image.[47] Perhaps he was too old, or his instrumental guitar music lacked the lyrics to create a fuller picture of teen life. In Dale's wake, it would be the harmonies of the Beach Boys that took surf music to the next level, singing evocative lyrics that captured the California youth experience.

In June 1963, *Billboard* pronounced the surfing craze "ready to splash across country to East's youth," calling it "the kookiest, wildest, and most refreshing fad within memory." Those unable to afford a board or whose "sole acquaintance with a body of water is the family bathtub" bought records to join the California crowd. "Surf disks are taking hold in landlocked markets," the article explained.[48] With the headline "Chicago Goes Surf," a July 1963 *Billboard* reported on the craze's "good, healthy appeal" in the Windy City. Despite their Lake Michigan location, young Chicagoans were "dressing like surfers, talking like surfers, even looking and acting like surfers."[49]

Radio stations and deejays across the country promoted surf records with tie-ins and contests. Capitol gave record retailers a "free surfing dictionary" to distribute to teenage customers, advertising records like *Sunset Surf* as music "chosen by the surfers themselves."[50] As *Billboard* explained, the expansion of the California sound was partly due to this "astute promotion and a dash of showmanship," with "big firms getting on the band wagon, even those located in the East."[51] In the summer of 1963, Del-Fi records sponsored a hearse giveaway, the preferred transportation for the hippest surfers and their boards. As the *Billboard* article reported, surfing "had created its own music, its own language and 'uniform,' and a thriving industry." The hearse promotion served to sell surf records alongside lifestyles.[52] The surf music craze was another fad in a long line of passing fancies for baby boomers, but its explosive popularity was not accidental or without meaning. It was carefully orchestrated by record company and media promotion to succeed in an environment tuned to California trends and images of youth.

Leaving instrumental surf music behind, the Beach Boys were well positioned to make a splash with their brand of the California sound, and they continued to capitalize on the surfing craze.[53] The cover for *Surfin' USA* featured a lone surfer braving a gigantic wave, while the album heralded the "brawny, fun-tanned fivesome" as the "Number One Surfing

Group in the Country." The album claimed the Beach Boys had "started the surf-dancing craze . . . even in places where the nearest thing to surf is maybe the froth on a chocolate shake." The liner notes went on to proclaim the group "nationwide symbols for the exhilarating sport that has taken America by storm." The tunes were "rockin,' sweet rollin' tunes, just right for dancing, singing-along, or listening, wet or dry." For curious record buyers, the album notes provided a mini glossary of surfing terms.[54]

The album featured covers of Dick Dale hits and original surfing compositions, including the title song "Surfin' USA," which borrowed the guitar melody and lyric style from Chuck Berry's "Sweet Little Sixteen." "Surfin' USA" was their biggest hit yet, reaching number three on the *Billboard* chart. Its lyrics took listeners on a trip through California, offering a coastal lesson in teenage cool. For those unfamiliar with the California surfing landscape, the song named popular destinations; "Ventura County Line, Santa Cruz . . . Pacific Palisades, San Onofre and Sunset, Redondo Beach L.A., all over La Jolla." The song also described the surfer uniform and hairstyle, "wearin' their baggies, huarachi sandals too, a bushy, bushy blond hair-do," and expressed hope that everyone across the world could know the joy of being young in California. With simple lyrics, the Beach Boys communicated a universal image to youth in the landlocked middle; "If everybody had an ocean, across the USA, then everybody'd be surfin,' like California."[55] In an ad proclaiming the single to be "sweeping the nation from coast to coast," the Beach Boys were inset into an outline of the United States, literally reaching from one coast to the other.[56]

The album cover for *Surfer Girl*, released in September 1963, featured the group barefoot on the beach, carrying a surfboard and sporting matching khakis and Pendleton shirts. It included the songs "The Surfer Moon," "South Bay Surfer," "The Rocking Surfer," and "Surfer's Rule." The title track, according to the album, was "a new kind of song for the Beach Boys . . . fast becoming the romantic ballad of the day, and it's making thousands of new friends for the boys."[57] The Beach Boys expanded the confines of the genre, and their versatility made them more than one-hit wonders. At the same time, the success of the Beach Boys influenced and altered surfing's negative reputation, cleaning up the beach with soaring falsettos.

The single "Catch a Wave" from *Surfer Girl* reinforced the magic behind California living and the desire for all to become part of the young crowd at the beach. By joining the clique, the lyrics promised, they would catch that wave and be on top of the world.[58] The song clearly communicated the idea that to be a nonsurfer, or a non-Californian, was to lack something, an intangible superiority available only to native sons (and daughters) of the Golden State.

Record producers believed surfing songs appealed to a limited audience, despite the craze's documented appeal beyond the coast. To broaden record sales, the B sides of the Beach Boys' early Capitol recordings featured odes to the automobile. As *Seventeen* reported; "To most boys a car is something to get around in; to some, it's life itself."[59] Mobility defined the postwar period, with baby boom teenagers enjoying greater access to cars than any earlier generation. The car culture, while seen at its most extreme in California, roared throughout the country. It was a natural progression for surf groups to turn to automobiles as a source of inspiration. Songs that celebrated automotive prowess communicated freedom and a safe rebelliousness to their listeners, couched in a secret language of youth.

The surf music wave reached its height as car songs sped up the charts.[60] Hot rod music, "love songs to the carburetor," provided another piece of the California sound.[61] Both fads involved leisure and consumption with a definite California spin. The "transition from surf to road" was seamless for many surf groups because of these interconnections. The Beach Boys recorded automobile hits, according to *Billboard*, "without grinding gears, roaring from a string of surf hits to their first in the wheel and engine groove." As with surf music, hot rod tunes received the exploitation treatment from record companies and deejays, with press packets explaining the jargon while promoting clubs and magazines.[62] The Beach Boys continued the domestication of the automobile that began in the 1950s, making drag racing and hot-rodding harmlessly fun activities through their music.

The Beach Boys, for example, recorded "409." The title referred to 409 cubic inches, the space occupied by a large Chevrolet engine.[63] The recording featured real car sounds, and expressed the adolescent obsession for car ownership. Bragging about the car's abilities and features, the song employed hot-rod terminology for teenage listeners.[64] In a similar groove, the group released the album *Little Deuce Coupe* in October 1963 with the songs "Cherry, Cherry Coupe," "Car Crazy Cutie," a remake of "409," "Custom Machine," "Shut Down," "No-Go Showboat," and a tribute to James Dean, "A Young Man Is Gone."[65] "Shut Down" captured the feeling of a drag race and explained to listeners that to be shut down meant to lose.[66] "Little Deuce Coupe" contained more specific hot-rod jargon than anyone had heard in popular music before.[67] "Fun, Fun, Fun" offered a picture of rebellion, but one of youthful exuberance rather than societal danger. The song tells the story of a young girl who prefers the hamburger joint to the library. Her love of fast driving results in a parental grounding from her Thunderbird, and a willing boy chauffeur steps in.[68]

The group's salute to cruising, "I Get Around," reached number one on the charts, suggesting the pastime's widespread appeal.[69] "Drive-In" celebrated the outdoor movie theater as a teenage hangout, while "Little Honda" gave the motorcycle a makeover, the first of the genre to suggest a safer image. The song rehabilitated the traditionally negative stereotype of motorcycle riding, making the vehicle a teen's toy.[70] This tempered treatment of motorcycles was just one example of the group's lyrical method. The Beach Boys' music made safe all threatening aspects of youthful activities, harmonizing and canonizing California lifestyles.

The Beach Boys, in addition to their surfing hymns and cruising odes, recorded songs that captured the joys of teen California living. "Be True to Your School" sings of high school spirit, the rah-rah passion of a pep rally before a football game, and anticipates the sports victory. The singer letters in football and track and has a cheerleader girlfriend, enjoying the epitome of happy high school life.[71] Chronicling the ideal California high school experience, this image of adolescence had an angst-free tone, celebrating the joys of youth without the heartaches, disappointments, or rebelliousness that typified depictions of teenagers less than a decade earlier.

All Summer Long, released in July 1964, endeavored to stay "on the kids' wavelength with their interests."[72] To ensure the group's continued success on the charts, Brian Wilson tried to "keep up with what young guys and dolls are doing and thinking."[73] The album cover featured vignettes of beach fun; horseback riding, tandem biking, playing football, running along the beach, drinking Coke, barbecuing hot dogs, boy-girl flirting, and going to the drive-in. The title track detailed a reminiscence of a fun summer, describing typical young California summer attire – thongs, jeans, and T-shirts – and the activities they enjoyed.[74] With this song, the group imagined the perfect model of a carefree summer in California.

The *Summer Days (and Summer Nights!!!)* album included songs with appeals to other locales: "The Girl from New York City," "Salt Lake City," and "Amusement Parks U.S.A."[75] "California Girls" was their only 1960s hit to explicitly use the state's name in its title, summoning the power of the place that inspired their music. Brian Wilson called the song "a hymn to youth."[76] While the attractiveness of youthful beauty is an evident theme,

An early promotional picture of the Beach Boys. The group sports Pendleton shirts, the favored attire of the surfer, Levi jeans, and a surfboard, exuding a clean-cut and definitively California image.

(Michael Ochs Archives.com)

the song evokes historical connections. Explorers named California after a mythological land of beautiful Amazons in Spanish literature.[77] The song begins as a travelogue, referencing the Beach Boys tour experience, highlighting the attractions of the women of various regions. Despite the competition, they "couldn't wait to get back in the state" to the tans and bikinis of the girls back home. They "wish they all could be California Girls . . . the cutest girls in the world."[78] Travel served only to convince the group of their hometown superiority. California boasted the best leisure time activities, the top surfing spots, and the most beautiful people. This was not an original theme, but it resonated in a culture conditioned to think of young Californians as the best and brightest.

The marketing of the Beach Boys matched the content of their records. With casual clothing, striped shirts with open necks, Pendletons, and short hairstyles, the Beach Boys captured the era's ideal.[79] Despite their questionable credentials as surfers, the record sleeves of the Beach Boys' first forty-five hits all featured surfboards and the group in surfing scenes. For promotional material, album covers, and appearances, the Beach Boys posed as avid surfers and beachcombers. Their first album cover depicted the group at the beach, piled into a truck filled with palm trees, holding a surfboard and watching for the next wave. The Beach Boys gradually moved away from surfing fashion to a more general clean-cut image. On the sleeve for "Fun, Fun, Fun/Why Do Fools Fall in Love" the Beach Boys sported suits and ties.[80] The release "Don't Worry Baby/I Get Around" pictured the group in casual jackets, slacks, and button-down sweaters.[81]

The Beach Boys' image mirrored the cultural inroads of surfing fashion. As *Time* reported, surfing style influenced "everything from haircuts to swim-suits."[82] *Look*'s profile of Newport Beach's surfers described "young . . . athletic, sunbrowned and clear-eyed" enthusiasts, with their own style and language. Pictures showed beautiful young Californians modeling trunks with hip pockets to hold surf wax and nylon parkas for attending beach bonfires.[83] While the actual surfing experience could not travel, the accompanying lifestyle could be commodified. A surfer's uniform – chinos, Pendleton shirts, striped windbreakers, sandals, and boxer-style swim trunks – were worn by teenagers far from the coast. The Montgomery Ward 1965 catalog advertised "bold surfer styling" in swim trunks and the "California Surf Beauties Collection for women."[84] Clothing companies evoked surfing words and imagery in product design. Vogue shoes marketed footwear called the "Surfer." The shoe, shaped like a surfboard with "surfin' ropes" for laces, featured surfers in its advertising, pledging the wearer would "hot-dog it in the wildest, most stoked new shoe. . . . So don't wipe-out, fashion-wise, but lock on a heavy."[85] In the spring of 1965, Catalina designed a new swimsuit/parka combination, naming it "the surfer."[86] In the Midwest, teenagers bolted surfboards to the roofs of their cars, a status symbol despite their distance from the ocean.[87]

The Beach Boys appeared on television in guises reminiscent of their album covers, posed amidst the icons of youthful California and visually acting out the lyrics. For example, musical segments were staged at a beach party or with the group encircled by girls in swimsuits. For their first network television appearance in the spring of 1963, the Beach Boys performed "Surfin' USA" on *The Steve Allen Show* in front of a beach backdrop.[88] On *The Ed Sullivan Show* the group sang surrounded by automobiles.[89] For "I Get Around," the group was perched on a car's hood amongst palm trees. During a Bob Hope special, the group sang "California Girls" on a beach set that included a hamburger stand, a pier, and bikini-clad dancers.[90] Hollywood, especially those studios tuned to the youth market, hired the Beach Boys for special guest appearances. The group provided instrumental backup and vocal harmonies for Annette Funicello during the title sequence of the Disney-produced *The Monkey's Uncle* (1964). For 1965's *The Girls on the Beach*, they provided the title song and performed "Little Honda."[91] The poster for the film highlighted their appearance, with their music one of the film's selling points.[92]

The Beach Boys were not the only group charting the California sound, only the most successful. Jan and Dean's recording career predated the Beach Boys, but they were quick to capitalize on surfing's appeal and the power of the California setting. Jan Berry and Dean Torrance, born and raised in Los Angeles, developed their musical talents with high school friends and then with local recording studios beginning in 1958.[93] Both blond and six feet tall, Jan and Dean were not typical teen idols when compared to the reigning Philadelphia crooners. *American Bandstand*, the reigning popular music television program for teens of the late 1950s and early 1960s, often promoted a particular type of East Coast artist because of its geographic location. Broadcast from Philadelphia, young singers like Fabian, Frankie Avalon, Bobby Darin, Paul Anka, and Bobby Rydell shared a particular look as well as the *Bandstand* stage. In contrast, record producer Lou Adler signed Jan and Dean to a record contract because of their unique and "very West Coast Look." Their first hit came in 1959 with

"Baby Talk," a novelty song they performed on *American Bandstand*. Their California image was their persona, a clean-cut duo decked out in sweaters and jackets. Between recordings and engagements, Jan and Dean were university students and volleyball players.[94]

The Beach Boys and Jan and Dean met in early 1963 while performing together at promotional record hops and began a creative collaboration. Brian Wilson wrote the lyrics for Jan and Dean's biggest hit, "Surf City," the number-one song in the country for two weeks in July 1963, and the first surf song to reach the top of the charts coast to coast.[95] As the song explains, "Surf City" boasts fabulous surfing and abundant female companionship. Surfers travel to this teenage Eden looking to shoot the curl, find a party, and get a girl.[96] The album *Surf City* reached number-one status as well. An ad in *Billboard* featured a U.S. map with an arrow marked "surf city" pointing eastward toward surf music's area of conquest.[97] Jan and Dean hopped on the hot-rod bandwagon as well, recording "Drag City," "Dead Man's Curve," and "The Little Old Lady from Pasadena." "Drag City" was a hot-rod version of "Surf City," with surfing slang altered to car types and racing locales.[98]

Looking to California fads for hit-making possibilities, Jan and Dean discovered skateboarding. From a small-scale hobby in the early 1960s, skateboarding matured into a national craze.[99] Surfing demonstrations on the East Coast marketed the skateboard as an alternative to the land-locked.[100] *Life* reported that while "real surfing requires real waves," skateboarding could catch on in places like the Midwest "where there is much less surf than sidewalk."[101] *Newsweek* reported that "Skateboard country" stretched from Capistrano Beach, California, to New York City's sedate East End Avenue."[102] The nation's young people bought 50 million boards in the 1960s.[103] As one New York teenager explained, "There's no place you can surf, so this is the next best thing."[104] Jan and Dean took advantage of the trend, releasing "Sidewalk Surfin,'" a number twenty-five on the hit list in October 1964.[105] The song, written by Brian Wilson, took its melody from "Catch a Wave" and invited listeners to join the skateboarding mania.[106]

Jan and Dean's image found fans beyond the teenage record-buying public. *Atlantic Monthly* praised the pair for introducing "a note of humor" into "the sullen self-consciousness of adolescent music." Tall, white, and middle class, Jan and Dean were "eminently representative of California's rock and roll singers and a vivid contrast to the ghetto-bound youths who dominate Eastern rock and roll."[107] A *Life* columnist described their sound as "so perfectly West Coast that you can practically hear that they are tall and blond and have surfboards under their arms."[108] Jan and Dean represented rock and roll light, a welcome change from earlier conceptions of what the new music form represented. Adult-marketed magazines could applaud the duo and their songs, highlighting their West Coast identity as a source of wholesomeness.

The Beach Boys and Jan and Dean enjoyed hit after hit, while other California bands charted tunes on the same wave. Five high school students from Glendora, California, represent one such success story.[109] Calling themselves the Surfaris, the group recorded "Surfer Joe" in 1963, the tale of a blond-haired surfer, eventually drafted and forced to cut his hair. The flip side, "Wipe Out," was an instrumental that began with a maniacal laugh and continued with rolling guitars and drums mimicking the roll of the surf.[110] "Wipe Out" sold a million copies, topping the charts at number two.[111] The group fit nicely into the California mold of rock and rollers, with publicity photos featuring the group wearing loafers, slacks, white shirts, and ties.[112] The Surfaris also posed with the recognizable props of surfboards and hot rods.[113] The Chantays from Santa Ana hit number four on the *Billboard* chart with "Pipeline" in the summer of 1963.[114]

California natives like Jan and Dean and the Beach Boys ruled the charts, but artists living beyond the state's borders found fame with the California sound too. The Astronauts from Colorado, the Trashmen from Minnesota, and the Rivieras from Indiana recorded songs in the California mold.[115] Most notably, the Rivieras charted a number-five hit in 1964, "California Sun."[116] The lyrics revealed a fascination with the West Coast, expressing a desire to travel to the Golden State and a willingness to follow the California lead.[117] The song reflected a widespread aspiration. Whatever the craze or fad, teens nationwide were eager to imitate their California peers. The mystique surrounding life in the state exercised a unique influence with its siren call.

Other recording artists tried to get into the act, notwithstanding their weak ties to the genre. Chubby Checker released an album in the summer of 1963 entitled "Beach Party." The album's cover featured cartoon kids, all white, dancing on the beach, with a large picture of Checker, made to appear as a very tan Polynesian.[118] "Surf Party" from that album reached number fifty-five on the charts. Pat Boone recorded a cover of "Little Honda" with "Beach Girl" on the flip side.[119] A Henry Mancini album,

Banzai Pipeline, was advertised with the description, "He takes to the surf . . . and rides the crest of the craze."[120] Bo Diddley released a surf album.[121]

Surf music success inspired the relocation of *American Bandstand*. Attempting to remain current with trends in popular culture, Clark's move was linked to musical and entertainment developments in Los Angeles. Broadcast from urban Philadelphia for eight years, the show began recording in Los Angeles on February 8, 1964.[122] As Dick Clark later explained, the "land of perpetual sunshine" proved impossible to resist.[123] "Everybody wanted to have bleached blonde straight hair," Clark remembered, "even if you were living in Detroit."[124] On a return trip to Philadelphia a few months after the show's West Coast debut, Clark found "the kids there doing the California dances."[125] Musical influence radiated eastward. Clark's version of rock and roll catered to mainstream tastes, a close counterpart to the general tone of California-produced entertainment. The only surprising facet of the *Bandstand* migration was its lateness. By 1970 the music business had shifted to the West Coast and Los Angeles had emerged as the nation's recording capital.[126]

The popularity of the California sound heightened surfing's appeal. At the same time, the soundtrack supported the creation of positive images subsequently adopted by media outlets across the country. The national coverage the sport received seemed overkill, yet it insured that surfing would expand beyond California's borders. For example, *Life*'s summer 1964 coverage featured two picture essays on different faddish aspects of the sport.[127] Despite its "pure Californese" vocabulary, surfing had become the "in" sport, with recognized "sociological overtones."[128] National magazines served as boosters, eager to grant the sport a safe and positive spin. The sport's appeal was to young people, but the image making reassured adults. Dozens of articles proclaimed surfing's wholesome attributes and popularized the idea that the youth involved were "clean-cut" Californians.

As *Newsweek* reported in July 1964, the image had infiltrated the East Coast. A traveling group of surf champions visited the New York and Jersey shores, eliciting an "enthusiastic reception." Acting as cultural ambassadors, the surfers lent their image to the sport's cause. Their main draw, "the 12-to-20 set," eagerly gathered to enjoy demonstrations of surfing derring-do. The report hinted at the assimilation of California habits that predated the surfers' arrival. In the crowd were "several hundred bug-eyed teens and tanned adults, beside whom the Californians looked surprisingly pale."

Tour promoters argued that Eastern waves were in many ways superior to the West Coast brand. Their smaller size made tricks easier and surfboards more maneuverable.[129]

Time challenged the long-held belief that "surfing and the way of life it suggested was something that was practiced only by the golden boys and girls of the West Coast." "From Maine to Miami," thousands of young people made a summer pilgrimage to East Coast beaches. With such growth, the article postulated, "Before long, Eastern surfers may well outnumber those in the west." Photographs showed surfers at Gilgo Beach, New York, and Nahant, Massachusetts – warm spots for summer surfing due to the Gulf Stream. *Time* again reassured its readers about surfing's wholesome appeal in the Eastern version of the craze. "After their first alarm," the article reported, "local authorities have discovered that East Coast surfers are mostly clean-cut collegians whose hair is as short as their surfing history."[130] This sport found fans far and wide, even in New Jersey.[131] ABC television covered the National Surfing Championships held at Huntington Beach, California, in December 1964. As part of *Wide World of Sports,* TV *Guide* reported, the network brought to a national audience this "new breed" of sportsman: "clear-eyed, sun-bronzed, [and] bleach-haired."[132]

Not all surfers fit that mold. Despite the white-bread character of the sport and the music that accompanied it, *Ebony* spotlighted Frank Edwards from Hermosa Beach, "one of the minute number of Negroes who have taken up the sport of surfing." The article had a simple explanation for the small numbers of minority enthusiasts: "surfing is most popular on the beaches of Southern California and Florida – areas not too often frequented by Negroes."[133] *Ebony*'s inclusion of a surfing profile within its pages offers a fascinating glimpse into surfing's cultural reach. It also illuminates the exclusive nature of the sport and its limited appeal outside the white middle-class. Surfing represented a barrier as well as a tool, creating a blindness toward the multiethnic reality of life in the state and sharing that exclusivity with the California sound.

Contemporary analyses recognized the interconnections between the music riding high on the charts and the California-born crazes of surfing and cars. *Atlantic Monthly* noted the origin of the music makers and the region they celebrated, arguing that the California sound could be considered "authentic folk music." However, the article found the music's popularity curious, as "the process of riding a surfboard . . . would seem to be, at best, a matter of coastal interest." It was surprising that a music "typically Californian in form and content" had achieved "a bizarre popularity among the puberty set across the nation."[134] *Life* called the sound a reflection of "the surfing and hot-rodding life, a feeling of pounding waves and gunning motorcycles."[135] The music, "recorded by the Beach Boys," *Look* reported, was an integral "part of the [surfing] cult."[136] Although adults recognized surf music's appeal, their general antipathy toward rock and roll limited serious introspection about its cultural power. The *Saturday Evening Post* called teen California music the "dumb sound" where "non-singers . . . speculate enthusiastically about a United States which has been turned into an entire ocean."[137]

Rock and cultural historians, on the other hand, have explored the role the music played in manufacturing myths about life in the state, arguing that the music "earned more free publicity for the good life in California . . . than a dozen Disneylands."[138] Nik Cohn sees the Beach Boys' music as supporting the vision of California as "teen heaven," where "age is suspended at twenty-five and school is outlawed and Coke flows free from public fountains and the perfect cosmic wave unfurls endlessly at Malibu."[139] Bruce Golden, in his work on the Beach Boys, believes that the group "reworked the pastoral theme to capitalize on the idea of Southern California as the new pastoral paradise."[140]

In addition to explaining the music's powerful imagery, rock critics have recognized the gender, racial, and economic exclusion that typifies the California sound. Barney Hoskyns calls the Beach Boys' "California Girls" an "implicitly Aryan anthem."[141] Along with its whiteness, critics point to the music's "primarily male-oriented, sexist imagery."[142] As rock critic Dave Marsh has shown, "It isn't just blacks who disappear from the rock and roll world of the Beach Boys. . . . It's also everyone without a comparatively great deal of wealth and leisure."[143] In his 1985 summation of the Beach Boys' career, John Milward calls the Beach Boys and other similar groups "madrigal singers for an American age of limitless growth."[144] It was not only an American age that the Beach Boys spoke to, but also a California era.

The group revolved around Brian Wilson, who, as *Life* explained, had a keen "grasp of the teenage mind."[145] The young mind Wilson captured was undoubtedly that of a Californian, as place defined the group's songs and lyrics. The Beach Boys' hits served as cultural road maps, charting behavior and lauding the California ideal. Wilson's songwriting trick, according to the group, was to "picture the U.S. as one great big California." The vision of California drawn by their lyrics offered a white, middle-class version of youth, an exclusion recognized by the group. As the Beach Boys told *Time*: "We're not colored; we're white. And we sing white."[146]

The biggest Beach Boys' hits, through lyrical content and musical style, utilized the imagery of California as the ultimate locale for fun-loving, beautiful youth. Capitol record producer Nick Venet called their tunes "a new form of teenage music." "It had nothing to do," he said, "with your girlfriend, breaking up or driving off a cliff. It was a pure California phenomenon. The Beach Boys just represented California to the rest of the country . . . [creating a] fantasy that got triggered by the Beach Boys records."[147] Venet believed that "they got most of it from the movies," that the Hollywood influence was the main source of lyrical inspiration.[148] The Beach Boys did not simply borrow from the movies, nor did they originate the California dream. The group tapped into a rich vein of golden hopes and a postwar environment that glorified life in California, especially for its teenagers. The music did not create the fantasy; rather, it played upon an existing set of values and ideas about California's kids.

The Beach Boys and other artists expanded on multiple icons of California mythmaking, from the images produced on the big screen to the magazine profiles that depicted California as a teenager's paradise. Ideas about California's youth culture were well established before the emergence of the surf sound. Popular culture images, the Mecca of Disneyland, Gidget, the surfing craze, the car culture – these ingredients created marketable symbols and prepared the audience for the music. Its appeal lay in cultural timing combined with genuine musical talent and powerful imagery. Listeners across the country, and throughout the world, believed California to be a teenager's wonderland, providing a ready audience for the exclusive vision portrayed in surf music. The Beach Boys' success – reflected in chart-topping hits, television performances, and movie appearances – indicate the popularity of the group's lyrical content and its carefully groomed image. These were hymns to consumerism and leisure, tuned to the white, middle-class teenagers of whom they sang, created and packaged to fit predetermined images of youth.

By 1965, with the help of the California sound, the national diffusion of the surfing subculture was complete. It became a mainstream advertising image, keyed into California's youthfulness as "an element of the marketing picture." Pepsi used images of surfers and this pun, "Board members of the

Pepsi Generation," to advertise its soft drinks.[149] Chesterfield King ciga-
rettes showed surfers at Huntington Beach for its "Great Day, Great
Smoke" campaign.[150] Ads for 7-Up employed beach scenes and California
imagery to promote the "7-Up . . . Where There's Action" slogan.[151] Royal
Crown Cola featured a California state junior surf-boarding champion as
its spokesman in July 1963 with the slogan, "the goingest people go Royal
Crown."[152] Falstaff Beer used a surfer shooting the curl in its ad in *Ebony*,
proclaiming, "There's a man-size pleasure in that great beer taste."[153] Surfing appeared on television sitcoms like *Gidget* and even entered the plots of
shows like *Dr. Kildare*.[154] *The Endless Summer*, released in 1965, told the
story of two surfers traveling the world in search of a perfect wave. California was one of its stars, sharing screen time with Australia, New Zealand,
Hawaii, Tahiti, and Africa.[155]

In the wake of the surfing craze and the emergence of the California
sound, American International Pictures (AIP) produced beach and surfing
movies for appreciative teenage audiences, reinforcing marketable images.
While the Beach Boys celebrated the coast, defining a lifestyle and offering
an ideal, this minor film company turned that image into a major movie
star.[156] It was time to find box office success with the "fun in the sun"
environment celebrated by media image makers. This world resurrected
Annette and turned Philadelphia teen idols into beachcombers, presenting
California youth as wholesome surfers and cruising teens. The *Beach Party*
films exploited on the big screen what the Beach Boys set to music, a
cinematic version of young California that captured the imagination of
drive-in patrons everywhere.

CHAPTER SIX

Beach Blanket California

The surfing craze traveled far from the coast, and the California sound played hymns to white middle-class suburbia, mobility, and leisure on radios nationwide. California's fashion industry utilized these themes as well, making the beach a commercialized symbol of the magical kingdom. These images set the stage for a California youth invasion of the big screen.[1] It was a natural evolution from singing about the beach to making movies for drive-ins across the country. Filmmakers produced a new movie cycle to boost box office revenues, with teenagers providing a ready audience for California tales. Southern California, as the center of moviemaking, enjoyed a unique window on these lifestyles and their exploitation possibilities. As Gidget went to Rome, so ex-Mouseketeers and Philadelphia teen idols conquered the beach. Nearly every major and minor studio produced this brand of big-screen fun in the sun, a cinematic addition to the wholesome vision of California youth that had reigned since the late 1950s. Hollywood took advantage of its backyard, creating a beach version of the California dream while packaging images of the state's youth.

While Disneyland represented childhood adventure, it was California's beaches that most clearly contributed to the state's youthful mystique and influenced the fashion world. National magazines paid careful attention to industry trends for fascinated readers. With its emphasis on youth, beauty, and the beach, the state was the perfect home for the swimsuit industry, "California's big claim to fashion fame."[2] *Sports Illustrated* reported in 1955 that California's swimsuit manufacturers enjoyed "a year-round, nonstop four-season cycle which supplies most of the world."³ By 1959, led by industry leader Cole of California, the West Coast produced 82 percent of the nation's suits.⁴ Swimsuit makers began marketing complete lines of beachwear, making the "Western way of beach life" popular "with Atlantic coastliners."⁵

The bikini appeared first on the beaches of California. This new, scandalous type of swimsuit, *Seventeen* reported, was "worn more on the Coast than in any other section of the country."⁶ In response, Cole marketed a tamer version with its "Cole Scandal Suit Collection." The ad asked, "Isn't it about time somebody created an absolutely wild scandal for nice girls?" Their bikini, the company promised, "accomplishes more by baring less."⁷ While still employing the swimsuit's shock value, Cole domesticated the bikini, making it safe for young beachcombers and appropriate for California girls.

Coverage of California's fashion trends helped manufacture and reinforce the image of the Golden State as the ultimate teen leisure destination. In the 1950s and 1960s, *Seventeen*, from April to September, included dozens of features on beachwear, leisure activities, summer fashion, swimsuits, party advice, and photo layouts with a pronounced California spin.⁸ *TV Guide*'s fashion features promoted television stars while spotlighting California designers' clothing for the beach and beyond.⁹ A 1959 article photographed six young television actresses, including Annette Funicello, who "have the right idea for summer: cool water (the Pacific) and 'real cool' play clothes."¹⁰ A 1961 *Seventeen* feature posed models at Disneyland sporting "paled-down casuals" for a day at the "fairyland of fun." "Life in the West is casual" the article explained, highlighting other teen activities such as surfing, spring vacation, Sunday brunch, biking, and parties. At the beach, teens "work for perpetual, no-strap-mark tans."¹¹

Only the magazine's advertisers, who employed catchphrases and images of California youth to sell their products, matched *Seventeen*'s perennial obsession with beach leisure. Marina Del Mar, a Los Angeles clothier, promoted its suits with the words; "To sea and be seen . . . wear the Marina Del Mar swimsuits leading California Cover Girls do."¹² Another ad campaign for the company was headlined, "From California, Naturally . . . Marina Del Mar, California Swimsuits."¹³ Rose Marie Reid of Los Angeles manufactured a line of "Switcheroo swimsuits," promoting them with pictures of girls carrying surfboards on a California beach.¹⁴ Cole of California, as its name suggests, purposefully advertised the location of its headquarters, using beach photography, blond models, and the surf.[15]

Cosmetic companies, tuned to the swimsuit industry's techniques, utilized the state's romantic imagery and the allure of beach living. In May 1961, Merle Norman marketed its new shade of eye shadow by highlighting the company's birthplace. "From California," the ad read, "Sun-ripened Madera."[16] In 1962, Max Factor produced an eye makeup called "California Blues." Its ad copy waxed poetic about the state's uncommon assets: "It could only happen by the California sunlight – the birth of a new kind of blues in the light – like music to your eyes."[17] The following year the company introduced a new powder and foundation product: "From California Max Factor brings you the sunlit look of Creme Puff. . . . It could only have been created in California where light does such wonderful, warming things to the skin."[18] Another ad for the same product advised: "Carry the sunlit look of California, from here to everywhere. It's for gadabouts, girls who are mad about a clear, radiant skin, luminous with California sunlight."[19]

Only in California, the makeup ads implied, could such beauty be created. By wearing these shades, teenage girls could vicariously enjoy the magic of living there. The pervasive use of the California aesthetic in advertising campaigns is testament to the marketing success and consumer response that such tactics elicited. These promotions contributed to the predominant images of California youth: a suburban, white, middle-class clique dedicated to status quo pursuits and the mass consumption of stylish leisure clothing. The fashion and cosmetic industries packaged California's kids as a beautiful and wholesome generation living it up on the coast.

Hollywood borrowed the ploys of California-based fashion, exploiting the surfing craze, the fascination with the beach, and trends in popular music. In the late 1950s and early 1960s, the beach was not the locale for teenage frolic and fun. Instead it was used as backdrop in science fiction and horror films. Teen delinquency pictures also featured the beach; for example, *Rock, Pretty Baby* (Universal, 1956) contained several beach party scenes.[20] *The Careless Years*, a 1957 troubled-youth film, was promoted as "The Beach Party That Blew the Lid Off."[21] In films made after 1963, however, the beach became "America's dream backyard," partly the result of an altered cultural environment.[22]

American International Pictures (AIP), which carved out its niche catering to young moviegoers, first discovered the beach's cinematic possibilities. As the only new moviemaking venture of the 1950s, a decade of floundering studios and disappearing audiences, AIP specialized in movies with budgets under $250,000 and shooting schedules of less than two weeks.[23] Tuned to the new demographics of moviegoing, AIP advertised its orientation proudly: "The Young Company with Young Executives Presents Its Young Producers."[24] Its first films were exploitation pieces modeled on *Rebel Without a Cause*, films that used parent-teen conflict to help AIP become the most successful "major-minor" in the business.[25] Low cost was the studio's driving principle, and its movies utilized southern California's scenery as much as possible.

While focusing on the youth market, the studio devised a formula to maximize profits. Called "The Peter Pan Syndrome," it was a strategy devised to capture the largest segment of the teen audience. Executives at AIP believed younger children would view anything that an older child watched. A girl would attend any movie that a boy watched, but boys would not return the favor. Therefore, to win box office, the studio followed the maxim, "Zero in on the 19-year-old male."[26] The AIP brand of entertainment mixed rock and roll and rebellion, and the studio rode this boom until audience interest in delinquency tales waned.

By the end of the 1950s, teenage troublemaking disappeared. A reformation of attitudes about baby boomers resulted in more films like *Gidget*. Hollywood's depiction of white middle-class kids evolved "from wild to mild."[27] The mainstream press shifted from covering teenage troublemakers to embracing the good life in California. Popular music captured the ideal on the *Billboard* charts, while youth fashion highlighted the state's alluring attractions. Hollywood simply followed their lead. The beach party cycle emerged out of this transition, outperforming juvenile delinquency in its appeal to teenagers hungry for images of California lifestyles. The new role models on the screen found refuge in California's beach culture, the perfect setting for this revisionist vision.

With the proven success of *Gidget* and Metro-Goldwyn-Mayer's *Where the Boys Are*, a spring break adventure set in Florida, AIP gravitated toward the beach picture. Producers needed a new fad, and the popularity of surfing and the beach seemed an obvious exploitation prospect. Sam Arkoff and James Nicholson, the founders of AIP, tapped television director William Asher to create AIP's first offering for this new wave. In the planning stages, writers pitched the film as another middle-class youth crime story about dangerous surfers; the original *Beach Party* script included overt references to sex and drugs.[28] However, Asher suggested the studio employ a different filmmaking mantra.[29] He wondered why the company "couldn't do a picture about kids not in trouble."[30] Asher believed that moviegoers "bored with juvenile delinquency [would] welcome clean sex."[31] The TV director lobbied AIP executives, arguing that few moviegoers wanted to "watch mayhem in the city when they could watch the same thing at Malibu Beach."[32] Arkoff concurred, agreeing that American teenagers, "no matter where they lived . . . fantasized about romping on the beach." Therefore, Arkoff reasoned, the AIP version of beach life "would appeal to just about every young person," a huge potential film audience.[33]

Sensitive to mainstream aspersions and wanting Hollywood respect, AIP cleaned up its image while doing the same for the American teenager.[34] In his films, Asher told *Life*, he wanted to capture "the marvelous moment just after adolescence and just before facing responsibility."[35] Each beach picture shared similar themes and characters, resembling an episodic sitcom rather than individual big-screen tales. As Asher explained to the *New York Times*, "We take the same teenagers and put them into a slightly different experience in each picture. The plot may change but the faces stay the same."[36] The beach films offered a reassuring version of teenagers, comforting viewers with the predictability and familiarity of each series entry.

The studio's operating motto was the importance of image over actual content, a process that began with the choice of the film's title. As AIP president Nicholson explained to *Life*, "70 percent of a picture's initial appeal to an audience is in the title." Producer Arkoff believed linear narrative and logic unnecessary, as long as the visuals "move fast enough."[37] Although the ad campaigns for the film offered "peak-a-boo promises" of sexual situations, the films themselves never veered from hand-holding and innocent kissing.[38] As Arkoff later explained, "We gave the illusion of being daring, but there was a lot of teasing with no real payoff. . . . There wasn't anything much more wholesome on the screen than our beach movies."[39] Asher espoused a safe, conformist viewpoint in his films. He told reporters, "It's all good clean fun. No hearts are broken, and virginity prevails."[40]

For a dash of authenticity, AIP recruited extras from the beaches where filming took place.[41] As the *New York Times* described, these California young people became "members of a serious sort of cinematic repertory company" in their work as recurring background characters. They enjoyed "a rather idyllic way of life," leisure combined with minor-league stardom.[42] For its leads, AIP wisely chose known quantities and popular young actors while remaining within the constraints of their small budget. The studio cast Annette Funicello with Frankie Avalon, a synergetic pairing of Disney magic and safe rock and roll.[43]

Annette Funicello parlayed her *Mickey Mouse Club* fame into starring roles in Disney productions and Top Ten hits, remaining under contract to Walt Disney. Magazine profiles maintained their spotlight on Annette's "unspectacular" talent throughout the early 1960s, continuing to explore possible explanations for her appeal. *Seventeen* featured the young actress in January 1962. The article expressed her displeasure at the constant interrogations, offering the explanation: "I'm just myself. I don't know how I got that way!"[44] In October 1963, *TV Guide* profiled the actress, theorizing that her lack of "larger-than-life qualities" contributed to her being "the sort of person today's teenagers see in themselves or wish they were."[45] Annette seemed ordinary, which was part of her charm. While she had grown up on television in front of millions, her natural style suggested a young woman uncorrupted by the Hollywood scene.

Beach Party was her first film away from the Disney studios. In choosing Annette, AIP made an astute casting decision, getting an actress who remained popular with teenagers, both fans of the children's show and admirers of her grown-up good looks. Annette's identity as a clean teen fit perfectly with the *Beach Party* films, which took advantage of her girl-next-door image. Annette was still under the aegis of Disney on the AIP set, and he insisted that her film appearance be contingent on swimsuit modesty.[46] Her role, both thematically and visually, was, as *Look* described, to be "the guardian of teen-age morals."[47]

While choosing Annette to play a California teen was a natural extension of her *Mickey Mouse Club* persona, AIP's casting of Frankie Avalon seemed superficially a strange choice. Avalon was a teen idol who first became famous on Dick Clark's *American Bandstand* in Philadelphia. His 1959 success with "Venus," the first of seven *Billboard* hits, had led to sporadic acting roles.[48] However, his fame as a teen crooner was not a product of the California music scene. In fact, the "antitype" casting of Avalon and Funicello, with their dark hair and Italian backgrounds, went against traditional images of blond beachcombers. Both AIP's beach films and their imitators cast these types of teen stars. While geographically distant, these eastern-based idols shared thematic ties with their California counterparts. They were the poster teens for a white version of rock and roll, with carefully orchestrated personalities designed to counterbalance the music's rebellious reputation.[49] These images meshed easily with the exclusivity of surfing and the beach. In addition, their disconnectedness invited "beach-starved inland teens" to identify better with characters on the screen.[50] Annette, Frankie, and their costars exuded a middle-class sensibility, allowing the actors to become honorary California teens, just like the ones celebrated in magazine profiles and music.

With characters cast in the California mold, AIP produced screen tales that employed a wide variety of the state's fashions and crazes. The *Beach Party* genre offered a strange mix of teenage fads, popular music, romance, comedy, surfing, and dancing. The films tossed into the formula every ingredient that had even the slightest potential teenage appeal: "outdoor barbecues, pie-throwing fights, Zen Buddhism, pajama parties, karate, rock and roll, skydiving, uninhibited dancing" – anything with which "adolescent moviegoers might identify."[51] "Keeping on top of trends" was the goal.[52] Each AIP production ended with movie trailers hyping the next installment, using this episodic structure to build a core repeat audience.[53] The films failed to win acclaim for their screenwriting or acting, but they popularized the pastimes of California's youth and influenced fashion as well. The bikini was a shocking outfit when first introduced, but it lost its scandalous reputation through repeated appearances on the big screen.[54]

The musical format of AIP's beach pictures supported the sales of sound-track recordings, adding another level of cultural influence by boosting teen record buying and bringing surfing acts to a wider audience. As a small studio with limited resources, AIP did not produce movie soundtracks, but recording companies released compilation albums featuring songs from the films padded with other surfing tunes. Dick Dale and the Del-Tones performed their hits as part of several *Beach Party* film installments. Annette recorded three albums on Disney's Buena Vista label.[55] One of these albums, *Annette's Beach Party*, featured the actress framed by a surfboard.[56] Avalon released an album for *Muscle Beach Party* on the United Arts label.[57] These records exploited their connection with the *Beach Party* films as well as the popularity of the California sound.

The films created an ideal teenage existence, marked by consumption, leisure, and little else. Purposefully ignoring the realities of adolescence, AIP created an exclusive and unrealistic ideal. As Arkoff explained to a *Life* reporter, the films featured "no parents, no school, no church, no legal or government authorities, no rich kids or poor kids, no money problems –

none of the things that plague the young people today."[58] A few corrupted youth appear, but unlike earlier incarnations, the wayward characters in the beach films are comic and nonthreatening. Misunderstanding adults eventually come to sympathize with youth, rather than forcing teens to conform.[59] The shockingly rebellious figures of 1950s films, motorcyclists, appeared in the beach films as objects of derision for the surfing kids.[60] As the *New York Times* noted, in the beach films, the "good guys who neither smoke nor drink, prevail in the end and, virtue rewarded, everyone heads back to the surf."[61]

The producers of the *Beach Party* films were very aware of their image-making power. As actor John Ashley remembered, "When we did the beach pictures, AIP was more cognizant of an image. We depicted the California surfing crowd as a bunch of fun-loving kids. Always Cokes. No beers."[62] Producer Arkoff told *Time* that the world created by the films was "a kind of never-never land in modern undress."[63] Annette later ascribed the popularity of *Beach Party* films this way: "[It showed] everybody's dream of what they would like their summer vacation to be, especially those kids who didn't live near water. Their big dream was to come out to Malibu Beach and to surf and dance on the sand, and to have weenie roasts every night. It also showed you that you could have fun without using vulgar language and without explicit sex scenes."[64] With a combination of budget restraints, business concerns, and intuitive luck, AIP found, as *Life* put it, "gold in corny films about surfing, beach life, and the joys of being young."[65] This leisure-filled, fantasy-based, image-conscious film-making – at its core silly and formulaic – enabled a young moviegoing public to revel in the California of their dreams. For the price of a movie ticket, they found fun in the sun without leaving home. The cultural environment that glorified California and packaged its young people guaranteed AIP's success.

Despite director Asher's assurance that moviegoing teenagers wanted to see good clean fun at the beach, AIP was unsure of the film's chances at the box office. During the summer of 1963, the studio launched a media blitz campaign to heighten interest in *Beach Party*.[66] Pictures of Frankie and Annette flooded the television airwaves, and the duo made public appearances. Local theaters held contests and promotional parties to hype the film. Landlocked drive-ins trucked in beach sand, placing it in front of concession stands.[67] The movie's poster promised excitement and California fun: "10,000 kids meet on 5,000 beach blankets! The inside story of what goes on when the sun's gone down . . . the moon's come up . . . and the water's too cold for surfin.' "[68] The response to the film surprised even those AIP executives who had pitched the film's premise. In Chicago, *Beach Party* outperformed the box office of the megastar, megabudget *Cleopatra*.[69]

Beach Party opens with a panoramic view of the California beach. Frankie (Frankie Avalon) and Dolores (Annette Funicello) drive an antique car, hauling surfboards and singing the praises of their anticipated vacation. Despite their harmonizing, the happy couple has very different ideas about what their vacation will entail. Dolores has invited the whole gang to the beach rather than spend time privately with Frankie. "I don't trust myself when I'm alone with you," she explains. Dolores refuses to get "any closer until I'm a wife." At the beach house, boys and girls sleep in separate rooms.

Meanwhile, a "developmental biologist and social anthropologist" (Bob Cummings) constructs a laboratory for scientific investigation in a neighboring beach house, observing the mating habits and culture of the California teens on the beach for his study, "Post-Adolescent Surf Dwellers." Erich Von Zipper and his gang, caricatures of the traditional biker rebels, plague the well-meaning surfers. A brawl between the surfers and the motorcycle gang ends the film with wholesome teenagers triumphant.[70]

Beach Party was a monster-size hit for the studio, providing the model for the genre's conventions. The use of an outside observer to comment on the goings-on would be a ploy used throughout AIP's *Beach Party* films: an anthropologist, a rich foreign countess, a covetous businessman, a rock and roll manager, or an advertising executive. These films lack dramatic tension, as the genre guarantees a happy ending, a departure from traditional teen movie territory. In juvenile delinquency movies of the 1950s, the outcome was always in doubt, as dangerous situations threatened the most innocuous of characters.[71]

The films establish "vacation" as a nebulous time frame, never revealing the exact age of the surfing tribe. Songs and dialogue mention school but do not offer any specifics. Characters are caricatures, types rather than fully developed parts of the story. The songs of Dick Dale and performances by Avalon and Funicello make up the soundtrack. The Peter Pan formula of AIP put girls in bikinis for the target male audience. Panoramic shots of the beach, ocean sunsets, and surfing scenes glue together plot segments and musical numbers. Each film ends with a cartoonish brawl between surfers and their adversaries.

Poor reviews were another element the beach films shared. *Beach Party*'s critiques highlighted the attraction of the California scenery but questioned the film's appeal to clear-thinking teenagers. The *New York Times* reviewer classified the film as a "musical" and praised the film's setting as "downright yummy, shot on a magnificent strip of California shoreline." However, the reviewer suspected "that the youngsters in the audience may find it all pretty laughable."[72] *Time*'s review of *Beach Party* sarcastically described the plot as the "coming-of-age-in-California shenanigans of a tribe of overripe adolescents."[73] Film critics chose Annette as the "least promising young performer" for both 1963 and 1964.[74] Reportedly, authentic southern California surfers attending the *Beach Party* premiere left in disgust.[75]

Variety praised the beauty of the setting but wondered whether unsuspecting adults in the audience "might find it a frightening manifestation of the culture of our age." For youthful viewers, it continued, the movie "has the kind of direct, simple-minded cheeriness which should prove well nigh irresistible to those teen-agers who have no desire to escape the emptiness of their lives."[76] What this reviewer misunderstood was the film's draw: mindless fun in the California sun, sexual teasing, and the lure of the beach tantalized teenage moviegoers.

Beach Party traveled the world, an ambassador of wholesome American youth on screens far and wide. Most of AIP's films earned close to a million dollars in Japan and Western Europe, making AIP dependent on foreign box office for about 20 percent of each film's profits.[77] Screening *Beach Party* abroad brought additional reviews from different perspectives. *Films and Filming*, the British film journal, wondered how "Britain's younger audiences will take to the sight of America's youth beating up the coastal resorts in the politest of manners." For the most part the review was positive, calling the film "slickly professional" and "done with style." The reviewer acknowledged that the "script may not be worthy of detailed examination" but responded favorably to the clean teen presented by the AIP studio.[78]

Beach Party's resounding box office success, despite the critical drubbing it received in its native country, inspired AIP to produce a quick sequel. *Muscle Beach Party* appeared in March 1964, with a similarly styled advertising campaign. Movie posters read, "When 10,000 Biceps go around 5,000 bikinis . . . you know what's gonna happen!"[79] Another poster evoked the success of the previous film to hype the next installment; "Remember what happened on those 'Beach Party Blankets'? Well here we go again with Biceps . . . Bikinis . . . Surf and . . . Sun . . . Music . . . Lovin' and beach time fun!"[80] *Muscle Beach Party*'s opening shot parallels *Beach Party*, showing happy young surfers on the highway. The plot featured bodybuilding and a rich countess entranced by the lifestyles of California youth. Spring break is the implied time, yet the lack of context suggests that these surfers are on a continuous holiday from responsibility.[81]

Fewer mainstream publications reviewed this second installment, partly a commentary on its lack of adult appeal. The *New York Times* proclaimed, "Never, anyway seldom, has so much idiocy cluttered a perfectly beautiful strip of California beach as in this dum-dum . . . a tangle of vigorous young people with beautiful bodies and empty heads."[82] Poor reviews failed to stop the beach party train from rolling profitably along. AIP released *Bikini Beach*, its third offering, in July 1964, less than four months after *Muscle Beach Party*. Again, the studio employed suggestive advertising copy; "The Girls are Bare-ing . . . the Guys are Dare-ing and the Surf's RARE-ing to GO-GO-GO!"[83] Very little about the film was actually daring, despite studio promises. *Bikini Beach* takes place during summer vacation. A businessman who wants the beach for a retirement community sensationalizes the surfer's hedonism, a "true subculture" of "potential delinquents," for the local paper. The film features Avalon in the dual role of both surfer and a pop star named "Potato Bug," a reference to the British musical invasion. Drag racing and "Little" Stevie Wonder play key roles as well.[84]

Beach Blanket Bingo, released in April 1965, included the standbys of the AIP genre, adding Deborah Walley of *Gidget Goes Hawaiian* fame to the mix. The poster summarized the simplistic plot: "The Beach Party Gang Goes Sky Diving!"[85] As the title suggests, this entry in the series offers more adolescent schemes and jealousy plots. Buster Keaton and a mermaid make appearances. The last frame warns, "Get Ready for the Next Beach Blast!"[86] While a popular addition to the genre, the film lacked the vitality and freshness of earlier entries.[87] Reviewers were not impressed. *Variety* asked the question: "Are teen-agers responding to such drivel as good-natured satire of themselves rather than identifying with it? Let's hope so."[88] The *New York Times* pulled no punches in its review; "We simply can't believe, no matter what the reports say, that teenagers buy such junk. It's for morons!"

The next "beach blast" appeared in August 1965. AIP promoted *How to Stuff a Wild Bikini* with this come-on: "For Beginners and Experts . . . An

A promotional picture for Annette
Funicello's album *Muscle Beach Party*,
released to promote the film of the
same name. The photo features all the
ingredients of the California beach
mystique; surfboard, surf, sand, and a
modest swimsuit.

(Hulton Getty/Archive Photos)

Interesting Course in The Birds . . . The Bees and Bikinis . . . In Six Very Easy Lessons." The plot involved the same beach and motorcycle gang high jinks that propelled the earlier films. Avalon, involved in another AIP production, is away on naval reserve duty. Stationed on a tropical isle, Frankie uses a witch doctor (Buster Keaton) to keep tabs on Annette. The film's outsiders are Madison Avenue executives looking to cast young people in motorcycle advertisements. The surfers represent commercial opportunity and profit to the cynical businessmen. This serves as an ironic plot point, as AIP made millions marketing its image of young California to the world.

The *New York Times* continued its disparagement of the series, calling it "the answer to a moron's prayer – the squealing young cuties, their gawking male counterparts, and the usual 'guest stars,'" adding, "The young folk cheerfully yelp the worst musical score since 1925 (the year before sound movies)." As one exhibitor explained, "Business was only average due to the fact that our teenagers here have seen all the beach films they want to see. When you've seen this one, you have seen them all."[89] This final entry in AIP's string of beach dramas was the least successful.[90]

However, moviegoers had not seen all the beach adventures Hollywood was ready to produce. Once AIP had demonstrated the cinematic potential of the California beach, the major studios, imitative and derivative, could not ignore AIP's success. The formula – "put some lithe teen-agers on a beach, turn on the rock 'n' roll music and let the cameras roll" – created what the *New York Times* called a "beach bonanza."[91] There was even talk of putting Frankie and Annette in an AIP-sponsored television series.[92] Established moviemakers joined the surfing crowd, despite having "once scoffed at what they called 'sand and sex epics,'" and actively challenged AIP's dominance of the teenage market.[93]

Hollywood released seven films in the *Beach Party* mold during 1964, and only three were AIP productions.[94] For the most part, the big studio beach movies failed to rival AIP's box office. While using the same locale and similarly attractive casts, the major studios added parents, teenage angst, and a more serious tone.[95] The derivative films, while not following the genre's exact rules pioneered by AIP, tapped into the fascination for California teen adventures.

Twentieth Century-Fox produced two AIP-inspired films. *Surf Party* (1964) told the story of three girls from Phoenix traveling to Malibu Beach.[96] Film advertisements copied the standard AIP campaign, promising "When Beach Boys meet Surf Sweets – it's a real swingin' splash of Fun,

Fun, Fun!" *Wild on the Beach* appeared in 1965. The film's plot revolved around a beach house mistakenly rented to both a male and a female contingent of teenage sun worshippers. Paramount directly challenged AIP with its ad campaign for 1965's *The Girls on the Beach*: "The jet action surf-set hits the beaches and captures a love-load of bikini beauties – It takes off where the others leave off."[97] The film is set during Easter vacation, when a sorority mistakenly believes it has booked the Beatles for a fundraiser. The Beach Boys perform the title song, "Little Honda," and "Lonely Sea."[98]

Paramount's *Beach Ball* (1965) was unusual for its ambitious exploitation of California crazes. The studio promised exhibitors "[the] 5 hottest groups in the whole beach-lovin' nation all rock 'n rolled into one picture – with a campaign that hits the surf ridin' skin divin' sky jumpin' drag racin' set where they play."[99] The film showcased appearances by the Four Seasons, the Supremes, the Righteous Brothers, and the Hondells.[100] The film's director worried about the genre's longevity even as he profited, commenting, "There's a great danger that too many of these films are being made."[101] While saturation of the market concerned studio executives and directors, only box office failure would stop production.

United Artists entered the fray with *For Those Who Think Young* in 1964, borrowing the Pepsi slogan and exploiting promotional tie-ins with the beverage. The picture starred *Gidget*'s James Darren in his return to the surf, Nancy Sinatra, and Bob Denver.[102] Columbia's *Ride the Wild Surf* was the only beach picture with Hawaiian surfing footage. Jan and Dean provided the title track. Shelley Fabares, Tab Hunter, and Barbara Eden played young Californians on vacation in Hawaii, changing locations but not theme.

Minor studios surfed for their piece of the big wave. *The Horror of Party Beach* appeared in 1963, marketed for the drive-in crowd as "the first horror monster musical." This *Beach Party* rip-off warned "of the dangers of nuclear waste management." Filmed in Stamford, Connecticut, the plot involved killer zombies created by radioactive waste eventually being defeated by sodium. United Screen Arts produced *A Swingin' Summer* in 1965, with the slogan "Spread out the Beach Towels . . . Grab Your Gals." Despite the campaign and surfboards on the movie poster, the movie actually took place on the shores of Lake Arrowhead, not the Pacific Ocean. U.S. Films released *The Beach Girls and the Monster* in 1965, cashing in on the craze with scenes of surfing, monsters, and death. Long surf instrumentals accompany the rampages of the rubber monster, along with a Frank Sinatra Jr. tune "Monster in the Surf."[103]

Popular magazines paid close attention to the explosion of beach movies. While the *New York Times* continued to call the beach films "idiocy," other publications included "pro-beach" articles on the genre.[104] *Life* called the beach films "corny," headlining its July 1965 story on the genre, "Peekaboo Sex." The magazine did not damn the "corn" content that served as the brand "trademark" but instead praised the camera techniques employed to make "the viewer feel he is watching good-looking, vibrant youngsters through one-way glass."[105]

Look examined the phenomenon in November 1964, calling it "Hollywood's Teenage Gold Mine." The article compared the film version of beach life with teenage reality. In this "fantasy world of teenage movies," the article observed, "the premium is on the human body and the happy witless outdoor life." Protagonists are "never faced with a decision more serious than whether to play volleyball or caress one another." The characters fail to make any improvements or changes, remaining the same beach-bound postadolescents.[106] Despite the article's challenge to AIP's version of teen life, the pictures accompanying it resembled publicity stills rather than serious journalistic investigation. While attempting to debunk *Beach Party*'s conventions, the magazine's photographs reinforced the AIP image.

In July 1965, the *Saturday Evening Post* called the "teen-oriented sand-surf-and-sex musicals" the "most successful California export since the orange." The article highlighted AIP's invention of the genre, and the ingredients that made it such a "galvanizing offshoot of rock and roll." Ironically, Annette, the "queen of the beach," didn't share her character's love for the seashore. "The only part I don't like about filming them is . . . the beach," Annette explained. The "king," Frankie Avalon, attracted the teenage audience not as an idol but as an inferior peer. As one of his costars argued, "Every kid thinks he can sing as well as Frankie, and they know they can surf as well as he can. . . . They don't laugh with him, they laugh at him. It makes them feel superior."[107]

While magazines profiled the beach movie trend, explaining its success proved more difficult. *Esquire* quoted AIP scriptwriter Deke Haywood's interpretation: "We do not hold a mirror up to nature." A true reflection of life in California was not the goal of filmmakers. From a simple measurement of box office, *Esquire* noted, "The kids they are made for seem to like them." It was "the kids themselves, those hard young bodies having fun being in the movies" that enthralled moviegoers and drove the *Beach Party* cycle.[108] Teens wanted to see the idyllic life of California youth. Judging from the critical reviews, the quality of the movies was unimportant.

Why did popular magazines include profiles of the beach movies? Their appearance in the pages of *Look*, the *Saturday Evening Post*, and *Esquire* was not accidental. These "pro-beach" profiles, aimed at an adult readership, offered a vision in keeping with companion articles about life in California, helping package and promote particular images. The *Beach Party* films represented the perfect opportunity to profile movies, California, and baby boomers under the same umbrella. These films codified beliefs about the state's young people – a tanned, vacationing, happy, content cohort in California – and by extension influenced the image of the nation's baby boomers.

How might one explain the short but influential reign of the clean California teen on the big screen? Some film chroniclers view these films as no more than interesting artifacts from a simpler time, silly and inconsequential to a larger cultural understanding of the 1960s. Film critic Ethan Mordden calls the *Beach Party* films a desperate throwback, belonging to "a cinema so old they make the 1950s look New Wave."[109] The genre, Marjorie Rosen argues, removes the complexities of adolescence in favor of a simplistic and sensationalistic appeal to moviegoers.[110] Another critic sees this falseness seeping into the beach locale, in real life crowded with thousands of visitors but deserted in these films. The environment provides a "locus of adolescent optimism, leisure, and social mobility." In this space, Annette strove to conform, to realize the middle-class dream of home and spouse.[111]

The assertion that these films are mere fantasy does little to explain their box office success. One critic supposes a swinging pendulum that governs popular culture, arguing that the large number of juvenile delinquent films that appeared in the 1950s required "a further wave of youth movies that placated and domesticated" the image.[112] Alan Betrock, in his analysis, heralds the "escapist fun" with "no parents . . . a fantasy vision of life." Betrock maintains that these film images, especially those visions in conflict with real life offscreen, were increasingly important as safe havens for baby boomers. He explains, "For millions of kids this worldly change was threatening and confusing, and though a large percentage of youth was caught up in these changes, another significant group fought steadfastly to hold onto what was safe, fun, and familiar."[113]

Gary Morris also argues that the beach culture was a reaction to "the troubling social, racial, and sexual barriers" in American society. By utilizing the "open space" of a frontier, filmmakers glorified white middle-class youth. The "employment of an environment as a tonic" was an attempt to manage and contain the growing uneasiness in society. As a result, he asserts, the films are "noticeably schizoid, typical of a period of social flux." Stevie Wonder's appearances in *Bikini Beach* and *Muscle Beach Party* avoid civil rights issues, and his performances are without political context.[114] The beach made both rock and racial issues noncontroversial. Motown acts singing surf songs made everyone a part of the beach culture, despite the evident incongruities. In addition, the presence of older actors, especially those from the silent era, such as Buster Keaton, point to a moviemaking attempt to bridge the generations and appeal to adults as well as teenagers.[115]

These examinations reveal important elements that drove the *Beach Party* genre. However, they ignore what some contemporary reviewers recognized as the films' most important ingredient: environmental determinism, the showcasing of California's beautiful people in a setting that attracted moviegoers. The films did not "hold a mirror up to nature," yet they mirrored the glorification of California then taking place in American culture. As a California mythmaker recently pointed out, the "real star of all beach movies was Southern California anyway. . . . Frankie Avalon in a bathing suit only made a viewer aware of what a troubled place Philly must be."[116] These films, in their silliness and slapstick, celebrated the California image, selling the dream at the drive-in. While not as popular with older moviegoers, the *Beach Party* films and their copycats represented an ideal image well articulated in other adult venues. National magazines heralded California as a wonderful place for baby boom youth. The beach films were the teen version, an image shaped and packaged for the big screen, passed down and popularized by adults for younger minds. Annette and her fellow cast members represented an ideal, making a last stand on the beach, the outermost edge of the western frontier. This cinematic portrayal of a leisured, white middle class lacked realism and inclusiveness, to be sure. In reality, the experience of California youth on the beach was not all fun and games. As *McCall's* reported in 1962, vacation havoc on both coasts was the rule. "If parents live, to some degree, in fantasy, so do their adolescent children," the magazine explained.[117] What was genuine was the films' popularity, a success fostered by mass media hype and Hollywood influence.

Millions migrated to California, but popular culture images moved in the opposite direction. The baby boom generation grew up in an environment pervaded by media forces, and California was the birthplace of many cultural trends. Images of California youth, carefully crafted by dozens of media venues, provided Hollywood with attractive and exploitable lifestyles. The *Beach Party* films glorified wholesome California teenagers in the golden sun, taking cues from popular music and a media environment that heralded the beach as the ultimate in fashionable leisure spots. Not all California's kids, however, were on vacation. Nineteen sixty-four was the year the first baby boomers, schooled by postwar popular culture, entered college. The most portentous challenge first appeared on the Berkeley campus of the University of California, shattering the reigning images of California youth. In Watts, a suburb of Los Angeles, miles of cultural distance away from the beach, a violent threat to the mythmaking was on the horizon.

CHAPTER SEVEN

Berkeley and Watts

The images of California youth packaged and sold in the postwar period represented belief in the frontier magic of the Golden State and hope for the future of the baby boomer generation. The moralistic youngsters of *The Mickey Mouse Club*, the wholesome Gidget, the surfing craze, the Beach Boys sound, and the leisured and fashionable Annette and Frankie combined to celebrate white middle-class youth, relieving societal anxiety about postwar changes with comforting imagery of consumerism and suburbia. In this environment, the disruptive appearance of the Berkeley Free Speech Movement in 1964–65 staggered and surprised the nation, while the Watts riot in 1965 helped destroy the image of California as a prosperous, untroubled land.

The actual events at Berkeley and the issues raised by the Free Speech Movement are not the focus of this examination. Similarly, the Watts rioting and the chain of events leading to the violence are not the main concern. Rather, the purpose of this analysis is to look at the extreme negative responses to the Berkeley trouble and the Watts uprising, responses that reveal cultural beliefs about California's young people. These challenges to the vision of conformist, happy, middle-class members of society had revolutionary consequences for postwar America. In the mid-1960s, California became "a study in contrasts," as predominant images gave way to contradictions and disputes. The "romantic reputation" of California changed to an image marked by "unprecedented social ferment."[1]

California had experienced free speech movements and racial troubles in its past.[2] Yet, the postwar environment did not evoke that history, and those earlier radical movements had not been the activities of middle-class children of the suburbs. Many Californians of the 1950s and 1960s were recent migrants or too young to recall previous outbreaks of civil unrest. In addition, these past troubles were part of a history that was largely ignored in contemporary snapshots of life in the state. The prevailing image of California was a land of new possibilities, unhampered by old inequalities or haunted by earlier conflicts. The blindness inherent in this view made trouble all the more surprising. The disturbances in Berkeley and Watts shocked the sensibilities of Californians, and of Americans as a whole, as they had been conditioned to see California as a land apart and its youth as contented and suburban.

California youth portrayals remained conventional throughout the early 1960s, as if the *Beach Party* films were documentaries rather than fantasies. These films echoed the descriptions in magazines and news media of a generation marked by apathy and leisure rather than political agitation. The baby boomers, it seemed, were "silent," content with the world presented by mass marketing and their opportunities within it. California's kids appeared the worst offenders in this regard, the epitome of the trend. *Look*, in its 1959 California cover story, compared the state's young people to "cellophaned fruit . . . [who] seem to have no tang."[3] The good life provided no ammunition for revolt or challenge. In 1963, the *New York Times Magazine* assessed the political climate of the Golden State this way: "The present is so sunny, euphoric, and pleasant that it seems subversive to worry about the future. In this sense, California has very, few subversives."[4] Most notably, a complacent white middle class ignored the warning signs that indicated this new decade would veer from the well-marked path of the previous one.[5] Many Americans, conditioned by mass-mediated popular culture, viewed the baby boom generation in an unrealistic, idealized way.

Before Berkeley, if California kids were portrayed as proactive citizens, it was rarely for questioning the status quo. In 1960 *American Mercury* profiled the "Torchbearers," a patriotic club organized by Los Angeles teens. These young people, "concerned with the suspicion that school history courses might not be making the most of the thrilling story of how our people struggled to build our Republic," gathered materials for their own library and sponsored parades. The club maintained patriotic and religious requirements for membership.[6] Many predictions about the children then matriculating in California shared this conservatism. As Clark Kerr, president of the University of California, said in 1959, "Employers will love this generation. . . . They are going to be easy to handle. There aren't going to be any riots."[7]

Typically, the complaints about young people in the late 1950s and early 1960s pointed to their lack of idealism.[8] The student icon in the early 1960s mirrored characterizations of California's youth, marked by a "conformity and willing acceptance of the standards of the affluent society."[9] In 1957, the *Nation* sponsored a symposium on the "silent generation." For its California section, the article quoted a professor of English who observed "far too little sense of excitement" in the rising generation. He feared that without drastic developments, "the undergraduate generation following this one may well never escape from childhood involvement with the . . . mass media."[10]

Baby boomers might have tried limiting their media consumption, but young Californians often found themselves the subject of media portrayals. National magazines employed California teens as baby boomer archetypes. For example, the *Saturday Evening Post* sponsored a Gallup opinion poll of the nation's youth in December 1961. The magazine chose for its cover a photograph of youngsters piled into an automobile, a "carload of high-spirited teen-agers in Glendale, California" reflecting "the casually groomed, untroubled look of the Cool Generation." For some critics, these young people were "indifferent and distressingly bland," while fans defended "them as self-assured and realistic individuals." As the *Saturday Evening Post* explained: "No one can say that the American youth is going to hell. He's not. But he is a pampered hothouse plant. . . . The Beatnik is a rarity, the delinquent a minority. In general, the typical American youth shows few symptoms of frustration, and is most unlikely to rebel or to involve himself in crusades of any kind. He likes himself the way he is, and he likes things as they are." The magazine also spotlighted Suzi Monahan, part of the "stay-at-home generation . . . satisfied to remain a hometown girl in Laguna Beach, California."[11]

For a 1963 article, *Life* profiled a young California high school student, Jill Dinwiddie. A "golden girl" from Monterey, Jill enjoyed the beach, cheerleading, and her role as "queen bee of the high school." The article was somewhat critical of her trivial goals and blindness to a world outside her own. A sociologist countered this criticism, acknowledging that while Jill might deserve reproach, society beyond the high school clique rewarded these behaviors and pursuits. He argued:

> I see little evidence that the kinds of young persons who are most committed and dedicated to the values we find missing in the golden girls are any healthier, securer, or less anxious. I see even less evidence that we appreciate them when they turn up. The young people who care about the things the popularity queen does not care most about are the young people disdained as beatniks, or who picket the White House, or who go to Cuba without passports, who stage sit-ins in offices of politicians, go on freedom rides and cause disturbances at hearings of the House Un-American Activities Committee. There is nobody better equipped than Jill to live in a society of all-electric kitchens, wall to wall carpets, dishwashers, garbage disposals, color TV, new cars in the garage, new boats in the dock, and old horses in the stable.[12]

In the world of California and in postwar America as a whole, the kids being celebrated were not making trouble or questioning the world, but taking advantage of the booming economy. In mid-1964 *Life* argued, "Given the choice, we'll take noisy wrongheadedness before gray-flannel silence any day."[13] The majority of Americans, however, did not support disruption. The cultural environment disdained its challengers, preferring to celebrate middle-class kids living it up in California.

A high school teacher living in the "mild, mild West" wrote a letter to the *New York Times*, responding to a story on California. In the West, the teacher noted, the students were "better behaved, kinder and friendlier." On the downside, she complained, "They're all alike, they rarely react."[14] This lack of social involvement permeated the college scene as well. *U.S. News & World Report* profiled higher education in February 1964. The article claimed, "A lot of the rah-rah spirit has gone out of the colleges of this country." West Coast educators expressed a concern for their suffering, "ulcerous and neurotic" students, whom they viewed as motivated by a "compulsive competitiveness" rather than a love of learning. One faculty member at San Francisco State College identified a politically conservative trend among his students.[15]

There were some prescient observers who identified a different course. In yet another attempt to name the aging baby boomers, *Look* dubbed them "The Explosive Generation" on its January 1961 cover. It argued that young people, having been "tarred with epithets ranging from 'mediocre and conformist' to 'fat, dumb, and happy'" were finding causes to join. The fight against racial discrimination was one such cause; another was political injustice. As an example, *Look* described the 1960 protests against the House Un-American Activities Committee (HUAC) meeting in San Francisco. Commenting on these events, a professor in the University of California system told the magazine, "There has been a genuine rebirth of student political activity. The last few months have been damned exciting around here." These rumblings, *Look* argued, merited a "fresh look at the new generation." "Young Americans," it explained, "want the fruits of material prosperity. They also want something more."[16] In California, where more to wish for seemed impossible, conflict was unthinkable.

In particular, California's educational system was an unlikely place to find student discord. Baby boomers in the Golden State made up the largest cohort in the nation, spawning a need for more high schools and colleges to house the growth. By 1961, due to continued immigration and high birth rates, California boasted the largest population of school-age children in the nation, making education "the state's biggest business."[17] In 1962, *Life* called the state's schools an "exemplary system of mass education that is unmatched anywhere in the country for its combination of magnitude and excellence." The article quoted one California coed, Virginia Trimble, who lauded the opportunities afforded her; "No matter what you want to know there's someone here to tell you where to find it."[18]

Peter Schrag, in his book on the nation's public schools, noted that Californians enjoyed the "most universal system of public education in the world," yet it was not without its flaws. Schools provided "education for the Good Life, for weekends on the beach and in the pool, for identity in a society that provides little, education for morals, patriotism, and religion, education to be charming, handsome, successful." This brand of instruction faced difficulties adapting to minorities and the underprivileged.[19] Despite that fact, many Californians looked to education to solve these problems. The state's higher education system in particular was a source of pride to its residents and a wonder to the nation.

The University of California (UC) complex housed 64,620 students and boasted seven campuses. Within this "truly vast" institution, impersonality was inevitable.[20] At the helm was Clark Kerr, the most vocal proponent of this type of mass education. In early 1964, Kerr published *The Uses of the University*, based on a series of lectures he gave at Harvard.

Coining the term "multiversity," Kerr argued that the modern world required the ambitiousness of an educational organization like the UC system, a "knowledge industry" for the masses. At the same time, Kerr recognized the difficulties faced by students, who "wanted to be treated as distinct individuals." Looking to the future, Kerr described a "general public concern with 'morality' on the campus: with the so-called beatniks, with the young radicals, with cheating and with sex."[21] Universities across the nation saw their role not just to educate but also to help students become "conventional adults."[22]

The University of California at Berkeley was the state's flagship, the leader among public universities.[23] Berkeley attracted the upper echelons of California's student achievers as well as the nation's top scholars.[24] The proximity of Berkeley to San Francisco influenced its political character, creating difficulties for administrators who wanted to turn out conventional graduates. Historically, the San Francisco Bay Area hosted California's most radical cultural insurgents, and the city maintained its reputation for "easy hospitality" to disparate groups. In 1964, *Life* recognized the city's notoriety as the "gay capital" of the United States.[25]

The Beats, a small literary and cultural movement of the 1950s, called San Francisco their home as well. In 1953, bohemianism traveled west with Jack Kerouac and Allen Ginsberg, with two enclaves established in California – one in North San Francisco and one in Venice Beach near Los Angeles.[26] The headlines of an obscenity trial brought the West Coast branch of Beatdom to the national stage in a case involving Ginsberg's *Howl* and a San Francisco bookstore. Calling it the "James Dean school of poetry," *Life* reported on the controversy in September 1957, quoting Ginsberg and other Beat poets.[27] *Esquire* called San Francisco "the Paris of this generation."[28]

Most national publications mocked the Beats' questionable cultural influence, focusing instead on salacious details about their lifestyles. In August 1958, *Look* featured an in-depth article and picture profile of the San Francisco scene, the "international headquarters of the so-called 'Beat Generation.'" The author described the mantra of the beatniks as "the average American's value scale – turned inside out." He concluded that the "overblown national furor and fascination" surrounding the Beats was a reflection of the nation's boredom rather than a testament to the group's allure.[29] In February 1959, *Time* called the Beats a "pack of oddballs who celebrate booze, dope, sex, and despair."[30] Later that year the magazine reported on the "brisk sales of Beat books" by the "unwashed minstrels of the West." The article maintained, "The beat blather certainly is not literature. But it can be amusing."[31]

Newsweek commented on Venice Beach hostility in August 1959, describing a community conflict between the "beatniks" and long-standing Venice residents. When this "handful of shaggy, arts-dedicated" beats settled in the area, disturbed property owners became increasingly concerned. One hotel manager, employing every Beat stereotype, described his neighbors as "a dirty bunch of people," complaining, "They drink and every night is debauchery. They make free love practically in the streets, play bongo drums."[32]

In November 1959, *Life* called the "Shabby Beats" the "Only Rebellion Around." Characterizing the United States as "the biggest, sweetest, and most succulent casaba ever produced by the melon patch of civilization," the author compared the Beats to troublesome "fruit flies," claiming their existence as a movement was possible only "in part as a result of the very prosperity it rejects." The majority of Americans, he argued, saw the Beats as "simply dirty people in sandals."[33]

Teenagers paid some attention to the Beats, at least superficially. In September 1959, *Life* featured three young women from Hutchinson, Kansas, who proposed a student exchange with Beats in Venice, California. The trade of lifestyles never occurred, but the article revealed beatnik stereotypes. The Kansas girls aspired to the "far-out freedoms" of the cats in California: "I'd like to do what I want to do and say what I want to say, and know it wouldn't effect me in the future."[34] The October 1960 *Seventeen* featured an article explaining the language and characteristics shared by "all truly Beat people." Along with their uniform – "sandals, blue jeans, and faded blue shirt" – Beats sported long hair for girls, beards for boys. The article featured a glossary of Beat terms and a list of questions to help determine whether the reader was a candidate for Beathood. Activities likely to qualify one for candidacy included expressing sympathy for underdogs like Don Quixote and Robin Hood, writing love poetry, debating the merits of the Kingston Trio, and taking off high-heeled shoes in restaurants.[35]

In May 1961, the *Nation* chronicled the "rise and fall of the Beats," calling the movement largely one of mass media exploitation. The Beat generation's image, "the beard . . . sloppy clothes and dark glasses," became a sensationalized product sold to the American public.[36] Made into a commodity and largely ridiculed, the Beats were not taken seriously as a cultural vanguard by the mainstream press. The Beats enjoyed media attention but were a source of humor rather than fear. Treated as fads, the Beats' poetry reading and weak challenges to middle-class values appeared as objects of derision.[37] The popular press, facing a dearth of societal challenges to exploit, used the Beats "as figures of revolt in a very docile age."[38]

While San Francisco provided many of the Beat thinkers and writers with a base, their limited access to the mainstream and their advanced age, beyond the teenage years, made them less connected to California's young baby boomers. Their California locale did not necessarily tie them to themes of prosperity and suburbia. Magazines used the Beats as narrative color, dismissing them as a lunatic fringe most pronounced in California but outside the bounds of serious discourse about life in the state. The stereotypes of the Beats – the derogatory imagery of the "beatnik" as unclean, darkly clothed, and morally bankrupt – would resurface with a vengeance in criticism of Berkeley students.

The University of California at Berkeley shared San Francisco's reputation for fostering dissent. By 1960, the Bay Area had a long history of student activism and public discord. The mainstream press muffled that notoriety. *Life*, always ready to showcase cheerleaders and good-natured youth, featured the Berkeley campus in May 1960. The article's focus was the construction of new male and female dorms that faced each other across a grassy quadrangle. In these residence halls, "students found a ready-made gambit for getting acquainted": men and women used the sixty-four big windows on the eight-story buildings as chessboards, creating large playing pieces for contests. In addition, flickering lights at night served as a dating Morse code.[39]

However, there were stirrings of a different kind of campus activity. In 1960, students from Berkeley supported the protest against a HUAC meeting in San Francisco. Locally, this inspired banner headlines that shook the image of happy conformity on college campuses. Jessica Treuhaft, a close observer of West Coast campus activities, chronicled these events in a 1961 article for the *Nation*. She argued that these ripples of discontent were "mirrored in varying degrees" around the country, with California at the forefront of national trends. University students also rallied in support of Caryl Chessman, a San Quentin inmate sentenced to death. Berkeley students joined the Congress of Racial Equality boycott of the Woolworth's chain. Treuhaft predicted that those activists beginning "to taste the sweet fruits of success in their efforts" would not "subside into silence" again.[40]

The *Los Angeles Times* reported in June 1962 that the rising college generation was "coming awake and finding its voice" in a "renaissance" of political activity. While the "great mass of students remain quiescent and uncommitted," it noted, a few small groups were beginning to agitate on the left and right of the political spectrum. The newspaper interviewed Katherine A. Towle, the dean of students at Berkeley, who said, "I think this is the most interesting college generation I've seen."[41] A follow-up article described an atmosphere where "the yeast appears to be rising on the campuses of California and the nation." The focus of most protest, the article explained, was "mild rebellion against long-accepted restrictions and administrative authority." Yet the "sleeping student giant awakening," motivated mainly by campus issues, foreshadowed future action.[42]

Sensitive to student concerns, Clark Kerr held a "gripe seminar" in the winter of 1964 to hear the complaints of UC student leaders. The students voiced complaints "not of wrath" against administration policy.[43] Polled before the start of the school year in 1964, 80 percent of students expressed contentment with their education.[44] At that time, the University of California system was reportedly "probably the freest of any major university in the U.S."[45] Yet portentous events were in store for Kerr in the 1964–65 academic year. In hindsight, it seems clear that the outbreak of discontent at Berkeley was born in the growing student involvement in political affairs.[46]

In 1964 the first baby boom cohort entered college.[47] Berkeley enrolled nearly 27,500 students, 6,000 of those from out of state, and the surrounding campus community housed 3,000 nonstudents.[48] Before the commencement of fall semester 1964, to a majority of Americans "student demonstrations" suggested postgame celebrations of victory.[49] Observers of campuses across the nation were "accustomed to the more frivolous outbursts of youth on the rampage in panty raids, football riots, and faddish activities such as hula-hooping." In contrast, student protests regarding "their education, their society, and their world" surprised Americans.[50] What began as "an apparently simple dispute between activist students and university officials – which everyone in the state would have been relieved to think of as a kind of glorified panty raid" became the most notorious campus movement of the 1964–65 school year.[51]

Trouble at Berkeley began over the issue of political advocacy. University officials, community members, and politicians were sensitive to issues surrounding the presidential election and the civil rights movement. Not wanting the university to appear a training ground for militant radicals,

Dean Towle decided to remove recruitment and literature tables from campus. Specifically, the new university rule banned the tables traditionally situated on Bancroft Way, the edge of campus and disputed territory between the school and the city.[52]

Representatives from eighteen student groups formed a United Front to challenge the ban, setting up tables and circulating petitions. The administration disciplined the students manning the tables, eventually suspending suspected ringleaders.[53] Among those suspended was Mario Savio, a 21-year-old philosophy student who had spent his early years in Catholic parochial school in New York.[54] His "Sicilian-immigrant" parents had moved to California in 1963, joining millions of other relocated Americans in the trek west.[55] He had transferred to Berkeley as a junior philosophy major in 1963 and spent the summer of 1964 as part of a civil rights movement freedom school in Mississippi.[56]

On October 1, 1964, police arrested Jack Weinberg, a former student staffing a table for the Congress of Racial Equality. Students surrounded the police car, sitting down and making an exit impossible. This began a 32-hour standoff between students, police, and state officials. Many students used the top of the police car as a platform, spouting diatribes against university policy. Savio was the most popular speaker during the siege, using humor to frankly criticize the multiversity.[57]

While Weinberg remained in the police car and students gathered, the crowd sang, enhancing solidarity. As protesters offered choruses of "We Shall Overcome," other students mocked their peers, singing *The Mickey Mouse Club* theme in response, spelling out the icon's name over and over, "M-I-C-K-E-Y M-O-U-S-E."[58] These "anti-demonstrators" answered the song of the civil rights movement with one from a children's television show.[59] The contested singing was part of a larger struggle between the two groups, which involved egg throwing, swearing, and shouting.[60] During this police car protest, a cultural battle in microcosm occurred. A new tribe, the protesting students, was challenging the old conformity that characterized their membership in the baby boom generation. The students at Berkeley were at war over cultural capital as much as over university policy; they were challenging the Disney version of themselves.

On October 2, Savio and others negotiated with the administration, demanding the release of Weinberg, immunity for sit-in participants, a committee to discuss campus free speech limitations, and justice for the suspended students.[61] There was a certain urgency to settle the conflict, as the following morning was "Parent's Day," a university-hosted event for parents, families, and taxpayers.[62] A compromise was reached, which ended the first crisis, but it fomented the creation of a new student organization, the Free Speech Movement (FSM). Except for Savio, the key leaders of FSM were Jewish. As William J. Rorabaugh has argued, this changed the character of traditional student politics, usually dominated by exclusionary fraternities, and the group's tactics perplexed the predominant "white, Anglo-Saxon, Protestant administration."[63]

After the police car episode, President Kerr recognized that the measures that had ended the sit-in were stopgap. He predicted more protests on campus due to the presence of a minority who were willing to push beyond the "bounds of law and order."[64] The October 2 agreement was an unstable settlement. Suspensions decreed by the administration were viewed as unfair, and questions about free speech limitations went unresolved. The FSM held daily rallies on campus, circulated petitions, and distributed pamphlets. Songs became a vital part of the movement, expressing the indignity of being treated like children and the alienating influence of the university system. For example, the FSM satirized Christmas carols, selling 15,000 copies of the parodies as a fundraiser. One tune, sung to the melody of "Jingle Bells," had these lyrics: "Oski Dolls, Pompom Girls, UC all the way! Oh, what fun it is to have your mind reduced to clay! Civil Rights, politics, just get in the way. Questioning authority when you should obey."[65]

Fire fights over political tables and recruitment continued. Throughout October and November, the FSM multiplied its student and faculty support. Disciplinary actions against FSM and the perceived duplicity of the administration angered student activists, and the growing campus endorsement inspired more drastic measures. In response to the sense of crisis, the FSM planned a takeover of the administration building, Sproul Hall.[66] On December 2, at a rally preceding the sit-in, Savio inspired the crowd with these words: "There is a time when the operation of the machine becomes so odious, makes you so sick at heart, that you can't take part; you can't even passively take part, and you've got to put your bodies upon the gears and upon the wheels, upon the levers, upon all the apparatus and you've got to make it stop. And you've got to indicate to the people who run it, to the people that own it, that unless you're free, the machines will be prevented from working at all."[67]

Once inside Sproul Hall students studied, watched movies, sang songs, and waited for administrative reaction. It came in the form of the California Highway Patrol, under governor's orders. The FSM was the largest student protest movement on a single campus in the history of American education, and the sit-in at Sproul Hall in December resulted in the "biggest mass arrest ever made in California."[68] As a final protest, sit-in members resisted arrest by going limp to slow the process down. The tactic worked, with the last students arrested at 4:00 in the afternoon on December 3.[69]

Governor Edmund G. "Pat" Brown, a politician who prided himself on his "liberal image," ordered the mass arrests and the use of police power against the students.[70] Brown defended his actions, pointing to the seriousness of the campus challenge. "We're not going to have anarchy in California," Brown told reporters.[71] The *Los Angeles Times* reported that the sit-in reached "new heights of rebellion, vocal warfare, and chaos," employing a large-type headline usually reserved for wars and assassinations. The *Times* revealed that of those arrested, 72 percent were students, with the remaining number employees, student spouses, and other nonstudents.[72] Other estimates of student involvement ran as high as 85 percent, and the majority of protesters came from middle-class backgrounds and had no history of radical activity. To the dismay of Kerr, the grades of the activists were higher than the university average.[73] It would prove difficult for officials to blame outside agitators or riff-raff for the disturbance.

After the sit-in, FSM leaders called for a student strike on Friday, December 4. Many faculty members, upset by the use of police force at an institution of higher learning, lent their support. Approximately 60 percent of classes were canceled. The Academic Senate brokered a deal between the beleaguered parties, which revised controls on free speech and disallowed disciplinary measures against sit-in participants. After three months of struggle, the FSM challenge succeeded, changing Berkeley's political atmosphere and demonstrating the possibilities of protest.[74]

In the spring of 1965, the campus erupted again. *Time* reported on the latest outbreak, the "Filthy Speech Movement," describing it as a disturbance involving "a handful of cause-hunting students and some off-campus beatniks . . . shouting obscene words into a public address system and displaying them on signs."[75] *Life* also covered what it called a "bizarre, shocking turn" of events, stressing the key role of nonstudents. A photograph accompanying the article showed instigator John Thomson practicing "yoga meditations" in old, torn clothes and disorderly hair.[76]

The student movement demobilized, unable to muster the fervor that had made headlines the previous fall. Savio appeared on a New York television talk show in December and spoke at university rallies at Harvard, Michigan, Columbia, Queens, and Brandeis.[77] *Life* gave Savio a forum in February 1965, naming him "California's Angriest Student."[78] But national fame could not save the FSM's fragile coalition; Savio resigned as leader in May 1965.[79] In August 1965 the charges of trespassing and resisting arrest resulting from the Sproul Hall sit-in became jail sentences (most suspended), fines, and probationary periods. Half of the accused refused probation, as it included a conditional ban on future illegal demonstrations.[80]

The events in the Free Speech Movement have been well chronicled by contemporary writers, sociological investigators, and historians, but attention to the tone of coverage in the mass media and the response it engendered has been less visible. The extensive magazine coverage editorialized its reporting, revealing the national mood toward the protests. The sit-in at Sproul Hall and the mass arrests that followed were for many Americans their first glimpse of unfolding events at Berkeley, and they caught the news media largely by surprise. The new icon that emerged forever changed images of California youth.

How could it happen in California, the land of sunshine and happy baby boomers? This question shaded much of the mass media coverage of Berkeley. *Life* captured the startling nature of the Berkeley events and their inherent challenge to the predominant college student image with its headline, "Panty Raids? No! Tough Campus Revolt!" The tone reveals the presumed nature of campus unrest, a panty raid, while reporting on a new variant, a "tough campus revolt."[81] The *New York Times Magazine* asked, "What turned the University of California's world-renowned campus here into a snake pit of unrepressed animosities?"[82] Some observers found Communist inspiration in the troubles. Kerr told the *Los Angeles Times* that "organizations having Communist influences" were seducing students. A further explanation, according to Kerr, was "the permissiveness that's come to pervade our society."[83] *U.S. News & World Report* headlined its first story on Berkeley, "A Campus Uproar That Is Blamed on Reds."[84] Others dismissed this explanation as "marginal or irrelevant."[85]

Mario Savio offered his own rationale for the "revolt among white middle-class youth." He argued that the forces of political activism were strongest in Berkeley, attributing the outbreak partly to the "political character of the Bay Area" and the growing concern for civil rights. These lessons, Savio argued, contradicted university training, where students were taught "just what is so good and only marginally improvable in today's pluralistic, democratic America." Even in the privileged university environment, students were part of "an oppressed white middle-class."[86]

That these events were taking place in California, and at the state's most prestigious campus, forced newspapers and magazines to take notice. Berkeley's influence radiated, serving as inspiration for like-minded young people around the country and as a warning to educators, parents, and politicians.[87] These were dangerous times, since "throughout the world, the University of California [was] looked upon as the shape of educational things to come."[88] *Look* wondered whether trouble at the state's "flagship campus" had "exposed a serious flaw in the heart of the multiversity." The danger posed by this "California uprising" was an escalating conflict that had "deeper implications that no parent, student, or educator can ignore."[89] The tone of coverage varied depending on the news organization – dismayed, suspicious, supportive, surprised – but the conclusions reached did not. All agreed that these were portentous events that merited attention. If California was the future, trouble on its campuses suggested that the entire nation was due for a reckoning.

Those ideologically opposed to the protesters' goals and unsympathetic to FSM noted the "nonstudent" or "non-Californian" identity of the troublemakers. Max Rafferty, the state superintendent of public instruction, told *U.S. News & World Report* that the majority were not "legitimate, genuine students" at all. "Many of them," he said, "are what you might call fugitives, from eastern and midwestern colleges and universities." Asked if he would "describe them as misfits in society," Rafferty replied: "Some of them are. You see the typical 'Peter the Hermit' types with long, lank, greasy hair, the collection of beards and pimples." What made the trouble at Berkeley most acute, he believed, was the surrounding "low cost rental property" that allowed "Bohemian hangers on" easy access to the campus.[90]

Anxious to dismiss Berkeley, some journalists downplayed the number of students involved. Fred M. Hechinger argued in the *New York Times* that a "small, dissident, and anti-authority minority among the students" was the heart of the rebellion.[91] *U.S. News & World Report* explored the issues raised by "rebellious collegians," explaining to its readers that only "3 percent of the student body" supported the struggle to promote off-campus causes; according to its report, social and political agitation sponsored by "the so-called 'beatnik' generation from California" had disturbed the "quiet, academic atmosphere of the campus."[92] *Life*, however, recognized that the FSM had "managed to inflame one of the largest collections of young brains in the U.S., caused a shutdown of classes, brought 500 cops to Sproul Hall to make 782 arrests, [and] got nearly 10,000 signatures on a petition to the Regents."[93] This indicated widespread support beyond a core group of agitators.

Newsweek described Sproul Hall during the takeover as a "fortress under siege . . . [which] sounded like a Saturday night hootenanny." Largely sympathetic to the protesters, the article called the students a "well-disciplined army of occupation." Berkeley, it concluded, the "very model of the modern university," had suffered a "staggering blow to its prestige."[94] Another supportive telling appeared in the *Nation*, highlighting the courtesy of the protesters, who were "careful not to block doorways" and opened locked restrooms by "carefully . . . removing the hinges." In contrast, the policemen dragged limp protesters harshly down the stairs, and once in jail, violated many students' civil rights. "When the university has to be turned over to the Oakland police," the article argued, "something must be seriously wrong."[95] The article, "The Students Strike at California," suggests an interesting double meaning. The students were on strike, but by their actions also striking "at" California, the image of silent college students happy with the status quo.

In descriptions of the protesters, reporters and editors used the Beats as a frame of reference. This was partly an explanatory tool as well as an attempt to brand the students as outside the mainstream. Beatnik imagery quickly entered the Free Speech Movement lexicon. Descriptions made sharp contrasts between the normal California student (clean-shaven, sporting casual middle-class styles, practicing personal hygiene) and protesters (long-haired, wearing black, bearded, barefoot, unclean). For some publications, the news reflex was to disparage activists as "unwashed beatniks, bunch of rowdies, [and] forlorn crackpots."[96] Photographers expressed bias through the subjects they chose, seeking out "the one or two bearded, longhaired students in a group" rather than taking pictures of "the majority of respectable looking boys and girls in the crowd" who did not conform to preconceived images.[97]

A *Life* editorial characterized Berkeley students as a "scruffy-looking bunch, fond of flowing hair and beards, ponchos and Army shoes."[98] The *New York Times* noted, "The student body at this campus is unusually picturesque in its dress and grooming." At the sit-in, it was reported, "The beards and long hair and guitars were much in evidence. . . . At least one young man came in barefoot."[99] With its sarcastic headline, "To Prison

A widely circulated photo of the crowd at
the University of California Berkeley during
the Free Speech Movement in December
1964, this image editorializes its subject by
placing a bearded youth at the forefront
while allowing more clean-cut youth to fade
into the background. Pictures and coverage
like this helped foster the impression of
Berkeley as a "beatnik" haven.

(AP/WIDE WORLD PHOTOS)

with Love," *Time* characterized the students involved in the sit-in as "guitar-laden . . . bearded" troublemakers. Its short article about the mass arrests featured photos of Mario Savio and folk performer Joan Baez, and described the FSM as "dominated by civil rights militants, Trotskyite groups, and members of a Communist front."[100] As Superintendent Rafferty explained to the *New York Times*: "What you have there are a few of these . . . bearded, unwashed characters, with sandals and long hair who normally would be regarded sort of tolerantly as a lunatic fringe which you put up with but not necessarily encourage and in effect the campus has been turned over to these characters."[101]

An editorial cartoon by Gibson Crockett that appeared in the *Washington Star* captured the reigning image of the Berkeley student. It depicted the office of the president, with a college banner on the wall clearly indicating "California." At the president's desk sits a student reminiscent of the beatnik stereotype: bearded with hair unkempt, his sandaled feet on top of the desk as he leans back in the leather chair. As the ungainly student smokes a cigar, he murmurs, "Now this is more like it!"[102] The implication of the cartoon was clear; students like these typified the average protester.

A sports writer for the *Berkeley Gazette* argued that academic standards should be relaxed to allow more area athletes into the university. This, he believed, would raise the "morale" of the university while ridding it of some of its more troublemaking elements. He wrote: "The demonstrators have used their soiled bodies and foggy intellects only to tear down the reputation of this citadel of learning . . . New Yorkers retched in disbelief to see on TV their bodies, a melange of beards and black socks, piled up like cattle across the corridors."[103]

As FSM leader, Savio provided a symbol of the campus "beatnik." A *San Francisco Chronicle* story with the ominous headline "Savio Takes on the State," profiled Savio as "unshaven, disheveled, but aflame as always with passion." The article described Savio's expanding litany of institutions to attack, this time the entire state of California.[104] In a sense, Savio was a challenge to the state's image, a creation of specific ideas about the proper and proscribed activities of California youth. *Newsweek* characterized Savio at a demonstration as "unaccustomedly outfitted in suit, tie, and clean shirt, and with his steel wool hair combed into a semblance of order."[105] The article emphasized the appearance of Savio, the media-appointed leader of the movement, suggesting to the reader that despite his temporary sporting of the safe, middle-class look, his bohemian tendencies lay just beneath the

—Crockett in "Washington Star"

"Now this is more like it!"

This cartoon by Gibson Crockett originally appeared in the Washington, D.C., newspaper *Washington Star*, and was reprinted nationally in *U.S. News and World Report* in December 1964. After the trouble at Berkeley, "California" (note its appearance on the banner) conjured up images of trouble-making students, a stark contrast to earlier portraits of the Golden State's young people.

(Credit *Washington Star*, 1964)

surface. Later, in its account of the sentencing in August 1965, *Newsweek* made special note of Savio's "bride of two months . . . visibly pregnant." The article included a picture of the couple – Suzanne with dark glasses and pale face, Mario with wild hair and an angry demeanor.[106]

All this media coverage had left an "indelible impression," in the words of *Sports Illustrated,* on the average American. The California student image, "a sort of scrofulous beatnik affecting sandals and a moth-eaten beard bearing a sign denouncing the American way of life," had been "clearly engraved on the public mind."[107] In newspaper editorials across the country there loomed "the specter of shaggy-bearded beatniks, anarchists, and even hard-core Communists inciting innocent and pure-minded students to riot and insurrection against their elders."[108] This impression traveled all over the world, becoming synonymous with the state's higher education system. As a British scholar reported in *Harper's,* "The University of California is identified as Berkeley."[109]

The majority of news stories, one letter to the *Nation* argued, were "edited to stress the colorful and the dramatic, at the expense of objective reporting."[110] Not all observers blindly accepted this image. As a university student's letter to *Life* explained: "Granted, there are a lot of beards and grubby-looking clothes. But one demonstrator asked me, 'Would you wear your best clothes to sleep on the floor and get dragged downstairs?' A shave and a haircut do not equal good citizenship, and have never been an accurate measurement of sincerity and devotion to one's ideals. I speak as one with short, nonflowing hair and a clean-shaven face."[111] News outlets and magazine editorials highlighted the beatnik image of the student protester, despite the fact that the majority of participants did not fit that mold. Utilizing the images surrounding the Beats, reporters could quickly construct a visual image, however false, until it became a type of self-fulfilling prophecy. Soon the majority of young activists would fashion themselves farther outside the mainstream.

Print journalism offered biased commentary, yet it was not the only media outlet to play the game. In 1965, CBS news produced a television documentary, "The Berkeley Rebels," and the journalistic shenanigans behind the scenes revealed the networks' concern about explosive subject matter. Executives insisted that a scene about a fraternity party, employed as contrast, be excised because of its "slander against nice kids." For "balance" they asked the producer to interview professors, obtaining quotes like, "The kids are immature and impatient. It will all blow over." Producers added condescending introductions and conclusions voiced by newsman Harry Reasoner, influencing the tone of the documentary and domesticating the subversive images.[112]

With California considered representative of the nation's future, the breakdown of order at Berkeley did not auger well. An editorial in *Saturday Review* contended that California's campus troubles had national significance. While educators had "deplored the passiveness and political lethargy of the American student," Berkeley had produced nostalgia for the "silent generation."[113] In September 1965, *Fortune* called campus uprisings "a troubled reflection of the U.S.," arguing California was "the hyperbolic state of the western world, experiencing many phenomena of change sooner and more intensely than the rest." Berkeley's observers could track "a conflict of national scope and historical magnitude . . . early warning signals of a deep-seated conflict between present U.S. society and its outdated image of itself."[114] *Holiday* called the university "the mirror on the wall to assure the Californian that he is the fairest of them all." Events at Berkeley, it said, had "cracked the mirror."[115] The image of baby boomers as status quo consumers apathetic toward political change was no longer the reflection.

At a conference of the American Council on Education in October 1965, the key issue discussed was student uprisings, as "the Berkeley tremors . . . had grown to a nationwide quake felt in hundreds of administrative offices."[116] In December 1965, *Saturday Review* explored the causes of the "student revolution" that by this time had erupted all across the country. These events that began in California challenged images of youth, making people "aware how far from the truth is the stereotype of the happy-go-lucky, golden college years."[117]

The consequences of Berkeley, despite the recognition of its national ramifications, were felt most keenly inside the Golden State. The California press "dealt with the story as though it were a kind of academic Western," using the language of battle, standoff, siege, mob, law and order. The events at Berkeley were also "editorialized in pictures," which were sympathetic to the police and administration while framing students as un-American rabble. The *Oakland Tribune* altered a photo of a student carrying an assigned class text, obscuring every word except "Marxism." The caption read, "A textbook on Marxism was among the crowd."[118] California public opinion polls revealed that 92 percent of those polled had heard or read about the demonstrations and 74 percent felt a "disapproving attitude toward them." This "clear majority" shared an impression of the students that was marked by violence, beatnik immorality, and Communist influence.[119]

California Monthly, the magazine published for UC alumni, devoted its entire February 1965 issue to the crisis. Calling the sit-ins "tragic . . . a virtual civil war without arms," the issue's editorial proclaimed, "The vast majority of alumni and citizens of this State . . . will not countenance the disruption of educational activity."[120] In a message to the magazine's readers, President Kerr argued that Berkeley had become the "focal point for such activity – a special aspect of the so-called 'westward tilt.'" With 46 percent of the nation under twenty-five, Kerr believed, the Berkeley campus "must rise to even greater heights for its own sake and for the sake of the whole University and the state of California."[121] Kerr might have taken his dominoes one step further. The safe and secure baby boomer vision, shattered by Berkeley, suggested a weakening of California and therefore the nation.

Letters to the editors of *California Monthly* revealed a concern about Berkeley's influence on the state's image. One alumnus called for the establishment of standards of dress and decorum: "The University of California at Berkeley is becoming more and more identified with demonstrations, radical behavior and viewpoints, and students who dress and act much like the much-publicized beatniks of the fifties."[122] Another former student placed blame on incitement by "out of state trash which come because they like the 'pinko' atmosphere." These outsiders, he complained, had ruined the reputation of "our best California youth, which includes football players, who wouldn't be caught dead playing for a 'pinko school.'" An alumnus who had traveled out of state returned with this news of California's image: "One hears distasteful things about California. . . . If these are true, the image of California has surely degenerated."[123]

Historians have pointed to events at Berkeley as the demarcation line that begins the tumultuous sixties. It was on this California campus, it is argued, that "the Eisenhower decade came to a belated end."[124] These events seem small in comparison to larger, later upheavals. Why was the fragmented and ultimately short-lived movement on one UC campus so important? The explanation lies in the powerful imagery that surrounded California's baby boomers. The Berkeley conflict challenged one of the most powerful and reassuring myths of the postwar period, altering the images of California's young people that had pervaded popular culture. California was viewed as the good life, the aspiration of millions personified. Its children were the recipients of golden opportunity. Here then were thousands rejecting those goals and dreams, questioning the rightness of the system, the machine, that surrounded them. Berkeley came to represent "the depths of disaffection in Nirvana."[125]

The protesters' opposition to mass education, the struggle against impersonality, could be viewed as a resistance to mass consumerism and to the constructed image of California youth in popular culture, the exclusionary imagery that appeared in magazine profiles, in television commercials and programming, on *Billboard* charts, and in Hollywood productions. A segment of the image's target audience, the baby boomers, destroyed it, turning California youth into a universal codeword for troublemaking baby boomers. The shocked surprise and disbelief that greeted the appearance of these new images is testament to the power of the older myths representing California's youth. Despite the small minority of youth directly involved in campus protest, students in California no longer appeared in the media as happy consumers schooled in the ways of conformity.

The new images of California youth were as deceiving as the earlier incarnations. In place of wholesome, middle-class lifestyles there emerged new images, less tied to the status quo but quickly adopted and supplied by mainstream manufacturers. Media coverage of the FSM helped shape perceptions, exaggerating the radicalism and influence of this cultural challenge. The events in California did provide new guides for living, just as earlier trends emerging from the state had provided models of consumption. The icon this time, however, was a challenge to society, subsequently adopted and imitated by large numbers of middle-class youth.[126]

In 1965, Berkeley shared the spotlight with another California trouble spot, a place more violently disaffected with the California dream.[127] Los Angeles was suburbia, the ultimate example of postwar prosperity. The city's reputation was tied to this projection of golden opportunities and modern lifestyles, its long history of strife left out of the mass-mediated picture. Freeways surrounded the city, with the beach and Disneyland its borders. The children of Los Angeles, according to popular culture, enjoyed their leisure time in suburban enclaves, devoid of difference or challenge. The Watts riot in August 1965 was unthinkable in this world of California, as the carefully constructed image left out the city's minority residents.

California attracted large numbers of African Americans with its golden promise, but for those trapped in the freeway-bordered ghetto, those dreams appeared as mirages in the land of plenty. Freeway construction created division, and restrictive housing covenants encouraged segregation. Racial rioting in Los Angeles, the "least expected and most incongruous" outbreak of the 1960s, helped destroy the California myth.[128] More important to this analysis, the rioting was an uprising of California's black youth, an invisible group of baby boomers frustrated by their lack of inclusion in the dream and reality of California life. In the western Eden, minorities were unrepresented and unsung, while their white counterparts commanded every privilege.

The middle-class suburban world was available to Watts only through television and film, which beamed images of the good life along with commercial "teases" showing the "goods that pour out of the American cornucopia."[129] While white suburban teens celebrated an "endless summer," overshadowed minority youth experienced "a winter of discontent."[130] Magazine profiles heralded the wonder of the expansive highways, ignoring the destruction, dislocation, and exclusion of minorities that accompanied their creation. Both African Americans and Hispanics found their communities ignored, bordered by prosperity and the rush of automobiles.[131] The postwar boom in California created very different worlds in close proximity, while the state's racial history was paved over by the freeway and glossed over by postwar dreaming.

Ominous signs in the early 1960s hinted at an increasingly volatile situation. They were largely ignored.[132] In June 1956, *U.S. News & World Report* examined black migration from the rural south. While many newcomers found "better houses and jobs," the "Los Angeles melting pot" faced difficulties providing opportunity as the "booming Negro population" continued to grow.[133] A *Saturday Evening Post* article noted the city's "Negro tensions." A massive influx of new residents without ready access to the California dream created "not what you would call a stable community."[134]

Prosperity obscured many problems, and the myth of California exceptionality reigned.[135] In 1964, the Urban League surveyed sixty-eight cities and proclaimed Los Angeles the most attractive city for minorities to live and work in.[136] This ranking was awarded despite the presence of Proposition 14 on the 1964 ballot, a measure that sought to overturn the Rumford Act passed by the state legislature, which prohibited racial discrimination in rental dwellings.[137] In an interview for the *Los Angeles Times*, police chief William H. Parker pronounced the city immune to the "racial conflict that is raging in the United States today." He maintained that Los Angeles was "ten years ahead of other major metropolitan areas in assimilating the Negro minority."[138] Mayor Sam Yorty considered the city impregnable to civil rights protests. He rejected the need for a "human relations commission" established during World War II, believing the California environment capable of ameliorating racial discontent.[139]

Despite the mayor's objections, the Human Relations Commission continued to operate in Los Angeles County. In October 1964, *Reader's Digest* featured the commission's efforts at pulling the "fuse from virtually every threatened racial explosion among the county's several million citizens." The commission dealt with prejudice in housing and employment faced by Asians, blacks, and Hispanics and attempted to dispel racial myths that supported such discriminatory practices. One commission member called Los Angeles "a miniature of the nation," hopeful that if the group's tactics proved successful, "they ought to work anywhere."[140] *Ebony* featured similar community outreach efforts in March 1964. The magazine profiled an African American policewoman, highlighting her contributions in improving relations between the police and the city's minority citizens. The article also included her work in establishing a "juvenile unit" in the Watts area.[141]

In the summer of 1964, *U.S. News & World Report* conducted an interview with police chief Parker and questioned him about racial conflict. This "internationally noted" lawman dismissed widespread charges of police brutality across the country and rejected the idea that Los Angeles was susceptible to similar racial violence. He stated, "We don't believe the situation will arise."[142] In the winter of 1964–65, Chief Parker rejected predictions that Los Angeles might experience violent upheaval, calling such prognosticators "false prophets [who] fail to consider that any condition which contributed to chaos in other parts of the country would not exist in Los Angeles."[143] In a summer 1965 *Reader's Digest* article Parker proclaimed, "There can be no race riots in Los Angeles."[144] The Cardinal Archbishop of Los Angeles was equally adamant, insisting "with full Episcopal dignity that there was no race problem in his city."[145]

Beyond Los Angeles, the threat of urban summer rioting preoccupied many politicians and federal agencies as 1965 approached. In July 1965, the *New Republic* reported on efforts spearheaded by Vice President Hubert Humphrey and the Community Relations Service to devise plans for stemming racial conflict. The agency targeted eight northern cities, none in

California. Los Angeles and Oakland, where few predicted racial trouble would occur, received nominal help from the program.[146] California was not the focus of anti-riot planning, offering the nation an exception to the rule. California's myth of racial harmony had become official government policy.

Most Californians suffered from a blindness to the problems rumbling just below the surface. Watts did not resemble the traditional picture of a ghetto slum, the tenements of eastern cities or the shacks that typified the rural south.[147] In 1964, *Sunset Travel* described Watts as an "industrial community," best known as the home of Sabatino Rodia's towers. This trio of steel rods, 104 feet high, stuccoed with cement and decorated with glass, tile, old dish materials, pebbles, and sea shells served as the area's only tourist attraction.[148]

Watts residents faced many obstacles that blocked access to California's other wonders. An inefficient bus system serviced Watts.[149] A tangle of freeways surrounded the community yet isolated thousands of black residents.[150] Four out of ten families in the area lived below the poverty level. Watts' housing was old and in desperate need of sanitary and structural improvements. Partly a result of limited opportunity and poor schooling, unemployment in Watts between 1960 and 1964 rose to 20 percent.[151] Joblessness especially plagued young people.[152]

Watts was a hidden region in the nation's most celebrated landscape. One reporter from the South noticed the tendency for "white men [to] ride the freeway" and avoid looking at the neighborhoods beyond the road's barricades.[153] The reputation of California as a "palm-lined Eden" obscured the problems of Watts, and prejudicial news reporting decreased its media visibility.[154] Writer Budd Schulberg argued that its invisibility was due to white residents "looking north and west while hundreds of thousands were sweating out poverty, hunger, unemployment, the lack of education, transportation, recreation" in the south and east.[155]

To the world, Los Angeles represented a vacationer's paradise, the home of Disneyland, beaches for surfing, hot rodders, and the good suburban life. Freeways bordered but did not welcome visitors to communities outside those boundaries. While northern cities had experienced racial violence in the hot summer of 1964, Los Angeles was believed safe from such catastrophes, an opinion underscored by civil and religious authorities. California's predominant images, in short, did not accommodate race. Rioting in the golden land caught the vast majority by surprise.

It was a California Highway patrol traffic stop that ignited the tinder of Watts. On August 11, 1965, police stopped 21-year-old Marquette Frye under suspicion of intoxication. In this locale, with its long history of police brutality and accompanying anti-police sentiment, crowds gathered to monitor the arrest and express their hostility toward the police. Violent altercations between the arresting officers and the growing mob resulted, and word of this most recent incident spread like wildfire. Mobs gathered, destroying property, and police made more arrests. The next morning, looting began. By the next day, police had lost control of the southern portion of Los Angeles.[156]

The *Los Angeles Times* reported on the Frye arrest on August 12 with the headline, "1000 Riot in LA: Police and Motorists Attacked."[157] As the rioting continued into the second day, Los Angeles coverage reflected the deepening crisis. With photos "reminiscent of wartime," the August 13 edition described the entry of National Guard troops into the area. "Young people were blamed for much of the trouble. There were twelve juveniles among those arrested," the article reported.[158] The *New York Times* featured the trouble on its front page, finding the riot difficult to explain due to its sunny location. Watts, the article argued, maintained "a pleasantly suburban aura . . . despite the low income of most of its residents."[159] The *New York Times* covered the riot as front-page news for four straight days, using large headline type to convey the situation's gravity.

Governor Brown, on a vacation in Greece, immediately flew home when informed of the trouble. "Nobody told me there was an explosive situation in Los Angeles," he explained to reporters. Brown believed California to be "a state where there is no racial discrimination."[160] The *Los Angeles Times* mirrored that sentiment in an editorial on Sunday, August 15: "There are no words to express the shock, the sick horror, that a civilized city feels at a moment like this. It could not happen in Los Angeles. But it did."[161] President Lyndon Johnson described the riot as "tragic and shocking" and sent two administration officials to help stop the violence.[162]

At rioting's end, the mayor, chief of police, thousands of news organizations, millions of listeners to radio and watchers of television had discovered Watts.[163] It was no longer invisible; indeed, pictures of Watts became intertwined with images of the city. Television, which in its fiction had ignored the city's minority population, could not disregard it now. Most Americans experienced the riot through the media, "the damnedest television show ever put on the tube."[164] Helicopters carried the riot live, and state and city officials used television to plead with residents for calm and a return to law and order.[165]

The impact and scope of the violence stunned the country. The Watts riot killed 34 people, injured 1,000, resulted in the arrest of over 4,000, and caused $200 million in damage. Thirty-five thousand people were involved in rioting, with an estimated 72,000 acting as spectators. The National Guard sent 16,000 troops into the area, while the Los Angeles Police and the California Highway Patrol deployed large numbers of officers to the scene.[166]

Watts made front-page news in most major magazines and newspapers across the country. The riots in Los Angeles were a dangerous indicator of nationwide problems. *Life* headlined its cover story "Arson and Street War – Most Destructive Riot in U.S. History." Inside its pages, *Life* described Watts as the place "where the golden dreams of California have turned most sharply to dross." The cover captured a young African American fleeing his burning home with a few possessions.[167]

Even more disturbing than the violence was the riot's location. *Time*'s cover story, "The Los Angeles Riot," described the ideological effect on Californians' peace of mind. "One evening white Angelenos had nothing to worry about but the humidity," the article explained, only to wake up to the worst riot in U.S. history. This "trigger of hate" occurred in "the City of Angels, the 'safe city' as the boosters like to call it, the city that has always taken pride in its history of racial relations."[168] The riot occurred in "the least expected" place, according to *Ebony*. "Why then, in God's name, was there a riot in Los Angeles, California?" the magazine asked. As the article explained, "For if it could happen in Los Angeles, it could happen anywhere." The result was a loss of surety: "It will be a long time before the city – and the nation – sleeps easy again."[169]

Newsweek described the riot as "The Fire This Time," highlighting the destruction and death in America's third largest city. The article included a map of the rioting area for its readers, showing the close proximity of Watts to Hollywood, two suburbs with disparate identities.[170] In a subsequent issue, *Newsweek*'s cover asked, "Los Angeles: Why?" How could Los Angeles, "that most American of mid-century cities – spawn the fire this time?"[171] Governor Brown expressed the incredulity of many Californians: "Here in California, we have a wonderful working relationship between

THIRTY-FIVE CENTS   AUGUST 20, 1965

TIME

THE WEEKLY NEWSMAGAZINE

THE LOS ANGELES RIOT

VOL 86 NO. 8

Both *Time* and *Life* featured the Watts Riot on their covers in August 1965. This *Time* cover features a different type of joyride, a burned-out car, and some wayward teens rioting and looting in the streets rather than sunning at the beach. (TimePix) whites and Negroes. We got along fine until this happened."[172] The governor shared the blindness that plagued both public policy and popular culture.

Why Watts? How to explain the impossible? Significantly, similar questions were not evoked during rioting in more traditionally segregated locales. A chorus of explanations pointed to the suddenly revealed frustrations of Watts' residents. A *Los Angeles Times* editorial attributed the violence to the disillusionment of those who "came hopefully to the promised land only to have their expectations dashed." Governor Brown compared Watts to "a prison riot, where the people in their frustration have just destroyed things."[173] Residents were trapped, physically and economically, incarcerated with little room for escape. *Newsweek* argued that the rioters, living in what "might look like the Promised Land," compared their situation to the rest of "super-America of Southern California" and found it lacking. Residents felt surrounded by the "lush life of Hollywood boulevard, the beaches of Santa Monica, and the affluent traffic of the Harbor Freeway."[174] This frustration fomented a desire to "direct . . . anger at the only white men they ever see: the shopkeeper, the landlord, and most of all, the cop."[175]

Part of that frustration was materialistic; rioters wanted their chance at the commercial utopia from which they were barred but lived amidst. Many commentators pointed to the disparity between expectations of life in California and the reality that many African Americans faced.[176] The *Saturday Evening Post* described the riots as evidence of "the width of the gulf that separates these young men from the secure and comfortable life that most white Americans live."[177] Historian Milton Viorst noted the irony of the geography, as Watts' nearby suburb Hollywood "produced the reminders for nightly television of a better world out of reach."[178] Writer Thomas Pynchon characterized the culture that surrounded Watts as unreal, existing "chiefly as images on a screen or TV tube, as four-color magazine photos . . . basically a white scene, and illusion is everywhere in it." Within this realm of fantasy sat Watts, "a pocket of bitter reality."[179] The riot offered some in Watts the opportunity to acquire "possessions which TV commercials identify to them as essential parts of the American Way of Life."[180] Some rioters took the chance during looting to grab, as *Newsweek* described, "the merit badges and necessities of consumer society" that eluded them.[181]

Interviews reflected the frustration that rioters felt toward their more prosperous neighbors. One black Watts resident explained: "Some nights on the roof of our rotten falling down buildings we can actually see your lights shining in the distance. So near and yet so far. We want to reach out and grab it and punch it in the nose."[182] Another rioter expressed his dissatisfaction with the California dream: "Everywhere they say, 'Go to California! California's the great pot o'gold at the end of the rainbow.' Well, now we're here in California, and there ain't no place else to go, and the only pot [is] the kind they peddle at Sixtieth and Avalon."[183]

Who were the riot participants, those who acted out their frustrations violently? Watts exhibited a typical riot pattern, in that the actions of teenagers provided the spark, and the community's youth played a key role. During the riot, police arrested 500 youngsters under the age of eighteen.[184] One study indicated that "the most outstanding characteristic of the riot participants was youth."[185] *Time* described the majority of rioters as "packs of youth . . . commanding the streets, defying anybody to challenge them."[186] Mayor Yorty blamed the outbreak on the "riff-raff," the unemployed youths of Watts left to wander the streets.[187] The *New York Times* headlined one of its reports on the riots, "Youths Run Wild." The front-page picture accompanying the story showed looting kids running "from the sacked stores in Watts."[188]

The median age in Watts was sixteen, giving the community an unusually large teenage population. Close to two-thirds of 12-year-olds starting the seventh grade never finished high school.[189] These "seemingly doomed youth" faced family difficulties, school obstacles, and employment hurdles.[190] The national media and the city's boosters ignored these California youth. For this reason, despite the destruction and death, some participants characterized the rioting as a victory. As one rioter exclaimed, "We won because we made the whole world pay attention to us. We made them come."[191] Within the community, rioters were "heroic guerrillas where people never had an identity before the uprising."[192] A letter from Chicago to *Time* magazine expressed it this way: "Being a Negro, I realize that the rioters of Watts were rebelling against themselves, or rather the false image of themselves that they wanted to destroy."[193]

Participants revolted against an exclusionary image and a public invisibility that plagued and limited the community. In hindsight, the shock Los Angeles experienced seems surprising. The youth of Watts, the riot underscored, were also part of California, an ignored component of the cultural landscape. The riot forced a reevaluation of the state's special status and its mythological place in the nation's psyche.

Events damaged Los Angeles' reputation, and there was an outcry to fix blame. Chief Parker charged civil rights activists and the tactic of civil disobedience for fostering disrespect for the law. Telling *U.S. News & World Report* he had expected the outbreak, Parker concluded, "When you keep telling them they are being badly treated and abused, they're going to react."[194] *Commonweal* made the connection less directly, arguing that the riot was the result of "gradual progress [that] increases unhappiness because it reveals more starkly the contrast between possibility and reality."[195] In the riot's wake, support for the civil rights movement dwindled, as observers of the riot connected the cause to the violence.

Governor Brown appointed a special commission to discover the riot's causes, a political maneuver and an effort to avoid future violence. John McCone, a former head of the Central Intelligence Agency, chaired the group. Brown cautioned investigators about the importance of their task: "The fate not only of Los Angeles but of other cities in California and the nation may well depend on your findings."[196] The McCone Commission report, released in December 1965, attempted to explain the riot and offer solutions to avoid future disturbances. Entitled "Violence in the City – An End or a Beginning?" the report recommended employment and educational support for the community.[197] The report pointed to the dashed dreams that plagued the thousands who traveled to California and dismissed the idea that California was special and could avoid the problems troubling northern cities.[198]

The report asserted that many of the rioters were recent arrivals, mostly from the South. However, later evidence indicated that half of the arrested teenagers were California natives, and over three-fourths had lived in California for more than five years.[199] As in the Berkeley controversy, there were many who wished that those involved in the riots had simply been outsiders. The large numbers of youth involved in the rioting sparked government agencies to offer aid programs with an "accent on youth." These included work projects, training programs, and child care centers.[200]

After the riot, some California residents expressed incredulity that they had been oblivious to the worsening crisis. The white community that surrounded the ghetto had somehow ignored "the forgotten slum," maintaining a "universal unawareness of the squalor and misery" in their midst.[201] A

Time reader from Los Angeles responded: "I must express my embarrassment and humiliation as a result of the terrible violence in Watts. We in Los Angeles had felt proud of the way the racial situation had been handled; we must have been blind not to see the melting pot of hate bubbling in the Negro sectors of this great city."[202]

Coverage of Watts removed the community's anonymity, if not its systemic problems. In a content analysis of the city's newspapers before and after the riot, sociologists discovered that "black invisibility" characterized press coverage prior to August 1965. After the initial explosion, press focus soon returned to a "pre-riot level."[203] A month after the riot, *Time* reported that Watts remained "as much as ever a far country, inaccessible, invisible, and incomprehensible" to the white majority.[204]

Despite the sharp decline in media attention to minority communities, the negative impression of Los Angeles lingered long after rioting ended. *U.S. News & World Report* proclaimed that the fear and shock of the riots had damaged "the image of Los Angeles as a pleasant place to live in . . . perhaps irrevocably."[205] *Newsweek* reported that by the end of 1965 Watts had become "a world-wide symbol for all that is wrong with ghetto life for American Negroes."[206] By extension, all of California suffered a blow to its postwar image as the land of sunshine.

The outbreak of racial rioting in the city of Angels spawned apocalyptic predictions and increased attention to the myriad problems in California. *U.S. News & World Report* headlined a story after the riot, "Troubled Los Angeles – Race Is Only One of Its Problems." The article argued that recent events, combined with other "king-size troubles" – increased crime, urban sprawl, and rising taxes – indicated that "the easy life is coming to an end."[207] The end of the "easy life" had consequences for the other forty-nine states. An editorial in *America* acknowledged the extent of America's racial difficulties, "from Harlem to Long Beach," without an escape valve. Its headline, "And Now What," revealed a deeply troubled nation.[208]

California, the compass for the future, now offered a bleak example of what lay ahead for America. The combined effect of the upheavals in Berkeley and Watts shattered earlier images. Fears of future rioting and anxiety about campus morals pushed the state to the right politically. A stunned populace was ready to accept a message more in keeping with its anxieties and past myths. The result was a lessened sympathy toward civil rights goals and legislation combined with an antipathy toward campus free speech and the growing antiwar movement. The majority of Californians were unwilling to embrace contrary images, revealing a strong affection for ideas surrounding California's greatness, its exceptionality, the dream of the good life, and visions of its youth.

The riot brought to the fore another image: teenagers and young adults living in Watts, desperate, without hope, locked out of a consumer culture and the attractiveness of middle-class suburbia. Combined with the growing challenge of white middle-class kids on the campuses, the state faced an insurmountable challenge that demanded retreat. Counterculture hippies emerged on the horizon, a wide cultural leap from Mouseketeers, Gidget, and the Beach Boys. Californians wanted to return to the imagined suburban island promoted in the postwar period by popular culture visions. Rather than reevaluate their attachment to those images, Californians lent willing ears to conservative messengers.

CHAPTER EIGHT

Reagan's Conservative Wave

By the end of 1965, Berkeley and Watts were two California communities that carried special meaning. They were not the typical California suburbs portrayed in the movies, on television, in music, or by magazines, and their youth were not content with consumerism or a day at the beach. Both places challenged the vision of California as the happy harbinger of America's future. The futuristic component of California mythology remained, but a darker version of America's destiny shadowed it. Californians felt this most keenly, and in the gubernatorial election of 1966 they denied the trouble that had altered California's view of itself, opting for older images. Republican Ronald Reagan appealed to voters who were anxious about cultural change and focused his campaign on politicizing such attitudes. His victory reinforced the tenacity of these images and their ability to shape voting behavior. A new conservatism in the state foreshadowed the forces that captured the White House in 1968. California, the nation's trendsetter in many ways, was where these changing political forces made their earliest mark.

In the wake of the Berkeley and Watts disruptions, California newspapers headlined stories of student rebellion and violent racial riots in the golden land. Reagan, a newly minted politician, acted as force for right, a defender of morality, a proponent of a worldview that maintained California's hold on the good life. His campaign exploited a working-class and middle-class antipathy toward rebellious youth. As the *New York Times Magazine* argued, Reagan's appeal revealed that Californians were "not so bold and confident as the glossy magazines would have you believe."[1] In a time of cultural confusion, Reagan campaigned on a platform of traditional truths, championing a message that resonated with voters.

The reassurance offered by Reagan's hard-line stance spoke to Californians who were experiencing the first waves of 1960s upheaval. As *Time* described, "Any headache that afflicts any other state throbs even harder in California – and many of its quandaries have not even been invented elsewhere."[2] Reagan did not create new images nor manufacture public sentiment. The movie star, union leader, and corporate spokesman turned political speaker represented the last stand of the California dream. Reagan's emergence was the political story of the 1966 election year, profiled by dozens of magazines and columnists amazed at the suddenness of his candidacy. Before long, his name was bandied about as a possible presidential contender, evidence of his message's appeal beyond California's anxious audiences.

Reagan's opponent was popular incumbent governor Edmund G. "Pat" Brown, nicknamed "The Giant Killer" for his past election-day victories. Brown had served two terms, guiding the state through years of unprecedented growth. Liberal Democrats dominated state government during Brown's tenure, and their place in California politics seemed secure.[3] Governor Brown firmly believed in California's special nature and its ability to weather storms. He compared the aims of President Johnson's War on Poverty to his state's general high quality of life: "In Washington they call it the Great Society. We just call it California."[4] Visions of white, middle-class prosperity blinded state politicians, and Brown similarly was unable to perceive trouble on the horizon. He was an unquestioning believer in the shining image of his state projected in popular culture. This left him unprepared for the challenges of Berkeley, Watts, and Reagan.

The Berkeley incident damaged Brown across the political spectrum. His orchestration of the state highway police arrests of 800 students at Sproul Hall was "hardly an action to endear him to liberals, especially those with children of college age."[5] Conservatives, meanwhile, reviled Brown as an agent of the permissiveness that allowed "childish, selfish, and spoiled rich kids" to destroy the image of the university system and the state.[6] "Those damned kids," the golden recipients of state-sponsored education, seemed ungrateful to taxpayers.[7] Watts erupted while Brown was on vacation, and his first response to the violence revealed a governor caught completely by surprise. The *New York Times*, on the last day of the riots, foresaw that events in Watts would provide "a ready-made issue for next year's campaign for governor."[8] As one Brown aide noted, "No one blames Pat specifically for Watts. They just blame him generally." In addition, taxpayers balked at the high cost of the state's poverty programs, compounding the white backlash.[9]

Brown's 1958 and 1962 campaigns were variations on a theme: California as the "Promised Land," the first state of a great nation. Audiences, humbled by the twin shocks of Berkeley and Watts, seemed unreceptive to the 1966 version. Brown found "thousands of irritated, angry, and frightened Californians" ready to blame his administration "for all the crises, failures, and frustrations" of recent years.[10] Democrats found it increasingly difficult to contain what *Newsweek* called the "rightward drift of California politics . . . the palpable white backlash over the Watts riots and the furor over radical student excesses at Berkeley."[11] The stage was set for a Republican resurgence. As a 1965 poll revealed, the party was well positioned to seriously challenge Democratic control.[12]

California's turn to the political right predated Reagan's rise. To voters, troubling events fostered a growing sense that California was headed in the wrong direction. The ultra-conservative John Birch Society cultivated fertile ground, attracting recruits and the support of some state officials.[13] After Brown's defeat of Richard Nixon in 1962, California's Republican Party had moved to the right, following the lead of 1964 presidential candidate Barry Goldwater. Conservative political hopefuls were quick to see Berkeley and Watts as fodder for the 1966 campaign. There was a precedent for electing Hollywood stars to high office. Conservative George Murphy, an actor who was Shirley Temple's former co-star, defeated Kennedyite Pierre Salinger for the Senate in 1964. Ronald Reagan appeared on the political scene that year, making a name for himself in a televised speech for Barry Goldwater.[14] The Republican Party benefited from the statewide swing to the right and moved to secure the gains by prodding Reagan to run. Spencer and Roberts, a public relations firm, sponsored speaking engagements for him across the state.[15]

In May 1965, *New Republic* spotlighted Reagan's appeal to Californians, calling them, "Midwesterners who have fled the dreary heartland, but still love the simple virtues." These voters looked to the actor and listened to his rhetoric because, as the article argued, "Things are bad in the orange grove, and it will take men like Reagan to set them right again."[16] *Look* described Reagan's sway over California audiences as "awesome to see."[17] *Time* called

Reagan "the most magnetic crowd puller California has seen since JFK first stumped the state in 1960."[18] Although Reagan was a rich movie and television star, the campaign touted him as a man of the people, an everyday fellow aware of the issues facing his fellow Californians. His autobiography, *Where's the Rest of Me?* appeared in the fall of 1965, telling a "wholesome Midwestern story" of humble beginnings and Hollywood stardom.[19] Campaign literature highlighted his all-American background: student body president, captain of the swimming team, college football player, sports fan, rancher, and unassuming movie star. Characterizing himself as a "citizen politician," Reagan made his lack of political experience an asset.[20]

Reagan's pre-campaign travels also took him outside the state and into the welcoming arms of the national media. In October 1965, *Newsweek* described his stumping in New England under the headline, "Reagan Rides East." Despite a few missteps, the article read, Reagan had "brought the California sunshine right along with him." A follower among the "swarms of women" who turned out to see him predicted he would be "the next Republican candidate for president."[21]

After months of canvassing the state, feeling out public sentiment about his possible candidacy, Reagan joined the race for the Republican nomination. On January 4, 1966, sixteen television stations statewide broadcast his announcement. Reagan filmed his declaration in a studio designed to appear denlike, with a desk, bookcase, and fireplace. The speech began by calling California a "paradise lost," a place of great physical beauty, and home of the western migrant's dream for a hundred years. It was the state's government that was destroying "the very things that brought us here in the first place." Despite California's growing chaos, Reagan insisted, "We're here to stay and our children are native born and California's problems are our problems."[22]

Reagan had discovered the salience of the Berkeley issue during public forums before his entry in the race, when question-and-answer sessions revealed widespread anxiety about the state's campuses. Now, as a candidate for governor, he focused in on that issue. Media coverage of Berkeley fostered the impression that "beatnik" and "communist" students were taking over the university. Berkeley's disruptive influence loomed in the minds of many white middle-class and working-class Democrats whose children would soon be in college.[23] While the trouble failed to rank high in polls of public concerns, it grew as an "emotional issue with people," commandeered and amplified by the Reagan campaign.[24] Millions of Californians harbored negative thoughts toward the flagship campus. By 1965, a poll revealed an "overwhelming disapproval" of both the goals and methods of the Free Speech Movement.[25] According to his aides, it was the "Berkeley reference which always got the explicit, noisy reaction."[26] Reagan quickly energized crowds with strident calls for investigations and crackdowns.[27]

Reagan publicized a report by the State Senate Subcommittee on Un-American Activities, which charged that the campus was a "refuge for communism and immorality." He criticized Governor Brown for appointing regents to conduct the official investigation rather than the legislature, accusing him of a campus cover-up.[28] He called for the Watts Riot Commission chief to head a similar investigation into Berkeley, telling the Associated Press in May 1966; "It is my belief that the people of California have a right to know all the facts about charges of communism, sexual misbehavior, and near anarchy on the campus of the University of California at Berkeley."[29]

As *Time* reported, Reagan characterized the Berkeley trouble as a "simple morality play," with Brown enacting a policy of "appeasement of campus malcontents and filthy speech advocates."[30] He told audiences, "When that police car was surrounded and the police were roughed up by the students and nonstudents, officials should have restored order."[31] Reagan's oft-repeated solution to campus troubles, "Observe the rules or get out," never failed to elicit applause.[32] Reagan stressed the immorality of student protesters, describing them as "beatniks and advocates of sexual orgies, drug usage, and 'filthy speech.'"[33] He piqued curiosity by hinting at the scandalous details of campus behavior: "I could not tell you in this audience, they were too shocking."[34]

In Reagan's campaign rhetoric, "Berkeley" became the buzzword for campus unrest, both real and imagined, tapping into deep fears among voters.[35] In the Brown reelection camp, one campaign adviser noted that with Reagan's help, Berkeley had become "the most negative word that you could mention."[36] Another Brown campaigner remembered Berkeley as "the single most reactive word . . . [which] at that time meant longhairs, drugs, lack of order or even tidiness, hostility, sit-ins."[37]

While Reagan made references to Berkeley for political ends, he did not construct the image, nor did he manufacture the response it engendered. In the political climate of the mid-1960s, Berkeley became a symbol representing all that was wrong with California, things that could be righted by strong leadership. Berkeley was a challenge to the moral and sexual boundaries set by popular culture images. Reagan promised to return California to its days of greatness, and part of that evocation was tied to images of its youth. California kids were supposed to frolic on the beaches and joyride in their cars, not challenge the status quo.

Reagan employed Watts in his campaigning as well. The riot shook California, suddenly revealing the problems plaguing the state's minority communities. Reagan viewed legislative solutions to the riot's causes as another example of government interference and inefficiency: "Government has moved in so many administrators you would think they are going to trample the problem to death."[38] In interviews, Reagan contended that only 1 percent of Watts residents rioted in August 1965 and that those involved were mostly recent arrivals from the Deep South. These newcomers, Reagan explained, dreamed "that the streets were paved with gold," only to encounter disappointment with California's reality.[39]

Some observers noted the coded rhetoric of the 1966 election season. An article in the *Nation* characterized the election season as "one of the most subtle and intensive racist political campaigns ever waged in a Northern or Western state." The fear of Watts, coupled with anti–fair housing legislation, fomented an "undercurrent of racism" that Reagan exploited. Few Californians, the author argued, would admit "that the number one state may elect Ronald Reagan governor to 'keep the Negro in his place.' "[40]

The key issues of Berkeley and Watts provided the context for the June primaries. The *Nation* highlighted the influence of these "two highly explosive, emotional situations" on the political landscape: "It is fairly easy to tap resentment among middle-class voters by inveighing against students that don't shave, go in for eccentric hair-dos, wear sandals and levis, and now and then raise hell on campus. As to Watts, there was unquestionably a strong white backlash."[41] The political repercussions of these issues were felt in both parties, as the politics of symbols became a bipartisan practice. In the Democratic primary, Brown's main challenger, Mayor Sam Yorty of Los Angeles, confronted Brown on Berkeley and Watts. The votes against Brown in the primary were largely from Californians strongly against campus demonstrations and critical of the "softness" they perceived in Brown's handling of the Watts rioters.[42] Yorty was able to parlay his city's anti-riot sentiment into a respectable primary showing against the governor.[43] The mayor received nearly 1 million votes, 38 percent of the Democratic votes cast.[44] The 1966 campaign demonstrated that images of California youth, in this case mostly negative ones, were potent in the realm of politics, just as they were in popular culture.

In the Republican primary race, Reagan emerged the clear victor. A veteran political analyst explained in *U.S. News & World Report* that Reagan's win was the result of voters believing that "students at the University of California are immoral and that the university is run by a bunch of kooks."[45] *Newsweek* analyzed the state's "swing to the right wing" in June 1966. "For all the accent on the new and the young," the article explained, "California is going conservative." Reagan captured key districts in the south, "formerly moderate sections of Los Angeles." Party affiliation changes from Democrat to Republican registered mostly among "elder migrants from the Middle West and the young marrieds."[46]

After his decisive victory in the primary, Reagan gave a speech in which he evoked the pioneer history of the state. He made the transition from that proud tradition to the shameful goings-on in higher education, using the rhetoric of the mythic connection between California and the nation. He asked voters: "Is this the way we want it to be? We can change it. We can start a prairie fire that will sweep the nation and prove we are number one in more than size and crime and taxes. If this is a dream, it's a good dream, as big and golden as California itself."[47] Reagan echoed the chant of greatness that marked California politics in the postwar period, but he contrasted his vision with the one presented by challengers to the dream. He campaigned on a platform of reassurance, offering Californians hope while responding to current realities. These strategies were reflected in the tone of media coverage. For example, *Look* headlined its article on the governor's race "Ronnie to the Rescue."[48]

With Reagan's impressive margin of victory, *Newsweek* declared, "It may be too soon to say that the biggest state . . . is the U.S. trendsetter; yet it is now possible this new conservative bloc could provide Ronald Reagan with victory in California in 1966 – and in the nation in 1968 or 1972."[49] Reagan was the first Californian to be touted at such an early stage as the national standard-bearer for the party.[50] Incredibly, pundits identified Reagan as a possible presidential candidate before any political achievement. A *New York Times* article was the first to suggest the possibility, and other politicos followed suit. Shortly before the November 1966 election, *Look* predicted that Reagan "might well try next for the White House."[51]

While focusing on the two main issues of Berkeley and Watts, Reagan carefully cultivated an image that served to counteract his lack of governmental experience. This self-styled "citizen-politician" hearkened back to the days of the republic's founding, putting a new face on California's problems. Reagan's appeal was cross-generational but based on themes of race and class. He charmed voters of both parties with his vision of California's future and promises to confront the state's challengers. As the *New Republic* observed, "He looks strong, gives off a certain toughness, and his voice is one of the most familiar and reassuring in the country."[52] Without bold leadership and tough choices, Reagan argued, Californians would someday have to explain their moral acquiescence. His campaign mantra summed up the struggle against laxity and disorder, never failing to inspire patriotic clapping: "We better plan to tell our children what it was we found more precious than freedom. I'm sure they will want to know."[53] At one fund-raising dinner, the Voices of Faith Choir sang a campaign version of "California, Here I Come" with the new lyrics: "Ronald Reagan, here we are. You're the one we're hoping for."[54]

Key to Reagan's campaign was his exploitation of youth images. In his rhetoric he sensationalized Berkeley students while presenting in comparison a more comforting version of the state's youth. At rallies and fund-raisers, a bevy of "Reagan girls" accompanied the candidate, dressed in uniforms specially designed by wife Nancy with a 25-inch maximum waist measurement and fronts emblazoned with the Reagan name. The manual for these campaigners insisted that "Reagan girls represent the young, wholesome, vivacious, natural, all-American girl" and warned against smoking, chewing gum, drinking alcohol, or giving out phone numbers.[55] The girls, good "California kids," served as a visual contrast to competing images of youth on television and in the print media, reinforcing Reagan's appeal to frightened voters of all ages. The state that set the music, fashion, and movie trends for the nation looked to a trustworthy screen star to restore California's youthful, innocent image.

Tactics used by Reagan and Brown made for "one of the most bitter gubernatorial campaigns in California history."[56] Brown depended on California's economic growth and his proven experience to save him on election day. The appeal of his opponent bewildered him: "Reagan's an awfully nice fellow, very likable. But for the life of me, I can't see where he is the least bit qualified to be governor."[57] Brown found it increasingly difficult to control his disdain for his Republican challenger, attacking the man but unable to counter his message. "I've been a great Governor," Brown told

Ronald Reagan on the campaign trail
for governor in 1966. Pictured with him are
the "Reagan girls," wearing red beanies
and outfits designed by wife Nancy,
emblazoned with the Reagan name. These
"girls" acted as cheerleaders and stood
in stark contrast to the images of
trouble-making California youth that Reagan
often evoked during the campaign.

(Courtesy Ronald Reagan Library)

Time. He continued: "If you let this state go to a motion picture actor or anybody else after the things I've done, you ought to be ashamed of yourself."[58] Brown's campaign posters proclaimed "Governor Brown speaks to the future."[59] The future was not what Californians found appealing. In its place they longed for a greatness that seemed to be receding into the past and which Reagan pledged to restore.

A national media fascination with the governor's race helped Reagan's cause. These profiles reveal a candidate packaged according to the California myth. Reagan stood as a classic example of a democratic society, a self-made man rising from humble midwestern roots to Hollywood stardom. Photo essays depicted a patriotic and family-minded candidate, while his movie-world connections increased his familiarity and appeal. For example, the *New York Times Magazine* featured the actor in November 1965 on its cover, a flattering shot of Reagan backlit by a large American flag. Subtitled "Tom Sawyer Enters Politics," the author called Reagan "sincere, handsome, and articulate . . . central casting's ideal political candidate." The article described the campaign committee, "Republicans for Reagan," that formed to raise money and support his entry into the gubernatorial race. Conservative members of the Hollywood elite, including James Cagney and Walt Disney, pledged funds and support.[60]

Life profiled Reagan, describing him as "an overnight political sensation" soon after he announced his candidacy in January 1966. The article characterized his childhood as "all-American as a strawberry festival" and described his reputation within Hollywood society as "something of a square – but a clean-cut, Eagle Scout–type square." Interspersed amongst these characterizations were pictures of the Reagan family enjoying wholesome activities together.[61] The *Saturday Evening Post,* under the headline "Ronald Reagan: Can He Win California?" featured the candidate on its cover in June 1966. The article included photographs of the Reagan family playing checkers, taking a family ride in a jeep, and walking with their dogs on their California ranch.[62] A *Time* reporter called Reagan "Hollywood handsome and remarkably youthful in appearance," a candidate who had "rattled political seismographs from coast to coast."[63]

The conservative journal *National Review* profiled the Reagan campaign in January 1966, confident in his election day chances and cognizant of the nation's move to the right. Columnist William F. Buckley believed Reagan was well positioned to challenge "the creeping anarchy whose manifestations at Berkeley and Watts are the big issues in California this year."[64] The journal published a follow-up article in June, calling Reagan "A Light in the West." His popularity was a reflection of statewide antipathy, most pronounced in the southern portion, toward challenges to the status quo. "Ideas of social protest," the article explained, "do not survive here, on the beaches, or under the orange trees. Southern California, to its inhabitants, is Paradise already."[65]

In the campaign's closing months, Reagan's steadily rising poll numbers revealed an audience receptive to his message. He offered an angry litany of California's first rankings: in crime, welfare rolls, and campus disturbances.[66] The candidate hammered the governor on the so-called "morality gap" between them. "The overriding issue of this campaign," Reagan said, was "the abandonment of all the old rules we've lived by." As evidence of this desertion of tradition, Reagan cited this example: "Our young people are told, even in the classroom, that they should experiment with LSD." A *Life* reporter characterized Reagan's appeal as "a summons to return to the true, tested principles of patriotism, godliness, and self-reliance."[67] The October 1966 race riot in San Francisco, Governor Brown's hometown, did little to help his reelection bid. The uprising reminded voters of Watts, giving Reagan another chance to criticize administration policy. "It is obvious that the Governor has not profited at all from the experience of Watts," Reagan told reporters, "and has done nothing to forestall future disturbances."[68]

For Brown, the writing was on the wall by October. In a profile of the upcoming election, the liberal journal *Ramparts*, displayed Mickey Mouse on its cover and characterized Brown as "an almost pathetic figure." The answer to California's questionable future, it predicted, was Ronald Reagan, "a product, as carefully processed and packaged as Lucky Filters." Interspersed with pictures of Disneyland, the article described the unreality and strangeness of California's political environment, comparing the electoral landscape to the park's imaginary one: "Ronnie in Tomorrowland" appealed to voters whose "social fantasies clash" with uncomfortable realities, who were "restless because they can't control their environment."[69] Disneyland offered a nostalgic space. Similarly, Reagan hearkened to those images, which celebrated an illusory past and looked to a familiar future.

Reagan won the governorship by a large plurality, almost a million votes, attracting thousands of crossover Democrats. Brown made incumbent history, losing by one of the largest margins on record.[70] The most noteworthy aspect of the win was the "blurring of the north/south split" in election returns, with the center of power migrating to Southern California. Anxieties about juvenile delinquency, crime, drugs, campus unrest, and racial problems motivated Californians to cast their votes for Reagan.[71] At their core, these were issues about California's youth and the state's future.

His win also revealed the widespread concern about the perceived "decay of values" occurring in California, personified by troubled and rebellious youth.[72] After his victory, Reagan appeared on the cover of *U.S. News & World Report* and proclaimed California more than capable of fighting its problems: "There's nobody quite like us. . . . If we can prove that we can take care of our problems here in California, if we can do this thing, we can say to a lot of people back in the tired East – It works, this system of ours."[73]

Four years after his defeat, Pat Brown penned an analysis of the Reagan appeal, belatedly understanding the reasons behind his political failure. "Californians were angry about the student demonstrations and violence at Berkeley," he wrote. In addition, Watts caused "political attitudes . . . to sour." The polarization that resulted created a "two-dimensional politics," casting the election as suits and ties versus long-haired hippies. Reagan's keen understanding of the political environment, the "first, quick, superficial reactions to style and taste," boosted him into office.[74]

In a postelection article, "Paradise Reagan-ed," the *Nation* examined the "Eden image" the state enjoyed. The Californian's predilection for escape "from the cold blasts of the Midwest or the problems of the South or lack of opportunity" fostered this mythology, the writer argued: "[During the 1966 political season,] a time of rapid social change and increasing problems, the people of California fled reality. Instead, they indulged in a ritual cleansing, and brought in a totally inexperienced man who campaigned on the basis of being a political innocent. . . . But now all is simple and wonderful in a land 'where thinking makes it so.' . . . The Californians can look forward to eternities of joy, while the rest of America, in the land of Nod (East of Eden) must continue to struggle and sweat."[75] California's reputation as a carefree suburban island immune to the nation's troubles, so carefully nurtured in the 1950s and 1960s, faced critical challenges in Berkeley and Watts. The election of Ronald Reagan in 1966 was the result of California's political turn to the right. As a candidate, Reagan masterfully employed themes of morality and law and order to attack disruptive baby boomers, a testament to the tenacity and power of California youth images.

Historians have recognized the election of 1966 as both a turning point and an example of symbols and images in political discourse, correctly identifying the important roles played by Berkeley and Watts. California's brand of conservatism extended its influence in the wake of the Reagan landslide.[76] Reagan's 1966 campaign brilliantly took advantage of populist themes in its attack on Berkeley, highlighting his commitment to strong leadership and traditional values.[77] Under normal circumstances, political experience and economic prosperity should have guaranteed a Brown victory. However, the unsettling nature of Berkeley and Watts shook many Californians and their sense of "public morality," fostering a belief that the nation's dreamland was becoming nightmarish.[78] In his recent book, *The Right Moment*, Matthew Dallek points to the electoral moment of 1966 as the decisive turning point in the rise of postwar conservatism. He argues that the roots of Reagan's long-term political success lay in the specter of social disorder that seemed to threaten California and the nation, most notably the challenges of Berkeley and Watts.[79] In *Suburban Warriors*, Lisa McGirr traces the evolution of conservatism from right wing to mainstream, focusing on Orange County in Southern California. The troubles experienced by the Golden State increased the appeal of political conservatism to middle-class Californians, resulting in the election of Ronald Reagan to the governorship and eventually the presidency. The importance of conservative movements within California, McGirr argues, has been overshadowed historically and culturally by the attention given to left-wing and counterculture actions and attitudes in the state.[80]

Reagan did not invent the California dream or construct the predominant images of California youth. It was the power of these images that made the 1966 election a turning point and the special dream of California that made Reagan's rhetoric succeed. He brilliantly exploited an existing mythology in light of recent challenges. The hope for the future embedded in postwar California was tied to specific attitudes about the baby boom generation. Californians feared that their "good kids," and by extension the "good life," had gone bad. As the carefully constructed image of California's youth began to falter, they turned to leaders who promised to restore and maintain those icons in a world seemingly turned upside down.

During the campaign, Reagan told a *Life* reporter he wished he could visit Disneyland "more often."[81] His role in the park's 1955 dedication must have made an impression, as Reagan's inaugural gala was designed to resemble a Disneyland-like experience and shared the personnel and grandeur of that event. The inauguration's director of ceremonies had been part of the Disneyland team.[82] Other designers from Walt Disney Studios helped plan Reagan's inaugural celebration.[83] Ceremonies in January 1967 lasted nearly four days, adding to the pomp of government tradition a gloss of Hollywood-premiere glamour. Emblazoned with the title "Fiesta California," festivities included a grand ball, a symphony concert, a large parade, multiple receptions, a prayer breakfast, a 19-gun salute, and an inaugural address. Danny Thomas and other Hollywood stars were special guests, evoking Reagan's Hollywood past.[84] Many University of California students attended the inauguration, with the USC chamber choir singing "America the Beautiful."[85] In the midst of this well scripted pageantry, the new governor's extraordinary security arrangements indicated a surprising degree of anxiety about threats from those left out of the choir. The night of the inauguration, officials barred the public from the Capitol. For the first time during the parade, armed policemen accompanied the governor-elect, and at the ball over 200 law enforcement personnel were on hand.[86]

Reagan's inauguration was similar to the dedication ceremony of Disneyland in many ways. Both evoked military power. The use of the name "Fiesta California" implies a surface understanding of the multiethnic realities of the state, just as Frontierland entertained with a homogenized version of the western past. Hollywood stars were in attendance at both events. The appearance of California's young people in parades and concerts reinforced Reagan's campaign message. His inaugural speech echoed themes similarly employed by Walt Disney of the uniqueness and power of California and America: "California with its climate, its resources, and its wealth of young, aggressive, talented people, must never take second place."[87] Reagan evoked a hope in the baby boom generation as a positive source of California's greatness.

Voters preferred to conjure up popular culture images rather than news accounts. Millions of Californians responded to Reagan's promised crackdown on youth rebellion, restoring the image of a baby boom generation grateful for its unparalleled privileges and comforts. Reagan, an entertainer from the silver screen turned conservative politician, reminded California of its celebrated greatness in the postwar era and pledged to restore its virtue. A vote for Reagan in 1966 was a vote for a sunnier vision of the state's destiny and a vote against California's youth who had deviated from their defined roles, activities, and icons. The election results revealed the perseverance of and attachment to idealized images of California life, despite new and recently noticed realities. However, the rising generation's threats had disturbed the mythology created for the state over the previous decade, ending the unobscured vision of a baby boomer's paradise.

Californians favored a Golden State where problems remained invisible, a land of carefree suburbia and happy baby boomers. The dream of California captivated Americans as well, providing a secure haven where the nation might escape. When rebellious images emerged, many were unwilling to forget the golden past represented in popular culture visions. The nation experienced a backlash against its challengers, finding comfort in conservative camps. California was the harbinger of this conservative turn, as upheavals similar to Berkeley and Watts across the country pushed many voters to follow California's political lead. Nixon was Reaganesque in his 1968 presidential campaign, calling on traditional-minded voters, the "silent majority," to send him to the White House. While Berkeley and Watts signaled a new cultural and political radicalism, the reaction to those events supported a conservatism that was more powerful electorally, demonstrating the salient power of California youth images.

CHAPTER NINE

Endless Summer

Things had better work here, because here . . .

is where we run out of continent.

—Joan Didion, in Lustig, "Envisioning California"

California, the baby boomer's dreamland, offered powerful images of an American future in suburbia under sunny skies. The destinies and identities of these postwar creations seem linked, the state and the generation both serving to glorify a place and an ideal, a land of beautiful, wholesome children raised in the perfect locale. On television and in magazines, California appeared as a healthy landscape and a dream vacation destination. With few exceptions, these representations celebrated young Californians as a white, suburban, middle-class cohort enjoying consumer opportunities and pursuing happiness. These were media creations based on evasive truths, images reflective of cultural needs, produced in Hollywood and broadcast to an audience eager for glimpses of California living. From the mid-1950s to the mid-1960s, images of California youth acquired certain meanings, sharing with the Golden State a key place in the national consciousness.

Baby boomers were special guests of Disneyland, a fantasy landscape and television-shaped Mecca. The theme park represented an Adventureland for kids, offering visions of a past and future America. Another Disney creation, *The Mickey Mouse Club*, televised daily reminders of moral behavior through serials and cartoons. The show made young Californians stars and invited every child in America to join the club. Over the same period, film images evolved from stories of delinquency, like *Rebel Without a Cause*, to more benign representations of teen life, like that seen in *Gidget*, though both were tales of conformity and suburbia in the California sun. Through fashion and media attention to the surfing craze, California teens modeled for the world lifestyles of mobility and freedom. The Beach Boys lyrically promised an ideal teenage existence, while the California sound reinforced visions of carefree fun in the sun. Hollywood studios made formulaic films celebrating the beach, offering models of playful leisure for eager teenage moviegoers to enjoy.

The California dream in postwar America was multifaceted, and a celebration of its youth was an important ingredient shaping the cultural environment. These images, manufactured and sold, recorded and filmed, depicted the Golden State as the promised land. In content and context, they presented models of behavior, icons marketed to the nation, that defined the concepts of normal and good. California's children were comforting and reassuring figures, created, packaged, and most importantly, believed. The challenges that arose in California disrupted the mythmaking, demonstrating the political repercussions of images that shape perceptions and create meaning. The Golden State ultimately failed to provide a safety valve for postwar anxiety.

California played a central role in American ideology, conditioning the nation to see life in the state as "better than real." The disruptions of Berkeley and Watts shocked the nation, as America's "Tomorrowland" now seemed to foreshadow societal, political, and cultural upheaval. The uprising at Berkeley raised questions, while the riot in Watts violently introduced California's minority youth. The beach party for California was over. California continued to be "the Mecca of American Teenagers" but of a different sort.[1] As one observer noted, "If a youth revolt is in progress in our country, one can say that California and L.A. are its vanguard."[2] In the mid-1960s, the wholesome surfer and suburban teenager clashed with a more threatening vision. Instead of the "superkids" coming to maturity in the land of sunshine, California's youth appeared in the mass media as the most drugged-out and rebellious generation the nation had seen. The postwar California dream ended, accompanied by a national revival of concerns about juvenile delinquency combined with hysteria over drug use.

Some icons in the California landscape kept their cultural positions. Disneyland was one such place. Walt Disney passed away in December 1966, and his *Newsweek* obituary mentioned that theme park officials had refused entry to "more than 500 teen-agers because of shorts, beards, long hair, similar deviations from the norm" during the summer of 1966.[3] The "norm" in Disneyland refused to accommodate changing images of youth. Similarly, the park maintained its exclusion of minorities in its hiring practices. Disneyland did not employ African Americans in "people contact" jobs until pressured to do so in 1968.[4] Disneyland became the antithesis of Los Angeles, a bastion holding out against the cultural chaos surrounding it.[5] Cultural critics of the 1970s conceded that Disneyland was "indeed happier than anything in the real world."[6] In February 2001, Disney launched a new park next to the 47-year-old Disneyland, taking over the space of its parking lot. Named "Disney's California Adventure," the park celebrates the popularized California experience with three themed areas: Paradise Pier, Hollywood Pictures Backlot, and the Golden State. At its entrance is the word "California," spelled out in 11½-foot-high gold letters. The loudspeakers play the tunes of the Beach Boys as visitors are treated to a theme park vision of a visit to California. As one of the park's planners explained, "The whole idea is that we're celebrating the dreams of California – the special qualities that draw people here."[7] The Disney company still situates its parks in the iconic world of California.

The theme park survives because of its fantasy world appeal. In the world of popular music, however, the California sound of surfing and cruising failed to maintain its position on the charts, despite serious attempts to change with the times. Jan and Dean released *Folk n' Roll* in 1965, with liner notes inviting record buyers to join their protest: "Burkly students two for one."[8] On the album, the duo recorded a cover of "Eve of Destruction," a chasm of cultural distance from the world evoked by "Surf City."[9] The Surfaris hit "Wipe Out" was re-released in July 1966, but this time the maniacal laugh and rolling guitar line evoked images of a drug trip.[10] *Beach Boys Party!* the group's last album of 1965, featured three John Lennon–Paul McCartney tunes and a recording of Bob Dylan's "The Times They Are A-Changin.'"[11] Their 1966 release *Pet Sounds* left behind striped shirts, Pendletons, short haircuts, surfing, and automobiles. The result was a critical success but a commercial disappointment.[12] While the Beach Boys' music reflected and perpetuated the California ideal of innocence in the early 1960s, that cultural position eventually proved untenable. Recording artist David Crosby called the Beach Boys "the essence of California music": "They wrote about the beach and girls and cars."[13] The group was the essence of California, but only of a certain exclusionary brand. As would become evident in the next decade, the Beach Boys themselves were a falsehood, nonsurfers who maintained a facade of carefree musical creation, obscuring the realities of a tortured leader, family squabbles, and substance abuse.

The San Francisco music scene developed a different aesthetic away from the commercial mainstream in Los Angeles.[14] "Wah-wah and fuzz-tone" replaced the treble falsettos and harmonies of the Beach Boys.[15] "California Dreamin'" by the Mamas and Papas reached number four in early 1966, remaining on the charts for seventeen weeks.[16] The song's title evoked familiar themes, but with a markedly different tone, a minor key and a more wistful sentiment. The 1967 Scott McKenzie hit "San Francisco" mythologized the West Coast's peace and love.[17] At the Monterey Pop Festival in 1967, Jimi Hendrix set fire to his guitar and proclaimed, "Now we'll never have to listen to surf music again."[18]

The beach movies, emerging from the same cultural milieu that made surf music popular, faced a similar downturn in box office revenue.[19] In November 1965, AIP executive Arkoff announced to the *New York Times*, "The bikini beach cycle has had it," reporting that the studio was looking for "a new locale."[20] While never intended as representations of reality, the *Beach Party* films reflected core beliefs about California youth lifestyles. Annette and Frankie's romps on the beach ended as the images they helped create vanished. California's kids left behind mouse ears and the Beach Boys, adopting new figures to take their place. For example, *Esquire* anointed Bob Dylan, Mario Savio, and Joan Baez "the heroes of the California rebels," adding, "(and as Cal goes, so goes the rest)."[21]

As the 1960s continued, California came to serve as the cultural headquarters of the nation's hippies, providing models of dress, behavior, and attitude. The hippies shared attributes of the Beats but broadened their influence. Modeling a "counterculture," played out in defiance of earlier images, the hippies represented mainstream America's worst fears: sexual freedom, dangerous rock and roll, and drug use.[22] The wholesome teen look disappeared, and psychedelic colors and wild paisley patterns invaded middle-class closets.[23] By 1968, most Americans could readily identify the images of San Francisco's Haight-Ashbury district.[24] Like the previous lightweight version, this new California youth movement attracted the world's attention.[25]

In the south, teenagers transformed Los Angeles's Sunset Strip into a "new kind of playground . . . the perfect place for flaunting rebellion." Wearing bell-bottom pants and gyrating to folk rock, *Time* reported, these California kids were "a sight to behold." Despite a curfew law, those under eighteen took part in "weekends of wild rioting," throwing bottles and rocks.[26] *Look* called the Strip the "new teen-age nightclub capital of the U.S." for "rebel-rousing youth."[27] Local teens and runaways frequented the strip.[28] The *Saturday Evening Post* called the "newest tribe" of teenagers "free souls," marked by tattoos and go-go dancing.[29]

National magazines depicted both Haight-Ashbury and the Sunset Strip, the two youth culture capitals of the mid-1960s, as key centers of the drug culture. The media turned its attention toward the explosion of drug use among baby boomers, especially in the Golden State. For its cover story, "The Exploding Threat of a Mind Drug That Got Out of Control," *Life* profiled Los Angeles and San Francisco as hometowns of the "acid-heads."[30] At San Francisco State, *Time* reported, 35 percent of students had tried LSD.[31] A "Drugs on the Campus" report published by the *Saturday Evening Post* exposed the role of marijuana at colleges, especially those in California.[32] A follow-up article profiled Berkeley, reporting that half the student body "experimented with marijuana," which ensnared the rebellious clique as well as fraternity members.[33] In Los Angeles area high schools, *Time* reported, at least 50 percent of students tried the drug before graduation. California's high incidence of marijuana use was "so widespread that pot must be considered an integral part of the generation's life experience."[34]

California still represented the national pacemaker, but it offered less comforting glimpses of America's destiny.[35] *Look* examined California in a special June 1966 issue, arguing that the state was "a window into the future . . . good or bad, hope or horror."[36] California trends strongly influenced baby boomers but no longer reassured mainstream America.[37] The state's powerful role in American life frightened many *Look* readers. One Pennsylvanian wrote to the editor, "How much more of the USA is like the California you describe? Could we cut it away and let it drift off into the Pacific to some sheltered paradise?" A reader from Texas bemoaned the craziness of California: "Thank goodness for the other 49 states! We need them to counterbalance the insanity in California."[38]

By the end of the 1960s, California represented a cautionary tale instead of fairytale promise. In national polls, California's disruptions ranked high as a source of national concern, displacing earlier images of the good life.[39] A critical flood of anti-California skepticism, matching the tide of 1950s boosterism, appeared in the late 1960s and 1970s.[40] Anxiety about earthquakes in the Golden State spawned religious and astrological predictions of doomsday, with books like *The Last Days of the Late, Great, State of California* riding to the top of the bestseller lists.[41] With the titles *California: The Vanishing Dream* and *Anti-California*, writers sounded off on the loss of innocence and possibility. Newspaper headlines asked, "Has the Dream Gone Sour?" and depicted "[the] California Dream in a Bodybag." In these analyses, high hopes and too much sunshine were identified as the causes of California's tragic decline.[42] Rather than a healthy dreamland attracting the migration of millions, California came to represent "a dark precinct of social pathology."[43] As a result of the negative hype, a *Saturday Review* article reported, Californians were "moving out rather than rear their children there."[44]

The negative imagery surrounding California continued into the 1980s and 1990s, with chroniclers and critics tracing California's past struggles and the ascendant dark side of the promise. In large part the harsh critiques are a reaction to the blissful picture of the postwar period, a recapturing of a turbulent past and a warning about California's troubled future as well as a response to the "pseudo-history of the boosters."[45] David Wyatt, in his book *Five Fires*, places race, conflict, and natural catastrophes at the center of the California story.[46] Others focus on urban and environmental problems with an apocalyptic bent. Mike Davis, author of *City of Quartz: Excavating the Future in Los Angeles* (1990), continued his critique of Los Angeles with his 1998 work *Ecology of Fear*. Davis argues that Los Angeles has paid a heavy price due to a lack of environmental responsibility in development, leading to tragedies both in the natural world and in the human infrastructure. He points to the fires, floods, earthquakes, and rioting of the 1990s as indicators of social problems connected with environmental ones.[47]

In the 1960s, California lost its identity as a baby boom paradise, becoming instead a catchphrase for the nation's modern troubles and the youth showplace of racial rioting, drug use, and campus upheaval. The fashion and music, the costumes and soundtracks of the late 1960s appear as contradictions to earlier generational images. What contemporaries chronicled but did not recognize was the powerful juxtaposition of seemingly disparate visions of the decade.

The more radical turns of the 1960s threatened the safe celebration of baby boom youth. Yet, while carefully constructed images of wholesome suburbia were endangered, they did not disappear, despite the turn in California historiography. In the minds of many baby boomers who view the period through a nostalgic lens, these images maintain their power. After forty years, the mythmaking remains salient, creating a world where many still live or to which they want to return. Baby boomers grew up along with the state of California, both nostalgically clinging to a seemingly simpler age. Sharing a timeframe of influence, the generation and its adopted home state experienced a rebellious adolescence, with an eventual return to adult responsibility and a celebration of its younger days.

Popular culture's shaping of reality remains a touchstone of meaning. The film *American Graffiti*, set in 1962 Modesto in California's central valley, appeared in the early 1970s and purported to capture the era of cruising and sock hops. Nostalgic films produced for the baby boomer audience largely ignore the more troubling images of the late 1960s.[48] Millions of parents take their children on a pilgrimage to Disneyland. Baby boomers flock to concerts of aging rock and rollers, still able to recall the words of *The Mickey Mouse Club* theme song. In the 1980s, Annette and Frankie nostalgically returned in the Paramount film *Back to the Beach* (1987), while syndicated television cast a grownup Gidget in a new sitcom. In June 2001, Penguin Putnam reissued the original *Gidget* novel, which had been out of print since the early 1960s, for an entirely new generation of readers. Images of California's baby boomers seem to have been ultimately successful, fostering a group identity and instilling in many members of that generation a longing for that past filled with popular culture imagery. Many fondly remember their California childhood, regardless of whether they grew up in the state. It is the attachment to those visions of the past that continue to cast the late 1960s as a jarring, radical age, as boomers share the media tendency to smooth out the era's rough edges.

The 1960s are popularly understood as a decade of dramatic change and upheaval, a challenge to America's innocence. However, in many ways the decade was more conservative than radical, leaving the majority's conceptual maps intact. In the late 1960s, campus rebels, counterculture hippies, and antiwar protesters made headlines, giving a false tint to the decade's meaning.[49] California's postwar dreams were based on demographic trends, suburban developments, and economic opportunity – all genuine components of the celebrated lifestyle. For some baby boomers, adolescence in California was a consumer-oriented, leisured existence. Popular culture, however, fashioned those images as the only reality, making challenges seem more disruptive. At the same time, images from the late 1960s are also exclusionary, leaving out of the picture more conservative trends and coloring the decade broadly as a counterculture generational experience. The two views of the 1960s seem starkly different, turning perception into reality and often clashing with historical evidence. The two sets of powerful media images serve as integral parts of the narrative, both revealing and concealing, swaying political behavior and continuing to influence interpretations of the past.

In many ways, the counterculture imagery of the late 1960s was victorious culturally, shadowing the decade. However, the explosive combination of California youth images and the challenges that emerged inspired a conservatism whose political aftershocks continue to be felt. Rather than exercising their own political power, radical insurgents of the 1960s actually fostered an attachment to conservative and comforting images. Reagan's presidential campaigning in the 1980s evoked the images and rhetoric that won him the governorship, a recapturing of the American dream, California-style. In many ways, America is still experiencing the backlash that undermined liberalism, a backlash that employed both images of a more innocent America and the contrasting forces of disruption for electoral purposes. Now, in the twenty-first century, California retains its key place in the national psyche, a predictor of trends and a laboratory of social change, as it has since the end of World War II.[50] The Golden State exercises a unique power, still enjoying a small part of its postwar mystique, despite racial tensions, immigration conflicts, and economic hard times.

The brand of California dreaming that focused on youth captured the imagination of filmmakers, television producers, magazine profiles, and musicians. California lifestyles proved a salient vision in the postwar period, shaping the general view of baby boomers. While elusive as a reality, these images were tied into core mainstream values and ideas and into the needs of postwar America, helping define a generation. Trials came when the California "good life" came to be viewed as the entire picture, encouraging an inability to envision a world beyond the concerns of white, middle-class suburbia. This creation, this "innocent" California image, dismissed the state's multiethnic realities and complexities, until outsiders and pressures building from within tarnished the image of the Golden State and altered the picture of its golden youth. Yet, despite the challenges, the images survive, still influencing memories of the past and visions of the present.

INTRODUCTION

1. Postol, "Reinterpreting the Fifties"; McGregor, "Domestic Blitz"; and Sugrue, "Reassessing the History."
2. J. B. Gilbert, "Popular Culture," 148.
3. Hall, *Representation*, 1.
4. Grossberg, Nelson, and Treichler, *Cultural Studies*, 4.
5. Story, *What Is Cultural Studies?*, 3.
6. O'Connor, "History in Images/Images in History," 1200–1209.
7. Cullen, *Art of Democracy*, 12.
8. Foreman, *The Other Fifties*, 6.
9. Inge, *Handbook of American Popular Culture*, xxiii.
10. Balio, "Hollywood," 12.
11. L. Y. Jones, *Great Expectations*, 6–7, 43.
12. Doherty, *Teenagers and Teenpics*, 201.
13. Starr, *Americans and the California Dream*.
14. L. Y. Jones, *Great Expectations*, 80, 70.

CHAPTER ONE

1. Bean and Rawls, *California*, 16–17.
2. Avila, "Reinventing Los Angeles" (Ph.D. diss.), 2.
3. Starr, "California, A Dream," 19.
4. Meinig, "American Wests," 168.
5. M. Davis, *City of Quartz*, 30.
6. Quoted in Bunch, *Black Angelenos*, 9.

7. This negative imagery can be traced particularly in literature and commentary about Los Angeles. See Fine, *Imagining Los Angeles*; and M. Davis, *City of Quartz*.
8. M. Davis, *City of Quartz*, 38.
9. Rawls, "Visions and Revisions," 60.
10. Vance, "California and the Search," 204.
11. McWilliams, *California: The Great Exception*, 14, 17.
12. "California, the Nation's First."
13. "California Way of Life," *Life*, 105–16.
14. Stegner quoted in Morgan, *Westward Tilt*, 25.
15. I. Stone, "California: A Land to Build a Dream On," 43, 53.
16. Parsons, "Uniqueness of California."
17. Packard, *Status Seekers*, 7.
18. Bunch, *Black Angelenos*, 38.
19. Nash, *American West*, 220.
20. Poe, "Nobody Was Listening," 426.
21. Verge, "Impact of the Second World War," 289, 314 (*Times* quote).
22. "Population of 6 Million Forecast."
23. "Lady Named Los Angeles."
24. R. A. Smith, "Los Angeles, Prototype of Supercity," 99.
25. Bowie, "Cultural History of Los Angeles" (Ph.D. diss.), 281.
26. "Nation That Moved West," 6–7.
27. Stern and Stern, *Way Out West*, 193.

28. Flink, *Automobile Age*, 140.
29. Teaford, *Twentieth-Century American City*, 99.
30. Cort, "Our Strangling Highways," 357.
31. Avila, "Reinventing Los Angeles," 212–22.
32. "Introduction: California."
33. Nash, *American West*, 225.
34. "L.A. Traffic Reflects," 74.
35. Coffin, "California Is Bustin' Out," 28.
36. Hughes, "California – The America to Come," 454.
37. Rawls, "Visions and Revisions," 61.
38. Quoted in James, "New World," 27.
39. "California," *Look* 1962, cover.
40. Leonard, "California – What It Means," 96.
41. Farber, *Age of Great Dreams*, 53.
42. *Gallup Poll*, 2:1461.
43. Atwood, "How America Feels," 12–13.
44. "Los Angeles: A Race Relations Success," 25–27.
45. Horne, *Fire This Time*, 49–50.
46. Rand, *Los Angeles: The Ultimate City*, 125.
47. Perlmutter, "Dodgers Accept L.A. Bid."
48. "Baseball: The Gold Rush West," 84; and Daley, "Will the Dodger-Giant Gold Rush Pan Out?" 34.
49. Jacobson, *Awesome Almanac California*, 108.
50. Schwartz, *From West to East*, 393.
51. R. L. Wilson, "California: The Year's Most Important Election," 23.
52. "California's Increasing Importance in U.S."
53. T. H. White, "Gentlemen from California," 39–40.
54. Lubell, "Who Will Take California?" 35.
55. *Los Angeles Times*, 30 September 1962, sec. 1, p. 10.
56. Bean and Rawls, *California*, 520.
57. Dunne, "Eureka! A Celebration of California," 20.
58. Schrag, *Paradise Lost*, 27.
59. "California," *Look* 1959.
60. "Call of California," 56B.
61. "Number One State," 29.
62. Bliven, "East Coast or West – Which?"
63. "That California Way of Life," 27.
64. While, "I Hate Southern California," 20–21.
65. Sargent, "How to Face the Move," 70.
66. Fowler, "Los Angeles," 21.
67. "Weather."
68. Miller and Nowak, *The Fifties*, 143.
69. Deegan, "Unclosed Frontier," 534.
70. Coffin, "Great American Week End," 61, 69.
71. "Good Life," 12, 62.
72. "Los Angeles: The Art of Living."
73. Meinig, "Symbolic Landscapes," 169–71.
74. K. T. Jackson, *Crabgrass Frontier*, 265.
75. Hine, *Populuxe*, 49.
76. Clark, *American Family Home*, 211.
77. Meinig, "American Wests," 179–80.
78. Vance, "Revolution in American Space," 453.
79. Rice, *Elusive Eden*, 461.
80. Coffin, "California Is Bustin' Out," 28.
81. Rice, *Elusive Eden*, 475.
82. *Los Angeles Times*, 12 June 1962, sec. 10, p. 3.
83. "California – Too Much, Too Soon," 65.
84. "Nation That Moved West," 7.
85. "Introduction: California," 23.
86. Kuehnl, "What It's Really Like," 56.
87. "That California Way of Life," 29, 32.

88. James, "New World in the West," 25.
89. Vance, "Revolution in American Space," 453.
90. "California Way of Life," 106.
91. Burdick, "From Gold Rush to Sun Rush."
92. Turpin, "California Schools."
93. James, "New World in the West," 25.
94. L. Y. Jones, *Great Expectations*, 70.
95. "Kids: Built-In Recession Cure," 83.
96. "The Fun Worshippers."
97. "Number One State," 31.
98. Coffin, "California Is Bustin' Out," 27.
99. L. Y. Jones, *Great Expectations*, 70.
100. J. Gilbert, *Cycle of Outrage*, 3–7.
101. Maudlin, "What Gives?" 46.
102. "Teen-agers – Why They Go Steady," cover, 22.
103. Cameron, "I Rode Heartbreak Train," 38.
104. Bliven, "California Culture," 38.
105. Robbins, "Inside Story."
106. Hulse, "What Becomes of the Juvenile Delinquent."
107. "30 Teen-Agers Arrested."
108. J. Gilbert, *Cycle of Outrage*, 14.
109. "U.S. Teenager," 22.
110. "Our Good Teen-Agers," 69.
111. "Hi-Fi Citizens."
112. Schaftner, "When These Teen-Agers Say," 38.
113. "Teen-ager Makes Her Mark"; and "Janet's Going to the Prom."
114. "Physiques Pay Off."
115. La Barre and Seghers, "California – Teenagers' Paradise," 46, 52.
116. Honor, "Gifts from the Sun," 66, 68, 69.
117. Coffin, "California Is Bustin' Out," 28.
118. S. Gordon, "California Co-Eds," 68.
119. "California Lassie, Universally Classy."
120. Nadeau, *California: The New Society*, 128, 167, 145.
121. "Los Angeles: A Race Relations Success," 25.
122. "No Rock, No Mop," 67.
123. Atwood, "How America Feels," 12–13.
124. "Poll Shows Teen-agers Look Westward."

CHAPTER TWO

1. Chris, "Beyond the Mouse-Ear Gates," 5.
2. Lipsitz, "Making of Disneyland," 195.
3. Schickel, *Disney Version*, 85, 29.
4. Findlay, *Magic Lands*, 58.
5. *Disneyland: The First Quarter Century*, 29.
6. Weinstein, "Disneyland and Coney Island," 146.
7. K. M. Jackson, *Walt Disney: A Bio-Bibliography*, 52.
8. Hodgins, "What's Wrong with the Movies?" 97; and "Movies: End of an Era?" 99.
9. Jowett, *Film: The Democratic Art*, 475.
10. MacKay, "The Big Brawl," 17.
11. Houseman, "Battle over Television."
12. Boddy, *Fifties Television*, 67.
13. Gomery, "Failed Opportunities," 33, 25.
14. "Film vs. Live Shows."
15. McDonald, *One Nation Under Television*, 118.
16. "Boom in the West."
17. "Wonderful World," 61, 64.
18. Watts, *Magic Kingdom*, 360.
19. C. Anderson, *Hollywood TV*, 4.
20. Cotter, *Wonderful World of Disney Television*, 58.
21. C. Anderson, *Hollywood TV*, 10.
22. "Disney's 7-Year ABC-TV Deal."

23. "Disney to Enter TV Field in Fall."
24. "Wonderful World," 61, 64.
25. Thomas, *Walt Disney: An American Original*, 250.
26. K. M. Jackson, *Walt Disney Bio-Bibliography*, 88.
27. Cotter, *Wonderful World of Disney Television*, 59.
28. "Disney in TVland."
29. Marling, "Imagineering the Disney Theme Parks," 70.
30. Findlay, *Magic Lands*, 54.
31. Cotter, *Wonderful World of Disney Television*, 104, 59–60.
32. C. Anderson, *Hollywood TV*, 141.
33. "This Week in Review."
34. Quinlan, *Inside ABC*, 53.
35. "ABC's Chest-Thumping," 31, 34.
36. A. Gordon, "Walt Disney," 35.
37. P. F. Anderson, *Davy Crockett Craze*, 35.
38. Maltin, *Disney Films*, 293.
39. Simonette, "Walt Disney Programs" (Ph.D. diss.), 96–99.
40. Marling, "Disneyland, 1955," 202–3.
41. Hine, *Populuxe*, 151.
42. Boddy, "Studios Move into Prime Time," 29, 31.
43. "Tidal Wave," 24–25.
44. King, "Recycled Hero," 143–45.
45. "Wonderful World," 62.
46. O'Boyle, "Be Sure You're Right," 78.
47. King, "Recycled Hero," 148.
48. C. Anderson, *Hollywood TV*, 149.
49. P. F. Anderson, *Davy Crockett Craze*, 49.
50. "Boy, Age 7, Defends His Crockett Cap."
51. "Tidal Wave," 34.
52. "U.S. Again Is Subdued by Davy," 27.
53. "King of the Wild Frontier."
54. "Meet Davy Crockett."
55. Watts, *Magic Kingdom*, 316.
56. King, "Recycled Hero," 147.
57. Fischman, "Coonskin Fever" (Ph.D. diss.), 144.
58. P. F. Anderson, *Davy Crockett Craze*, 64.
59. McDonald, *Television and the Red Menace*, 137–38.
60. *Davy Crockett: King of the Wild Frontier* (television program).
61. P. F. Anderson, *Davy Crockett Craze*, 35.
62. "Decline of a Hero."
63. McDonald, *Who Shot the Sheriff?*, 40.
64. "Wide World of Disney," 50–51.
65. Marling, *As Seen on TV*, 123.
66. K. M. Jackson, *Walt Disney Bio-Bibliography*, 96.
67. "Here's Your First View of Disneyland."
68. "Disneyland," *McCall's*, 8.
69. Hill, "Disneyland Gets Its Last Touches."
70. "Kid's Dream World Come True."
71. "Disneyland," *Life*, 39.
72. "Disneyland," *Woman's Home Companion*.
73. Hastings, "All Aboard for Disneyland!" 4.
74. "Newest Travel Lure."
75. "Disneyland, Multimillion Dollar Magic Kingdom."
76. "Walt Disney – To Enchanted Worlds," 41.
77. A. Gordon, "Walt Disney," 29.
78. Ames, "Fans Await Debut of Disneyland."
79. Cotter, *Wonderful World of Disney Television*, 17.
80. "West Coast Activities."
81. Lipsitz, "Making of Disneyland," 180.
82. "Dateline: Disneyland."
83. "Gov. Knight to Head List."
84. "Dateline: Disneyland."
85. Marling, "Disneyland, 1955," 170.

86. Steiner, "Frontier as Tomorrowland," 3.

87. Hulse, "Dream Realized – Disneyland Opens."

88. "Dateline: Disneyland."

89. D. Smith, *Walt Disney Famous Quotes*, 23.

90. Cotter, *Wonderful World of Disney Television*, 17.

91. "Disneyland Dedication."

92. "California: Spectacular Plus," 32.

93. "Welcome to Disneyland," sec. 5, p. 1.

94. "Disneyland as Two-Headed Child of TV."

95. "Disneyland Gates Open."

96. King, "Disneyland and Walt Disney World," 121.

97. *Walt Disney's Guide to Disneyland.*

98. Bright, *Disneyland: Inside Story*, 239–40.

99. Real, *Mass-Mediated Culture*, 51.

100. Liston, "Land That Does Away with Time."

101. Bright, *Disneyland: Inside Story*, 104.

102. Wolfert, "Walt Disney's Magic Kingdom," 146.

103. Findlay, *Magic Lands*, 74.

104. Lipsitz, "Making of Disneyland," 192.

105. D. Smith, *Walt Disney Famous Quotes*, 27.

106. "Greatest Triple Play in Show Business," 69.

107. Adams, *American Amusement Park Industry*, 102.

108. Schickel, *Disney Version*, 19.

109. M. Gordon, "Walt's Profit Formula."

110. "Disneyland as Two-Headed Child of TV," 2.

111. "Topics of the Times."

112. Marling, "Disneyland, 1955," 172.

113. Hollis and Sibley, *Disney Studio Story*, 178.

114. Cotter, *Wonderful World of Disney Television*, 77, 32, 103, 120, 224–26.

115. "Disneyland Reports on Its First Ten Million."

116. "Their Happiness Castle."

117. "Show Business," 78.

118. Nestegard, "Reading Disneyland" (Ph.D. diss.), 170.

119. Cahn, "Intrepid Kids of Disneyland," 119, 22.

120. M. Gordon, "Walt's Profit Formula," 12.

121. Marling, "Imagineering," 168

122. "Disneyland and Son."

123. Lipsitz, "Making of Disneyland," 182; and *Disneyland: The First Quarter Century*, 59.

124. "Premier Annoyed by Ban."

125. Hill, "Never-Never Land Khrushchev Never Saw."

126. "Builders and Pioneers."

127. *Disneyland: The First Quarter Century*, 53.

128. Litwack, "Fantasy That Paid Off," 28.

129. Adams, *American Amusement Park Industry*, 96, 103

130. Findlay, *Magic Lands*, 97.

131. Nestegard, "Reading Disneyland," 169.

132. "Recreation: Disneyland East."

133. Marling, "Disneyland, 1955," 173.

134. Ciardi, "Manner of Speaking," 20.

135. Wallace, "Onward and Upward," 104, 114.

136. Halevy, "Disneyland and Las Vegas."

137. Bradbury, "Not Child Enough."

138. Bradbury, "Machine Tooled Happyland," 104.

139. Rafferty quoted in "Walt Disney Accused," 602.

140. Zimmerman, "Walt Disney: Giant at the Fair," 31.

141. Menin, "Dazzled in Disneyland," 70.

142. "Tinker Bell, Mary Poppins, Cold Cash," 74, 76.

143. Nestegard, "Reading Disneyland," 73–75.

144. Findlay, *Magic Lands*, 54.

145. Steiner, "Frontier as Tomorrowland," 9, 13.

146. W. L. Thompson, "Introductory," 5–6.

147. Bierman, "Disneyland and the Los Angelization," 281.

148. Marling, "Disneyland, 1955," 176–77.

149. Cahn, "Intrepid Kids," 119.

150. Marling, "Imagineering," 31, 85.

151. King, "Disneyland," 131.

152. Marling, "Disneyland, 1955," 185.

153. *Disneyland: The First Quarter Century*, 34.

154. Lipsitz, "Making of Disneyland," 190.

155. D. M. Johnson, "Disney World as Structure and Symbol," 157.

156. Nasaw, *Going Out*, 254–55.

157. Avila, "Reinventing Los Angeles" (Ph.D. diss.), 256–70.

158. Findlay, *Magic Lands*, 95.

CHAPTER THREE

1. Cotter, *Wonderful World of Disney Television*, 17.

2. Keller, *Mickey Mouse Club Scrapbook*, 22.

3. Schramm, *Television in the Lives of Our Children*, 11.

4. Watts, *Magic Kingdom*, 343–44.

5. Bowles, *Forever Hold Your Banner High*, 14.

6. D. Smith, *Walt Disney Famous Quotes*, 43.

7. Heylbut, "Disney Fun With Music," 59.

8. K. M. Jackson, *Walt Disney*, 58.

9. Thomas, *Walt Disney*, 274.

10. Ames, "*Mickey Mouse Club* Set for Debut."

11. Santoli, *Official Mickey Mouse Club Book*, xi.

12. Schneider, *Children's Television*, 17.

13. Kline, *Out of the Garden*, 166.

14. Stark, *Glued to the Set*, 55.

15. "Spectacular Mr. Disney."

16. A. Gordon, "Walt Disney," 35.

17. Santoli, *Official Mickey Mouse Club*, 55–56.

18. "*Mickey Mouse Club* Review."

19. Woolery, *Children's Television*, 335.

20. S. Davis, *Say Kids!*, 181.

21. J. Davis, *Children's Television*, 165.

22. Woolery, *Children's Television*, 335.

23. O'Boyle, "Be Sure You're Right," 70.

24. Hollis and Sibley, *Disney Studio Story*, 71.

25. Keller, *Mickey Mouse Club Scrapbook*, 24.

26. Bowles, *Forever Hold Your Banner*, 2, 11, 14.

27. Keller, *Mickey Mouse Club Scrapbook*, 30.

28. Cotter, *Wonderful World of Disney Television*, 183.

29. Watts, *Magic Kingdom*, 344.

30. D. Smith, *Walt Disney Famous Quotes*, 14.

31. Lipsitz, "Making of Disneyland," 193.

32. Bowles, *Forever Hold Your Banner*, 14.

33. "*Mickey Mouse Club*," *Variety*.

34. Keller, *Mickey Mouse Club Scrapbook*, 80.

35. "No Mothers Allowed," 6.

36. Watts, *Magic Kingdom*, 339, 41.

37. Woolery, *Children's Television*, 336.

38. "Birth of a Mouseketeer."

39. B. R. Wright, *Walt Disney's The Mouseketeers Tryout Time.*

40. Munsey, *Disneyana*, 294.

41. Watts, *Magic Kingdom*, 337.

42. M. Gordon, "Walt's Profit Formula," 12.

43. Santoli, *Official Mickey Mouse Club Book*, 85.

44. Thomas, *Walt Disney*, 275.

45. Munsey, *Disneyana*, 295.

46. *Sears, Roebuck* catalog, 296.

47. Munsey, *Disneyana*, 295–97.

48. Schneider, *Children's Television*, 12.

49. Kline, *Out of the Garden*, 123–24.

50. Schneider, *Children's Television*, 18–21.

51. Boy, *Barbie*, 43.

52. Kline, *Out of the Garden*, 124, 166–67.

53. "Mickey Mouse March," Words and music by Jimmie Dodd. © 1955 Walt Disney Music Company. All rights reserved, reprinted by permission.

54. "Wonderful World," 64.

55. Santoli, *Official Mickey Mouse Club Book*, 93.

56. Bowles, *Forever Hold Your Banner*, 21.

57. Hine, *Populuxe*, 174.

58. Woolery, *Children's Television*, 335.

59. Schneider, *Children's Television*, 17.

60. *The Mickey Mouse Club*, 1955–56 season.

61. *The Mickey Mouse Club*, 1957–58 season.

62. J. Davis, *Children's Television*, 164.

63. Munsey, *Disneyana*, 301.

64. Castleman and Podrazik, *Watching TV*, 103.

65. Munsey, *Disneyana*, 295.

66. "Be Sure You're Right, and Then Go Ahead." Words and music by Buddy Ebsen and Fess Parker. © 1955 Walt Disney Music Company. All rights reserved, reprinted by permission.

67. *Mickey Mouse Club*, 1957–58 season.

68. *Mickey Mouse Club*, 1955–56 season.

69. Watts, *Magic Kingdom*, 343–44.

70. "Pied Piper to Millions."

71. *Mickey Mouse Club*, 1957–58 season.

72. "Do What the Good Book Says." Words and music by Jimmie Dodd and Ruth Carrell. © 1955 Walt Disney Music Company. All rights reserved, reprinted by permission.

73. *Mickey Mouse Club*, 1957–58 season.

74. "Get Busy." Words and music by Jimmie Dodd and Tom Adair. © Walt Disney Music Company. All rights reserved, reprinted by permission.

75. *Mickey Mouse Club*, 1957–58 season.

76. "The Merry Mouseketeers," Words and music by Jimmie Dodd. © Walt Disney Music Company. All rights reserved, reprinted by permission.

77. *Mickey Mouse Club*, 1957–58 season.

78. Keller, *Mickey Mouse Club Scrapbook*, 35, 69.

79. *Mickey Mouse Club*, 1955–56 season.

80. "When I Grow Up," Words and music by Jimmie Dodd and Sonny Burke. © Walt Disney Music Company. All rights reserved, reprinted by permission.

81. Watkin, *Walt Disney's Spin and Marty*.

82. *Adventures of Spin and Marty*, 1955–56 season.

83. O'Boyle, "Be Sure You're Right," 4.

84. "*Mickey Mouse Club* Review," *TV Guide*.

85. Cotter, *Wonderful World of Disney Television*, 187.

86. *Adventures of Spin and Marty*, 1955–56 season.

87. Cotter, *Wonderful World of Disney Television*, 190, 192.

88. "*Spin and Marty*," *TV Guide*.

89. Hollis and Sibley, *Disney Studio Story*, 72.

90. Munsey, *Disneyana*, 296.

91. Cotter, *Wonderful World of Disney Television*, 91.

92. *Annette*, 1957–58 season.

93. Keller, *Mickey Mouse Club Scrapbook*, 70.

94. Watts, *Magic Kingdom*, 342–43.

95. Santoli, *Official Mickey Mouse Club Book*, 152–54.

96. "Fair Weather Ahead."

97. Nichols, "Stardom Bound," 72.

98. N. Anderson, "What is an Annette?"

99. Coy, "Why Did I Ever Let Him"; "Annette's Own Story"; and Baskette, "What Happened."

100. *Annette's Life Story*.

101. "So Long, Mickey."

102. Meyers, *Walt Disney's Annette*.

103. "Annette's Own Story," 85.

104. "So Long, Mickey."

105. Watts, *Magic Kingdom*, 342.

106. Coleman, "Fitting Pretty" (Ph.D. diss.), 16.

107. Bowles, *Forever Hold Your Banner*, 28.

108. Interview, "*Good Morning America*."

109. McDonald, *One Nation under Television*, 118, 66.

110. Thomas, *Walt Disney*, 287.

111. "*Mickey Mouse Club*," *Variety*.

112. Santoli, *Official Mickey Mouse Club*, 178.

113. Keller, *Mickey Mouse Club Scrapbook*, 80.

114. Munsey, *Disneyana*, 295.

115. J. Davis, *Children's Television*, 44.

116. Lipsitz, "Making of Disneyland," 194–95.

117. Kline, *Out of the Garden*, 123.

118. "Senate Committee Reports," 75.

119. "Calif. Making Study."

120. Stark, *Glued to the Set*, 14.

121. McDonald, *One Nation Under Television*, 92, 100.

122. Schramm, *Television in the Lives of Our Children*, 137.

123. Marc, *Comic Visions*, 16.

124. Marling, *As Seen on TV*, 129.

CHAPTER FOUR

1. J. Gilbert, *Cycle of Outrage*, 63.

2. Doherty, *Teenagers and Teenpics*, 51.

3. *Collier's* 136 (25 November 1955): 80.

4. J. Gilbert, *Cycle of Outrage*, 64.

5. Ibid., 163.

6. Andrew, *Films of Nicholas Ray*, 112.

7. Avila, "Reinventing Los Angeles" (Ph.D. diss.), 54.

8. Kreidl, *Nicholas Ray*, 100.

9. Considine, *Cinema of Adolescence*, 83.

10. *Rebel Without a Cause*.

11. Summons, "Censoring of *Rebel*," 56–63.

12. Barson and Heller, *Teenage Confidential*, 61.

13. MacCann, *Hollywood in Transition*, 188.

14. Hoskyns, *James Dean*, 114.

15. *Variety* 200 (26 October 1955): 10

16. *Variety* 200 (5 October 1955): 11.

17. "*Rebel's* Child-Parent Hostility."

18. Kreidl, *Nicholas Ray*, 99.

19. "*Rebel Without a Cause*," *Films in Review*.

20. "*Rebel Without a Cause*," *Time*.

21. "*Rebel Without a Cause*," *Variety*.

22. Crowther, "Screen: Delinquency."

23. Biskind, *Seeing Is Believing*, 200.

24. Leibman, "Leave Mother Out," 27.

25. Leibman, *Living Room Lectures*, 79, 141.

26. Roffman and Purdy, *Hollywood Social Problem Film*, 297.

27. Ray, *Certain Tendency*, 161.

28. Biskind, "*Rebel Without a Cause*," 35, 37.

29. Briley, "Hollywood and the Rebel Image."

30. Spoto, *Rebel*, 217, 264.

31. Thomson, *American in the Dark*, 29.

32. Sayre, *Running Time*, 111.

33. Marling, *As Seen on TV*, 158.

34. Roth, "Late James Dean," 63.

35. Mitgang, "Strange James Dean Death Cult," 111–13.

36. Dyer, "Youth and the Cinema," 29.

37. R. Clark, *At a Theater or Drive-In*, 52.

38. McGee and Robertson, *J.D. Films*, 61.

39. Considine, *Cinema of Adolescence*, 90.

40. Schultze and Anker, *Dancing in the Dark*, 91.

41. "Film Future."

42. Doherty, *Teenagers and Teenpics*, 196.

43. McGregor, "Domestic Blitz," 20.

44. "Gidget Makes the Grade."

45. Barson and Heller, *Teenage Confidential*, 77.

46. Kohner, *Gidget*.

47. Brode, *Films of the Fifties*, 260.

48. Scheiner, "Are These Our Daughters?" (Ph.D. diss.), 182.

49. *Gidget*.

50. Burchill, *Girls on Film*, 134.

51. E. Miller, "Sandra Dee Out West," 164.

52. "I Giggle," 104.

53. Steinberg, *Reel Facts*, 406–7.

54. Jennings, "Odd Odyssey of Sandra Dee."

55. Woodfield, "Bringing Up Mother."

56. Burt, *Surf City, Drag City*, 12.

57. T. White, *Nearest Faraway Place*, 118.

58. Aquila, *That Old Time Rock and Roll*, 205, 224.

59. *Seventeen* 18 (March 1959): 34.

60. "Gidget," *Variety*.

61. "Gidget," *Library Journal*.

62. "Screen: Sun and Surf."

63. Moss, "Gidget," 23.

64. Dyer, "Youth and the Cinema," 30.

65. Rosen, *Popcorn Venus*, 293.

66. Burchill, *Girls on Film*, 134.

67. Pendleton, "Assault on the American Dream" (Ph.D. diss.), 170.

68. Rosen, *Popcorn Venus*, 293.

69. "Hollywood Scene."

70. Scheiner, "Are These Our Daughters?" 210.

71. *Gidget Goes Hawaiian* (film).

72. "Gidget Goes Hawaiian," *Variety*.

73. "Gidget Goes Hawaiian," *New York Times*.

74. "Showing Now and Notable."

75. Stern and Stern, *Sixties People*, 7.

76. E. Miller, "Gidget Was Here," 95.

77. "Gidget Goes to Rome," *Seventeen*.

78. *Seventeen* 22 (August 1963): 33, 35.

79. "Gidget Goes to Rome," *New York Times*.

80. "Gidget Goes to Rome," *Variety*.

81. "Surf Boredom."

82. Steinberg, *Reel Facts*, 225.

83. Kohner, *The Affairs of Gidget, Gidget Goes to Rome, Gidget in Love, Gidget Goes Parisienne*.

84. Champlin, "Novel Origins of Gidget."

85. Eisner and Krinsky, *Television Comedy Series*, 294.

86. Luckett, "Girl Watchers."

87. Roddy, "Networks Turn to Teen-Agers," 36.

88. *Gidget* outline, Ackerman Papers.

89. Flippen, presentation, Ackerman Papers.

90. Ackerman to Dozier, Ackerman Papers.

91. *Gidget* television screen tests, Ackerman Papers.

92. Brooks and Marsh, *Complete Directory to Prime Time*, 397.

93. Raddatz, "Sally Field's Actually," 16.

94. "Sally Field: Gidget '65."

95. Philip Barry Jr. to Harry Ackerman, Ackerman Papers.

96. Kohner, new character proposal for *Gidget*, Ackerman Papers.

97. Kurland to Ackerman, Ackerman Papers.

98. Scherick, ASI test results, Ackerman Papers.

99. ASI test, Ackerman Papers.

100. Schrier to Scherick, Ackerman Papers.

101. Perry, *Screen Gems*, 93–94.

102. Publicity and promotion, Ackerman Papers.

103. Douglas, *Where the Girls Are*, 110.

104. "*Gidget*," *TV Guide*.

105. *TV Guide* 13 (6 November 1965): 49.

106. Raddatz, "Sally Field's Actually," 16.

107. Roddy, "Networks Turn to Teen-Agers," 36.

108. "Struggling with the Board of Education."

109. Kohner, "How It All Began."

110. Raddatz, "Sally Field's Actually," 17.

111. "Dear Diary – Et Al." *Gidget*.

112. *TV Guide* 13 (29 September 1965): 52.

113. Eisner and Krinsky, *Television Comedy Series*, 294–96.

114. "Is It Love or Symbiosis?" *Gidget*.

115. Eisner and Krinsky, *Television Comedy Series*, 294–96.

116. Hamamoto, *Nervous Laughter*, 78–80.

117. *TV Guide* 13 (8 December 1965): 46.

118. *TV Guide* 13 (10 November 1965): 50.

119. Bindas and Heineman, "Image Is Everything," 23.

120. *TV Guide* 13 (13 November 1965): 44.

121. *TV Guide* 14 (20 January 1966): 50.

122. G. Jones, *Honey, I'm Home*, 185.

123. Petition to Albert Sackheim, Ackerman Papers.

124. E. Miller, "TV Screen," 97.

CHAPTER FIVE

1. L. Brown, "You Gotta Have a Gimmick," 35.

2. Young, *History of Surfing*, 82.

3. "New Boom in Surf-Boarding."

4. Webster, "They Ride the Wild Water."

5. Weatherbee, "Surf's Up," 61.

6. "Surfin' Craze."

7. Loper, "They Go Down to the Sea."

8. "Mad Happy Surfers."

9. Severson, "Riding the World's Wild Giants," 24.

10. Weatherbee, "Surf's Up," 100.

11. "Your Letters."

12. "Recreation: Surf's Up!"

13. J. Miller, "13 Years on a Suburban Safari," 67.

14. Milward, *Beach Boys: Silver Anniversary*, 25.

15. "California, Here I Come" (song).

16. Ford and Henderson, "The Image of Place," 309.

17. Curtis, *Rock Eras*, 103.

18. Ford, "Geographic Factors," 266.

19. Blair, *Discography of Surf Music*, viii.

20. Dalley, *Surfin' Guitars*, 7–8, 328.

21. Wood, *Surf City*, 8.

22. Otfinoski, *Golden Age of Rock Instrumentals*, 123–24.

23. Parales, "Surfin' Again."

24. Blair, *Discography of Surf Music*, 127.

25. Shore with Clark, *History of American Bandstand*, 130.

26. Zhito, "Capitol Snags Dick Dale."

27. Otfinoski, *Golden Age of Rock Instrumentals*, 122.

28. Stambler, *Encyclopedia of Pop, Rock, and Soul*, 42.

29. T. White, *Nearest Faraway Place*, 90.

30. Leaf, *Beach Boys and the California Myth*, 28–29.

31. McFarland, "Understanding the Beach Boys," 23.

32. Wise, *In Their Own Words*, 61.

33. Stern and Stern, *Sixties People*, 82.

34. "Surfin'" (song).

35. Blair, *Discography of Surf Music*, 126.

36. Zhito, "Capitol Comeback."

37. Blair, *Discography of Surf Music*, 126.
38. Wood, *Surf City*, 30.
39. "Surfin' Safari" (song).
40. "Dick Dale Phenomenon."
41. Blair, *Discography of Surf Music*, 101.
42. "*Life* Visits Dick Dale."
43. Blair and McFarland, *Discography of Hot Rod Music*, 18.
44. "The King at 24."
45. Belz, *Story of Rock*, 96.
46. Wood, *Surf City*, 15–18.
47. Otfinoski, *Golden Age of Rock Instrumentals*, 125.
48. Zhito, "Surfing Craze."
49. Biro, "Sea or No."
50. Blair, *Discography of Surf Music*, 99.
51. "Wee Surf Disk Ripple Building."
52. "Surfing Scene."
53. Burt, *Surf City, Drag City*, 38.
54. Beach Boys, *Surfin' USA* (album).
55. "Surfin' USA" (song). Chuck Berry, © 1958 and 1963 (renewed) ARC Music Corporation. Used by permission, all rights reserved.
56. Leaf, Liner Notes, *Good Vibrations*, 4.
57. Beach Boys, *Surfer Girl* (album).
58. "Catch a Wave" (song).
59. "San Francisco."
60. J. L. Wright, "Croonin' about Cruising," 116–17.
61. Alexander, "Love Songs to the Carburetor."
62. Maher, "Hot Rod Trend."
63. Blair and McFarland, *Discography of Hot Rod Music*, xiv.
64. "409" (song).
65. Elliott, *Surf's Up*, 24–26.
66. "Shut Down" (song).
67. Curtis, *Rock Eras*, 105.
68. "Fun, Fun, Fun" (song).
69. "I Get Around" (song).
70. Blair and McFarland, *Discography of Hot Rod Music*, xviii; and Golden, *Beach Boys*, 25.
71. "Be True to Your School" (song).
72. Grevatt, "Songs for Swinging Surfers."
73. Wise, *In Their Own Words*, 59.
74. "All Summer Long" (song).
75. Elliott, *Surf's Up*, 46–47.
76. Wise, *In Their Own Words*, 25.
77. York, "California Girls," 33.
78. "California Girls" (song). Words and music by Brian Wilson, Mike Love. © Irving Music, Inc. (BMI). International copyright secured, all rights reserved, reprinted by permission.
79. Connikie, *Fashions of a Decade*, 17.
80. Elliott, *Surf's Up*, 15–18, 30.
81. Blair and McFarland, *Discography of Hot Rod Music*, 4–7.
82. "Shooting the Tube."
83. "West Coast Surfers."
84. Stern and Stern, *Sixties People*, 84.
85. *Seventeen* 24 (July 1965): 62.
86. *Seventeen* 24 (March 1965): 78.
87. Golden, *Beach Boys*, 21.
88. Elliott, *Surf's Up*, 309.
89. Leaf, Liner Notes, *Good Vibrations*, 7.
90. Leo, *Beach Boys: An American Band*.
91. Jenkinson and Warner, *Celluloid Rock*, 75, 82.
92. Leaf, Liner Notes, *Good Vibrations*, 5.
93. Stambler, *Encyclopedia of Pop, Rock, and Soul*, 267.
94. *Jan and Dean: Behind the Music* (film).
95. Bronson, *Billboard Book of #1 Hits*, 133.
96. "Surf City" (song).
97. *Billboard* 69 (3 August 1963): 9.
98. Wood, *Surf City*, 45.
99. Cassorla, *Ultimate Skateboard Book*, 13–16.
100. "Wave of the Future."
101. "Here Come the Sidewalk Surfers."
102. "Sidewalk Surfing."

103. Cassorla, *Ultimate Skateboard Book*, 17–18.
104. "Pavement Surfing Makes Splash."
105. Blair, *Discography of Surf Music*, 127.
106. "Sidewalk Surfin'" (song).
107. Bart, "California Sound," 142.
108. Alexander, "Love Songs to the Carburetor."
109. Burt and North, *West Coast Story*, 10.
110. Otfinoski, *Golden Age of Rock Instrumentals*, 127–28.
111. Blair, *Discography of Surf Music*, 127.
112. Blair and McFarland, *Discography of Hot Rod Music*, 76.
113. Burt and North, *West Coast Story*, 12.
114. Blair, *Discography of Surf Music*, 126.
115. Hoskyns, *Waiting for the Sun*, 57.
116. Aquila, *That Old Time Rock and Roll*, 310.
117. "California Sun" (song).
118. Stern and Stern, *Sixties People*, 91.
119. Blair, *Discography of Surf Music*, 127, 8.
120. *Billboard* 69 (1 June 1963): 2.
121. Otfinoski, *Golden Age of Rock Instrumentals*, 127.
122. Shore with Clark, *History of American Bandstand*, 116.
123. D. Clark with Bronson, *Dick Clark's American Bandstand*, 85–86.
124. J. A. Jackson, *American Bandstand*, 227.
125. "Clark Blames Game Show."
126. Blair and McFarland, *Discography of Hot Rod Music*, xvi.
127. "Surfing in Tandem"; and "Surfing Pizza Style."
128. C. Mitchell, "Fad and Fascination," 122, 126.
129. "Wave of the Future."
130. "Surfing: Go East, Golden Boy."
131. Santelli, "Catching a Wave," 51–52.
132. "Shooting the Curl."
133. "Surfing: Young Californian."
134. Bart, "California Sound."
135. T. Thompson, "Sound Flowed Out."
136. "West Coast Surfers," 57.
137. Aronowitz, "Dumb Sound," 92.
138. Edelstein, *Pop Sixties*, 8.
139. Cohn, *Rock From the Beginning*, 117.
140. Golden, *Beach Boys*, 19.
141. Hoskyns, *Waiting for the Sun*, 105.
142. Garofalo, *Rockin' Out*, 179.
143. Marsh, *Fortunate Son*, 121.
144. Milward, *Beach Boys: Silver Anniversary*, 49.
145. Alexander, "Love Songs."
146. "Rock and Roll," 87.
147. Quoted in Leaf, *Beach Boys and the California Myth*, 36.
148. Quoted in Hoskyns, *Waiting for the Sun*, 58.
149. Fink, *Conquest of Cool*, 25, 177.
150. "Taste of Action – Chesterfield King."
151. "7-Up . . . Where There's Action."
152. *Seventeen* 22 (July 1963): 26.
153. *Ebony* 20 (July 1965): 136–37.
154. "She Sure Doesn't Look Sick," 119–20.
155. Crenshaw, *Hollywood Rock*, 77.
156. Stern and Stern, *Sixties People*, 85.

CHAPTER SIX

1. Aquila, "Images of the American West," 420.
2. Fairchild, *Fashionable Savages*, 105.
3. "Sporting Look Well-Suited by the West," 54.
4. "Splashy Suits to Swim In."
5. "Beachwear: West Coast vs. East Coast."
6. "Pinky Pastels Are Flourishing in Los Angeles."
7. *Seventeen* 24 (May 1965): 54–55.
8. "All Ashore! Beach Party!"; and "A Two-Way Summer Set."

9. "Accessories for the Beach"; "Casual Clothes from California"; and "California Cottons."

10. "Seaside Fashions."

11. "Pinky Pastels."

12. *Seventeen* 18 (June 1959): 118.

13. *Seventeen* 20 (May 1961): 88–89.

14. *Seventeen* 24 (June 1965): 54.

15. *Seventeen* 24 (May 1965): 79.

16. *Seventeen* 20 (May 1961): 26.

17. *Seventeen* 21 (October 1962): 45.

18. *Seventeen* 22 (September 1963): 2.

19. *Seventeen* 24 (May 1965): 44.

20. Stacy and Syvertsen, *Rockin' Reels*, 11.

21. Barson and Heller, *Teenage Confidential*, 62.

22. G. Morris, "Beyond the Beach," 7.

23. Mast, *Short History of the Movies*, 287–88.

24. Doherty, *Teenagers and Teenpics*, 155.

25. G. Morris, "Beyond the Beach," 2.

26. Doherty, *Teenagers and Teenpics*, 157.

27. Grant, "Classic Hollywood Musical," 201.

28. G. Morris, "Beyond the Beach," 8.

29. R. Clark, *At a Theater or Drive-In*, 62.

30. McGee, *Faster and Furiouser*, 222.

31. Hoskyns, *Waiting for the Sun*, 58.

32. Staehling, "Truth about Teen Movies," 41.

33. Arkoff with Trubo, *Flying through Hollywood*, 129.

34. G. Morris, "Beyond the Beach," 2.

35. Levy, "Peekaboo Sex," 81.

36. Bart, "Hollywood Beach Bonanza."

37. Levy, "Peekaboo Sex," 81.

38. Denisoff and Romanowski, *Risky Business*, 120–21.

39. Arkoff, *Flying through Hollywood*, 131.

40. Edelstein, *Pop Sixties*, 142.

41. Arkoff, *Flying through Hollywood*, 129.

42. Bart, "Hollywood Beach Bonanza."

43. Parish and Pitts, *Great Hollywood Musical Pictures*, 39–40.

44. Funicello, "I'm Just Myself."

45. "She's the Idol."

46. Arkoff, *Flying through Hollywood*, 128–29.

47. "Hollywood's Teenage Gold Mine," 60.

48. Denisoff and Romanowski, *Risky Business*, 117.

49. Ford, "Geographic Factors," 265.

50. Stern and Stern, *Sixties People*, 85.

51. Arkoff, *Flying through Hollywood*, 132.

52. "Hollywood's Teenage Gold Mine," 60.

53. Denisoff and Romanowski, *Risky Business*, 117.

54. Lencek and Baker, *Making Waves*, 116.

55. Denisoff and Romanowski, *Risky Business*, 118.

56. Barson and Heller, *Teenage Confidential*, 83.

57. Blair, *Discography of Surf Music*, 94.

58. Levy, "Peekaboo Sex," 81.

59. R. Clark, *At a Theatre or Drive-In*, 62–63.

60. McGee and Robertson, *J. D. Films*, 99.

61. Bart, "Hollywood Beach Bonanza."

62. McGee, *Faster and Furiouser*, 218.

63. "Today's Teenagers," 58.

64. Burt, *Surf City, Drag City*, 98.

65. Levy, "Peekaboo Sex," 81.

66. Betrock, *Guide to the Teen Exploitation Film*, 100–101.

67. Arkoff, *Flying through Hollywood*, 130.

68. McGee, *Faster and Furiouser*, 218–19.

69. "Hollywood's Teenage Gold Mine," 60.

70. *Beach Party* (film).

71. Betrock, *Guide to the Teen Exploitation Film*, 111.

72. "Screen: *Beach Party*"

73. "Surf Boredom."

74. Steinberg, *Reel Facts*, 226.

75. Crenshaw, *Hollywood Rock*, 31.
76. "*Beach Party*," *Variety*.
77. "Hollywood's Teen-Age Gold Mine," 60.
78. "*Beach Party*," *Films and Filming*.
79. Ehrenstein and Reed, *Rock on Film*, 205.
80. Burt, *Surf City, Drag City*, 95.
81. *Muscle Beach Party* (film).
82. Betrock, *Guide to the Teen Exploitation Film*, 115–16.
83. Jenkinson and Warner, *Celluloid Rock*, 76.
84. *Bikini Beach* (film).
85. Betrock, *Guide to the Teen Exploitation Film*, 106–7.
86. *Beach Blanket Bingo* (film).
87. Crenshaw, *Hollywood Rock*, 29.
88. "*Beach Blanket Bingo*," *Variety*.
89. Betrock, *Guide to the Teen Exploitation Film*, 106, 113.
90. G. Morris, "Beyond the Beach," 7.
91. Bart, "Hollywood Beach Bonanza," 9.
92. Ransom, "Beach Blanket Babies," 108.
93. Bart, "Hollywood Finds Gold on Beaches."
94. Morton, "Beach Party Films."
95. Arkoff, *Flying through Hollywood*, 134.
96. Burt, *Surf City, Drag City*, 102.
97. Betrock, *Guide to the Teen Exploitation Film*, 119, 112.
98. Crenshaw, *Hollywood Rock*, 96.
99. Betrock, *Guide to the Teen Exploitation Film*, 106.
100. Burt, *Surf City, Drag City*, 97.
101. Lewis, "Swinging Beach Movies."
102. Betrock, *Guide to the Teen Exploitation Film*, 110.
103. Crenshaw, *Hollywood Rock*, 183, 220–21, 30.
104. Betrock, *Guide to the Teen Exploitation Film*, 102.
105. Levy, "Peekaboo Sex," 81–85.
106. "Hollywood's Teenage Gold Mine," 60.
107. Lewis, "Swinging Beach Movies," 87.
108. Ransom, "Beach Blanket Babies," 90–94.
109. Mordden, *Medium Cool*, 104.
110. Rosen, *Popcorn Venus*, 317.
111. Coleman, "Fitting Pretty" (Ph.D. diss.), 130, 160.
112. Romney and Wooten, *Celluloid Jukebox*, 3.
113. Betrock, *Guide to the Teen Exploitation Film*, 102.
114. G. Morris, "Beyond the Beach," 4, 7.
115. Ibid., 11.
116. Barich, *Big Dreams*, 398.
117. Grafton, "When Youth Runs Wild," 164.

CHAPTER SEVEN

1. Bean and Rawls, *California*, 400.
2. For a discussion of the IWW (Industrial Workers of the World) Free Speech Riots of the early twentieth century, see Carey McWilliams, *Factories in the Field: The Story of Migratory Farm Labor in California* (1949), and Don Mitchell, *The Lie of the Land: Migrant Workers and the California Landscape* (1996).
3. Coffin, "California Is Bustin' Out," 28.
4. Burdick, "From Gold Rush to Sun Rush," 92.
5. Lavender, *California*, 201.
6. Beardslee, "Teen-Age Patriots."
7. C. R. Morris, *Time of Passion*, 75.
8. Kerr, "Student Dissent," 3.
9. "More than Restless."
10. "Careful Young Men."
11. Gallup and Hill, "Youth: The Cool Generation," 65, 69.

12. Schapiro, "Golden Girl," 85.
13. Obear, "Student Activism in the Sixties," 17.
14. "Letters," *New York Times.*
15. "Changes in Today's College Students."
16. Leonard, "Youth of the Sixties," 17, 18, 20.
17. J. C. Stone, *California's Commitment,* 3, 95.
18. B. Ray, "Fever of a Mass Thrust."
19. Schrag, *Voices from the Classroom,* 191.
20. Trombly, "Exploding University," 23–26.
21. Kerr, *Uses of the University,* 103.
22. T. H. Anderson, *The Movement and the Sixties,* 100.
23. Viorst, *Fire in the Streets,* 276.
24. Draper, *Berkeley,* 13.
25. Welch, "Homosexuality in America."
26. O'Neil, "Only Rebellion Around."
27. "Big Day for Bards," 105.
28. Holmes, "Philosophy of the Beat Generation," 38.
29. Leonard, "Bored, Bearded and Beat."
30. "Manners and Morals."
31. "Bang, Bong, Bing."
32. "California: Heat on the Beatniks."
33. O'Neil, "Only Rebellion Around."
34. "Squaresville, USA, vs. Beatsville."
35. Hodges, "Beats Like I Think I Know Them."
36. Ross, "Rise and Fall of the Beats."
37. Maynard, *Venice West,* 3–5.
38. Cook, *Beat Generation,* iv.
39. "Big Campus Chess Game."
40. Treuhaft, "Rebels with a Hundred Causes."
41. J. Smith, "Silent Generation Finding Its Voice."
42. J. Smith, "Politics Stirs New Interest."
43. "Gripes – Not of Wrath."
44. C. R. Morris, *Time of Passion,* 87.
45. Feuer, "Rebellion at Berkeley," 5.
46. Heirich and Kaplan, "Yesterday's Discord," 32.
47. Baritz, *The Good Life,* 255.
48. "How Campus Discord Forced."
49. Foster and Long, *Protest,* v.
50. Sampson, "Student Activism," 1–2.
51. Poppy, "Human Cry Behind the Speeches."
52. Rorabaugh, "Berkeley Free Speech Movement," 200–201.
53. Goldberg, *Grassroots Resistance,* 175.
54. Feuer, "Rebellion at Berkeley," 9.
55. "When and Where to Speak."
56. Eynon, "Community in Motion," 51.
57. Rorabaugh, "Berkeley Free Speech Movement," 202.
58. Branch, *Pillar of Fire,* 505.
59. Heirich, *Spiral of Conflict,* 171.
60. "Chronology of Events," 41.
61. Goldberg, *Grassroots Resistance,* 177.
62. Draper, *Berkeley: New Student Revolt,* 52.
63. Rorabaugh, "Berkeley Free Speech Movement," 205.
64. Hartt, "Kerr Predicts More."
65. Rorabaugh, "Berkeley Free Speech Movement," 205–7.
66. Goldberg, *Grassroots Resistance,* 182.
67. Rorabaugh, "Berkeley Free Speech Movement," 209.
68. Draper, *Berkeley: New Student Revolt,* 13.
69. Rorabaugh, "Berkeley Free Speech Movement," 210.
70. Draper, *Berkeley: New Student Revolt,* 100.
71. T. H. Anderson, *The Movement and the Sixties,* 104.
72. Lembke, "801 UC Arrests."
73. Rorabaugh, "Berkeley Free Speech Movement," 210–11.
74. Goldberg, *Grassroots Resistance,* 186–88.

75. "Stiffening the Spine."
76. "Trouble Again at Cal."
77. "Savio Onstage."
78. Savio, "California's Angriest Student."
79. "Bonaparte's Retreat."
80. "Yesterday's Rebels."
81. "Panty Raids? No!"
82. Raskin, "Berkeley Affair."
83. Hartt, "Kerr Predicts More."
84. "Campus Uproar."
85. "Campus Agitation vs. Education."
86. Savio, "Why It Happened at Berkeley."
87. Ravitch, *Troubled Crusade*, 196.
88. Feuer, "Rebellion at Berkeley," 3.
89. "California Uprising."
90. "Cure for Campus Riots."
91. Hechinger, "Berkeley Story."
92. "When Students Try to Run a University."
93. "Campus Agitation vs. Education."
94. "Battle of Sproul Hall."
95. Marine, "No Fair!" 485.
96. Draper, *Berkeley: New Student Revolt*, 15.
97. Ibid., 58.
98. Alexander, "You Don't Shoot Mice."
99. Turner, "Berkeley Students Stage Sit-In."
100. "To Prison with Love."
101. *Berkeley in the Sixties* (film).
102. "When Students Try to Run a University."
103. C. Miller, "Press and the Student Revolt," 338.
104. Ibid., 333.
105. "Savio Onstage."
106. "Choices at Berkeley."
107. A. Wright, "To the Big Game," 50.
108. M. Miller, "Letter from the Berkeley Underground."
109. R. Gilbert, "Good Time at UCLA."
110. "Letters," *Nation*.
111. "Letters to the Editor," *Life*.
112. Gitlin, *Whole World Is Watching*, 64–65.
113. "Escalation in California."
114. Ways, "On the Campus," 131–34.
115. Morgan, "The State as a Campus," 121.
116. "Dysphoric Generation?"
117. Katz and Sanford, "Causes of the Student Revolution," 64.
118. C. Miller, "Press and the Student Revolt," 313–47.
119. Field, "UC Student Protests."
120. "Editorial," *California Monthly*.
121. Kerr, "Message to Alumni," 95–96.
122. "Letters to the Editor," *California Monthly*, 5.
123. Ibid., 8.
124. Hiyiya, "Free Speech Movement," 44.
125. Raskin, "Where It All Began."
126. Horowitz, *Campus Life*, 223.
127. Lavender, *California*, 207.
128. Schwartz, *From West to East*, 510.
129. Jacobs, *Prelude to Riot*, 102–3.
130. Hoskyns, *Waiting for the Sun*, 64.
131. Avila, "Folklore of the Freeway," 15–21.
132. Dewitt, *Fragmented Dream*, 207.
133. "West Coast, Too."
134. Lubell, "Who Will Take California?"
135. Fulton, *Reluctant Metropolis*, 225.
136. Viorst, *Fire in the Streets*, 309.
137. Schrag, *Paradise Lost*, 44.
138. Schiesl, "Behind the Badge," 163.
139. Abbott, *Metropolitan Frontier*, 100.
140. Deutsch and Deutsch, "How Los Angeles Eases Racial Tensions."
141. "Ambassador of Goodwill."
142. "Crisis in Race Relations."
143. Moser, "There's No Easy Place," 31.
144. Rossa, *Why Watts Exploded*, 13.
145. "Are We Listening?" 613.
146. "Long Hot Summer."

147. Rossa, *Why Watts Exploded*, 3.
148. Sunset Books, *Southern California*, 48.
149. Rand, *Los Angeles*, 125.
150. Horne, *Fire This Time*, 53.
151. Viorst, *Fire in the Streets*, 318.
152. Lapp, *Afro-Americans in California*, 78.
153. Moser, "There's No Easy Place," 33.
154. Sears and McConahay, *Politics of Violence*, 17, 136.
155. Schulberg, *From the Ashes*, 2.
156. Dewitt, *Fragmented Dream*, 208–9.
157. "1000 Riot in LA."
158. McCurdy and Beeman, "7,000 in New Rioting."
159. Bart, "New Negro Riots."
160. Rossa, *Why Watts Exploded*, 8.
161. "Editorial: A Time for Prayer."
162. Semple, "21 Dead."
163. Viorst, *Fire in the Streets*, 341.
164. Schulberg, *From the Ashes*, 1.
165. "The Riot."
166. Dewitt, *Fragmented Dream*, 209–10.
167. "Get Whitey! The War Cry."
168. "Trigger of Hate," 13.
169. Robinson, "This Would Never Have Happened," 114, 122, 124.
170. "Los Angeles: The Fire This Time."
171. "After the Blood Bath," 1, 15.
172. Viorst, *Fire in the Streets*, 309.
173. "Los Angeles Riots," 24.
174. "After the Blood Bath," 16.
175. "Los Angeles: The Fire This Time," 15.
176. Poe, "Nobody Was Listening," 431.
177. Alsop, "Watts: The Fire Next Time."
178. Viorst, *Fire in the Streets*, 310.
179. Pynchon, *Journey into the Mind of Watts*, 5.
180. Bullock, *Watts: The Aftermath*, 37.
181. Horne, *Fire This Time*, 71.
182. T. H. Anderson, *The Movement and the Sixties*, 134.
183. Rawls, "Visions and Revisions," 63.
184. "Get Whitey! The War Cry."
185. Sears and McConahay, *Politics of Violence*, 27.
186. "The Loneliest Road."
187. Abbott, *Metropolitan Frontier*, 101.
188. Bart, "Youths Run Wild."
189. Robinson, "This Would Never Have Happened," 118.
190. "After the Blood Bath," 15.
191. Viorst, *Fire in the Streets*, 341.
192. "When the Poor Are Powerless."
193. "Letters to the Editor," *Life* 59 (17 September 1965).
194. "End of a 'Quiet Summer,'" 6.
195. "Are We Listening?" 612.
196. "Fruits of Fire."
197. "McCone Report," 3–5.
198. "Why Negroes Rioted in Watts."
199. J. Q. Wilson, "Guide to Reagan Country," 38.
200. "Fruits of Fire."
201. McWilliams, "Watts: The Forgotten Slum."
202. Pearman, *Dear Editor*, 205.
203. Johnson, Sears, and McConahay, "Black Invisibility," 698.
204. "Los Angeles: The Far Country."
205. "For Shocked Los Angeles."
206. "Watts Today."
207. "Troubled Los Angeles," 58.
208. "Los Angeles: And Now What."

CHAPTER EIGHT

1. Langguth, "Political Fun and Games."
2. "Ronald for Real."
3. Putnam, "Half-Century of Conflict," 48.
4. Brown and Brown, *Reagan*, 8.
5. Seabury, "Antic Politics of California," 84.
6. Rorabaugh, "Berkeley Free Speech Movement," 215.

7. Brown and Brown, *Reagan*, 13–14.
8. Davies, "California Issue."
9. Kopkind, "Running Wild," 16.
10. "Ronald for Real," 32.
11. "California: Democratic Dissidence," 33–34.
12. "Polls Apart," 28.
13. Goldberg, *Grassroots Resistance*, 124–25.
14. Oulahan and Lambert, "Real Ronald Reagan Stands Up," 71.
15. Kopkind, "Running Wild," 18.
16. Kopkind, "Hooray for the Red, White, and Blue."
17. Broder, "California's Political Free-for-All."
18. "Ronald for Real."
19. Mitford, "Rest of Ronald Reagan," 31.
20. Schuparra, *Triumph of the Right*, 113, 127.
21. "Republicans: Reagan Rides East."
22. Ritter and Henry, *Ronald Reagan*, 39–40.
23. Cannon, *Ronnie and Jesse*, 82–83.
24. Schuparra, *Triumph of the Right*, 117.
25. Ravitch, *Troubled Crusade*, 196.
26. De Groot, "Reagan's Rise," 32.
27. Anderson and Lee, "1966 Election in California," 543.
28. Davies, "Berkeley Report."
29. Kiefer, *I Goofed*, 31.
30. "No Business Like It."
31. Litwack, "Ronald Reagan Story," 184.
32. Cannon, *Ronnie and Jesse*, 228.
33. "Cut and Thrust."
34. "Reagan for President?"
35. Cannon, *Ronnie and Jesse*, 229.
36. Schuparra, *Triumph of the Right*, 117.
37. De Groot, " 'Goddamned Electable Person,' " 443.
38. Phelan, "Can Reagan Win California?" 89.
39. "Exclusive Interview with Ronald Reagan."
40. McWilliams, "Reagan vs. Brown."
41. "California, There She Blows!"
42. Harris, "Analyzing the Swing to the Right Wing."
43. Brown and Brown, *Reagan*, 116.
44. M. Dallek, "Liberalism Overthrown," 48.
45. "Why Republican Hopes Are Rising."
46. Harris, "Analyzing the Swing to Right Wing."
47. Ritter and Henry, *Ronald Reagan*, 41.
48. Roddy, "California: Ronnie to the Rescue," 52.
49. Harris, "Analyzing the Swing to Right Wing."
50. Phillips, *Big Wayward Girl*, 282.
51. Roddy, "Big Contest Is in California," 41.
52. Duscha, "But What If Reagan Becomes the Governor?" 12.
53. Murray, "Ronald Reagan to the Rescue!" 117.
54. Brown and Brown, *Reagan*, 136.
55. De Groot, " 'Goddamned Electable Person,' " 440.
56. Becker and Fuchs, "How Two Major California Dailies," 645.
57. Rogers, "California: Pat Runs Scared."
58. "Parkinson's Law."
59. M. Dallek, "Liberalism Overthrown," 58.
60. Litwack, "Ronald Reagan Story," 47.
61. Oulahan and Lambert, "Real Ronald Reagan," 77–78.
62. Phelan, "Can Reagan Win California?"
63. "Up from Death Valley."
64. Buckley, "On the Right."
65. Clinton, "Ronald Reagan," 615.

66. Hill, "California: Barbecues and Other Trivia," 377.
67. Bonfante, "Reagan vs. Brown," 45.
68. "San Francisco Riot."
69. "Golly Gee! California," 12, 27.
70. Cannon, *Ronnie and Jesse*, 86.
71. Anderson and Lee, "1966 Election in California," 546, 550–54.
72. J. Q. Wilson, "Guide to Reagan Country," 45.
73. "Story of Ronald Reagan," 36.
74. Brown, *Reagan and Reality*, 12–14, 43.
75. "Paradise Reagan-ed."
76. R. Dallek, *Ronald Reagan*; Leamer, *Make Believe*; and Schuparra, *Triumph of the Right*.
77. De Groot, "Ronald Reagan and Student Unrest," 107.
78. M. Dallek, "Liberalism Overthrown," 40–46, 50.
79. M. Dallek, *The Right Moment*.
80. McGirr, *Suburban Warriors*.
81. Alexander, "Ronald Reagan – For Governor?"
82. Phillips, *Big Wayward Girl*, 272–73.
83. Wills, *Reagan's America*, 300.
84. Phillips, *Big Wayward Girl*, 272–73.
85. Cannon, *Ronnie and Jesse*, 130.
86. Boyarsky, *Rise of Ronald Reagan*, 16.
87. *A Time for Choosing*, 65–67.

CHAPTER NINE

1. "Going Together," 80.
2. Rand, *Los Angeles*, 150–51.
3. "Walt Disney (1901–1966)," 69.
4. Kotkin and Grabowicz, *California, Inc.*, 124.
5. Findlay, *Magic Lands*, 54.
6. Jewett and Shelton, *American Monomyth*, 136.
7. McLellan, "This Land Is Your Land."
8. Jan and Dean, *Folk 'n' Roll* (album).
9. Burt and North, *West Coast Story*, 13.
10. Blair, *Discography of Surf Music*, 127.
11. Elliott, *Surf's Up*, 52.
12. Gaines, *Heroes and Villains*, 149.
13. Fawcett, *California Rock*, 14.
14. Matusow, *Unraveling of America*, 296.
15. Morton, "Beach Party Films," 147.
16. Shore with Clark, *History of American Bandstand*, 135.
17. Aquila, "Blaze of Glory," 200–201.
18. Wise, *In Their Own Words*, 111.
19. R. Clark, *At a Theater or Drive-In*, 66.
20. "Film Company Seeks New Locale."
21. "28 People Who Count."
22. Stern and Stern, *Sixties People*, 149–50.
23. Morton, "Beach Party Films," 147.
24. Anthony, *Summer of Love*, 26.
25. Lobenthal, *Radical Rags*, 109.
26. "Youth: Sunset Along the Strip."
27. Poppy, "California: Vision of Hell and Heaven."
28. "The Teenagers."
29. Siegel, "Surf, Wheels, and Free Souls," 36.
30. "LSD: Turmoil in a Capsule."
31. "LSD and the Drugs of the Mind."
32. Goldstein, "Drugs on the Campus, Part I," 40.
33. Goldstein, "Drugs on the Campus, Part II."
34. "The Inheritor."
35. Cross, "America's Laboratory," 110.
36. Leonard, "California: A New Game."
37. Leonard, "Where the California Game Is Taking Us."
38. "Letters to the Editor," *Look*.
39. Funkhouser, "Issues of the Sixties."
40. Fallows, "California Dreaming," 13.
41. "Anxiety: Doomsday in the Golden State."
42. Rawls, "Introduction."

43. Rawls, "Visions and Revisions," 64.
44. Stegner, "California: The Experimental Society," 28.
45. M. Davis, *City of Quartz*, 83.
46. Wyatt, *Five Fires*.
47. M. Davis, *Ecology of Fear*.
48. Hurup, "Bridge Over Troubled Water," 57.
49. Patterson, *Grand Expectations*, 450, 454.
50. Salisbury, "Californication of America," 78.

※ *Bibliography*

ARCHIVAL SOURCES

Harry S. Ackerman Papers, American
Heritage Center, University of
Wyoming, Laramie
Ackerman, Harry, to William Dozier,
Columbia Inter-Office
Communication, 8 March 1961
ASI Entertainment (ASI) test, 12
January 1965
Barry, Philip, Jr. to Harry Ackerman, 11
March 1965
Flippen, Ruth Brooks, presentation to
Screen Gems, 22 September 1964
Gidget outline, 1961
Gidget television screen tests, 12
September 1964
Kohner, Frederick, new character
proposal for *Gidget*, November
1965
Kurland, Norman, to Harry
Ackerman, ASI *Gidget* Tests, 12
March 1965
Petition to Albert Sackheim, 30 May
1966
Publicity and Promotion Files, *Gidget*,
Box 14, File 18
Schrier, Joseph, to Edgar Scherick, ASI
Test Results, 18 March 1965
Scherick, Edgar, ASI test results, 15
February 1965

PERIODICALS

Atlantic Monthly
Better Homes and
Gardens
Billboard
Changing Times
Collier's
Coronet
Cosmopolitan
Ebony
Esquire
Harper's
Holiday
Life
Look
Los Angeles Times
McCall's
Nation
National Review
New Republic
Newsweek
New York Times
New York Times
Magazine
Photoplay
Popular Science

Ramparts
Reader's Digest
Saturday Evening
Post
Seventeen
Time
TV Guide
U.S. News & World
Report
Variety
Wall Street Journal
Woman's Home
Companion

BOOKS

Abbott, Carl. *The Metropolitan Frontier: Cities in the Modern American West.* Tucson: University of Arizona Press, 1993.

Adams, Judith A. *The American Amusement Park Industry: A History of Technology and Thrills.* Boston: Twayne, 1991.

Anderson, Christopher. *Hollywood TV: The Studio System in the 1950s.* Austin: University of Texas Press, 1994.

Anderson, Paul F. *The Davy Crockett Craze: A Look at the 1950s Phenomenon and Davy Crockett Collectibles.* Hillside, Ill.: R & G Productions, 1996.

Anderson, Terry H. *The Movement and the Sixties Generation.* New York: Oxford University Press, 1995.

Andrew, Geoff. *The Films of Nicholas Ray: The Poet of Nightfall.* London: Charles Letts, 1991.

Annette's Life Story. New York: Dell, 1960.

Anthony, Gene. *The Summer of Love: Haight-Ashbury at Its Highest.* Berkeley, Calif.: Celestial Arts, 1980.

Aquila, Richard. *That Old Time Rock and Roll: A Chronicle of an Era, 1954–1963.* New York: Schirmer, 1989.

Arkoff, Sam, with Richard Trubo. *Flying through Hollywood by the Seat of My Pants.* New York: Carol Publishing Group, 1992.

Barich, Bill. *Big Dreams: Into the Heart of California.* New York: Pantheon, 1994.

Baritz, Loren. *The Good Life: The Meaning of Success for the American Middle Class.* New York: Alfred A. Knopf, 1989.

Barson, Michael, and Steven Heller. *Teenage Confidential: An Illustrated History of the American Teen.* San Francisco: Chronicle Books, 1998.

Bean, Walton, and James J. Rawls. *California: An Interpretive History.* New York: McGraw-Hill, 1988.

Belz, Carl. *The Story of Rock.* New York: Oxford University Press, 1972.

Betrock, Alan. *The "I Was a Teenage Juvenile Delinquent" Rock 'n' Roll Horror Beach Party Movie Book: A Complete Guide to the Teen Exploitation Film, 1954–1969.* New York: St. Martin's, 1986.

Biskind, Peter. *Seeing Is Believing: How Hollywood Taught Us to Stop Worrying and Love the Bomb.* New York: Pantheon, 1983.

Blair, John. *The Illustrated Discography of Surf Music, 1961–1965.* Rev. ed. Ann Arbor, Mich.: Pierian, 1985.

Blair, John, and Stephen McFarland. *The Illustrated Discography of Hot Rod Music, 1961–1965.* Ann Arbor, Mich.: Popular Culture, Inc., 1990.

Boddy, William. *Fifties Television: The Industry and Its Critics.* Chicago: University of Illinois Press, 1990.

Bowles, Jerry. *Forever Hold Your Banner High: The Story of the Mickey Mouse Club and What Happened to the Mouseketeers.* Garden City, N.Y.: Doubleday, 1976.

Boy, Billy. *Barbie: Her Life and Times.* New York: Crown, 1987.

Boyarsky, Bill. *The Rise of Ronald Reagan.* New York: Random House, 1968.

Branch, Taylor. *Pillar of Fire: America in the King Years, 1963–1965.* New York: Simon & Schuster, 1998.

Bright, Randy. *Disneyland: Inside Story.* New York: Harry N. Abrams, 1987.

Brode, Douglas. *The Films of the Fifties: Sunset Boulevard to On the Beach.* Secaucus, N.J.: Citadel, 1976.

Brooks, Tim, and Earle Marsh. *The Complete Directory to Prime Time Network and Cable Television Shows,*

1946–Present. New York: Ballantine, 1995.

Bronson, Fred. *The Billboard Book of #1 Hits.* New York: Billboard Publications, 1985.

Brown, Edmund G. *Reagan and Reality: The Two Californias.* New York: Praeger, 1970.

Brown, Edmund G., and Bill Brown. *Reagan: The Political Chameleon.* New York: Praeger, 1976.

Bunch, Lonnie G. *Black Angelenos: The Afro-American in Los Angeles, 1850–1950.* Los Angeles: California Afro-American Museum, 1988.

Bullock, Paul, ed. *Watts: The Aftermath.* New York: Grove, 1969.

Burchill, Julie. *Girls on Film.* New York: Pantheon, 1986.

Burt, Rob. *Surf City, Drag City.* Poole, Dorset, U.K.: Blandford, 1986.

Burt, Rob, and Patsy North. *West Coast Story.* London: Hamlyn, 1977.

Cannon, Lou. *Ronnie and Jesse: A Political Odyssey.* Garden City, N.Y.: Doubleday, 1969.

Cassorla, Albert. *The Ultimate Skateboard Book.* Philadelphia: Running Press, 1988.

Castleman, Harry, and Walter J. Podrazik. *Watching TV: Four Decades of American Television.* New York: McGraw-Hill, 1982.

Clark, Clifford Edward, Jr. *The American Family Home, 1800–1960.* Chapel Hill: University of North Carolina Press, 1986.

Clark, Dick, with Fred Bronson. *Dick Clark's American Bandstand.* New York: Collins, 1997.

Clark, Randall. *At a Theatre or Drive-In Near You: The History, Culture, and Politics of the American Exploitation Film.* New York: Garland, 1995.

Cohn, Nik. *Rock from the Beginning.* New York: Stein & Day, 1969.

Connikie, Yvonne. *Fashions of a Decade: The 1960s.* New York: Facts on File, 1990.

Considine, David M. *The Cinema of Adolescence.* Jefferson, N.C.: McFarland, 1985.

Cook, Bruce. *The Beat Generation.* New York: William Morrow, 1971.

Cotter, Bill. *The Wonderful World of Disney Television: A Complete History.* New York: Hyperion, 1997.

Crenshaw, Marshall. *Hollywood Rock: A Guide to Rock and Roll in the Movies.* New York: Agincourt, 1994.

Cullen, Jim. *The Art of Democracy: A Concise History of Popular Culture in the United States.* New York: Monthly Review Press, 1996.

Curtis, Jim. *Rock Eras: Interpretations of Music and Society, 1954–1984.* Bowling Green, Ohio: Bowling Green State University Press, 1987.

Dallek, Matthew. *The Right Moment: Ronald Reagan's First Victory and the Decisive Turning Point in American Politics.* New York: Free Press, 2000.

Dallek, Robert. *Ronald Reagan: The Politics of Symbolism.* Cambridge: Harvard University Press, 1984.

Dalley, Robert J. *Surfin' Guitars: Instrumental Surf Bands of the Sixties.* Southern California: Surf Publications, 1988.

Davis, Jeffrey. *Children's Television: 1947–1990.* Jefferson, N.C.: McFarland, 1995.

Davis, Mike. *City of Quartz: Excavating the Future in Los Angeles.* New York: Vintage, 1990.

———. *Ecology of Fear: Los Angeles and the Imagination of Disaster.* New York: Metropolitan, 1998.

Davis, Stephen. *Say Kids! What Time Is It?*

Notes from the Peanut Gallery. Boston: Little, Brown, 1987.

Denisoff, R. Serge, and William D. Romanowski. *Risky Business: Rock in Film*. New Brunswick, N.J.: Transaction, 1991.

Dewitt, Howard. *The Fragmented Dream: Multicultural California*. USA: Kendall/Hunt Publishing, 1996.

Disneyland: The First Quarter Century. Anaheim, Calif.: Walt Disney Productions, 1979.

Doherty, Thomas. *Teenagers and Teenpics: The Juvenilization of American Movies in the 1950s*. Boston: Unwin Hyman, 1988.

Douglas, Susan J. *Where the Girls Are: Growing Up Female with the Mass Media*. New York: Times Books, 1994.

Draper, Hal. *Berkeley: The New Student Revolt*. New York: Grove, 1965.

Edelstein, Andrew J. *The Pop Sixties*. New York: World Almanac Publications, 1985.

Ehrenstein, David, and Bill Reed. *Rock on Film*. New York: Delilah, 1982.

Eisner, Joel, and David Krinsky. *Television Comedy Series: An Episode Guide to 153 Sitcoms in Syndication*. Jefferson, N.C.: McFarland, 1984.

Elliott, Brad. *Surf's Up: The Beach Boys on Record, 1961–1981*. Ann Arbor, Mich.: Pierian, 1982.

Fairchild, John. *The Fashionable Savages*. Garden City, N.Y.: Doubleday, 1965.

Farber, David. *The Age of Great Dreams: America in the 1960s*. New York: Hill & Wang, 1991.

Fawcett, Anthony. *California Rock, California Sound: The Music of Los Angeles and Southern California*. Los Angeles: Reed, 1978.

Findlay, John M. *Magic Lands: Western Cityscapes and American Culture after 1940*. Berkeley: University of California Press, 1992.

Fine, David. *Imagining Los Angeles: A City in Fiction*. Albuquerque: University of New Mexico Press, 2000.

Fink, Thomas J. *The Conquest of Cool: Business Culture, Counterculture, and the Rise of Hip Consumerism*. Chicago: University of Chicago Press, 1997.

Flink, James J. *The Automobile Age*. Cambridge: MIT Press, 1988.

Foreman, Joel, ed. *The Other Fifties: Interrogating Mid-Century American Icons*. Chicago: University of Illinois Press, 1997.

Foster, Julian, and Durward Long, eds. *Protest! Student Activism in America*. New York: William Morrow, 1970.

Fulton, William. *The Reluctant Metropolis: The Politics of Urban Growth in Los Angeles*. Point Arena, Calif.: Solano, 1997.

The Gallup Poll: Public Opinion, 1935–1971. Vols. 2 and 3. New York: Random House, 1972.

Gaines, Steven. *Heroes and Villains: The True Story of the Beach Boys*. New York: Nal, 1986.

Garofalo, Reebee. *Rockin' Out: Popular Music in the USA*. Boston: Allyn Bacon, 1997.

Gilbert, James. *A Cycle of Outrage: America's Reaction to the Juvenile Delinquent in the 1950s*. New York: Oxford University Press, 1986.

Gitlin, Todd. *The Whole World Is Watching: Mass Media in the Making and Unmaking of the New Left*. Berkeley: University of California Press, 1980.

Goldberg, Robert A. *Grassroots Resistance: Social Movements in Twentieth Century America*. Belmont, Calif.: Wadsworth, 1991.

Golden, Bruce. *The Beach Boys: Southern*

California Pastoral. Rev. ed. (Vol. 1 in *The Woodstock Series: Popular Music of Today.*) San Bernardino, Calif.: Borgo, 1991.

Grossberg, Lawrence, Cary Nelson, and Paula A. Treichler, eds. *Cultural Studies.* London: Chapman & Hall, 1992.

Hall, Stuart, ed. *Representation: Cultural Representation and Signifying Practices.* London: Sage, 1997.

Hamamoto, Darrel Y. *Nervous Laughter: Television Situation Comedy and Liberal Democratic Ideology.* New York: Praeger, 1989.

Heirich, Max. *The Spiral of Conflict: Berkeley, 1964.* New York: Columbia University Press, 1971.

Hine, Thomas. *Populuxe.* New York: Alfred A. Knopf, 1986.

Hollis, Richard, and Brian Sibley. *The Disney Studio Story.* New York: Crown, 1988.

Horne, Gerald. *Fire This Time: The Watts Uprising and the 1960s.* Charlottesville: University Press of Virginia, 1995.

Horowitz, Helen Lefkowitz. *Campus Life: Undergraduate Cultures from the End of the Eighteenth Century to the Present.* New York: Alfred A. Knopf, 1987.

Hoskyns, Barney. *James Dean: Shooting Star.* London: Doubleday, 1989.

——. *Waiting for the Sun: Strange Days, Weird Scenes, and the Sound of Los Angeles.* New York: St. Martin's, 1996.

Inge, M. Thomas, ed. *Handbook of American Popular Culture.* Vol. 3. New York: Greenwood, 1989.

Jackson, John A. *American Bandstand: Dick Clark and the Making of a Rock and Roll Empire.* New York: Oxford University Press, 1997.

Jackson, Kathy Merlock. *Walt Disney: A Bio-Bibliography.* Westport, Conn.: Greenwood, 1993.

Jackson, Kenneth T. *Crabgrass Frontier: The Suburbanization of the United States.* New York: Oxford University Press, 1985.

Jacobs, Paul. *Prelude to Riot: A View of Urban America from the Bottom.* New York: Random House, 1967.

Jacobson, Michelle, ed. *Awesome Almanac California.* Walworth, Wisc.: B & B Publishing, 1994.

Jenkinson, Philip, and Alan Warner. *Celluloid Rock: Twenty Years of Movie Rock.* London: Warner, 1976.

Jewett, Robert, and John Shelton. *The American Monomyth.* Garden City, N.Y.: Anchor Press/Doubleday, 1977.

Jones, Gerard. *Honey, I'm Home! Sitcoms, Selling the American Dream.* New York: Grove Weidenfeld, 1992.

Jones, Landon Y. *Great Expectations: America and the Baby Boom Generation.* New York: Coward, McCann, & Geoghegan, 1980.

Jowett, Garth. *Film: The Democratic Art.* Boston: Little, Brown, 1979.

Jurmain, Claudia K., and James J. Rawls. *California: A Place, a People, a Dream.* San Francisco: Chronicle Books, 1996.

Keller, Keith. *The Mickey Mouse Club Scrapbook.* New York: Grosset & Dunlap, 1975.

Kerr, Clark. *The Uses of the University.* Cambridge: Harvard University Press, 1964.

Kiefer, Frank, ed. *I Goofed: The Wise and Curious Sayings of Ronald Reagan, Thirty-Third Governor of California.* Berkeley, Calif.: Diablo, 1968.

Kline, Stephen. *Out of the Garden: Toys, TV, and Children's Culture in the Age of Marketing.* New York: Verso, 1993.

Kohner, Frederick. *The Affairs of Gidget.* New York: Bantam, 1963.

——. *Gidget.* New York: G. P. Putnam & Sons, 1957.

——. *Gidget Goes Parisienne.* New York: Dell, 1966.

——. *Gidget Goes to Rome.* New York: Bantam, 1963.

——. *Gidget in Love.* New York: New English Library, 1965.

Kotkin, Joel, and Paul Grabowicz. *California, Inc.* New York: Wade, 1982.

Kreidl, John Francis. *Nicholas Ray.* Boston: Twayne, 1977.

Lapp, Rudolph M. *Afro-Americans in California.* 2d ed. San Francisco: Boyd & Fraser, 1987.

Lavender, David. *California: A Bicentennial History.* Nashville, Tenn.: American Association for State and Local History, 1976.

Leaf, David. *The Beach Boys and the California Myth.* New York: Grosset & Dunlap, 1978.

——. Liner notes, *Good Vibrations: Thirty Years of the Beach Boys* (album). Capitol Records, 1993.

Leamer, Lawrence. *Make Believe: The Story of Nancy and Ronald Reagan.* New York: Harper & Row, 1983.

Lencek, Lean, and Gideon Baker. *Making Waves: Swimsuits and the Undressing of America.* San Francisco: Chronicle Books, 1989.

Leibman, Nina C. *Living Room Lectures: The Fifties Family in Film and Television.* Austin: University of Texas Press, 1995.

Lobenthal, Joe. *Radical Rags: Fashions of the Sixties.* New York: Abbeville, 1990.

MacCann, Richard Dyer. *Hollywood in Transition.* Boston: Houghton Mifflin, 1962.

McDonald, J. Fred. *One Nation Under Television: The Rise and Decline of Network Television.* Chicago: Nielson-Hall, 1990.

——. *Television and the Red Menace: The Video Road to Vietnam.* New York: Praeger, 1985.

——. *Who Shot the Sheriff? The Rise and Fall of the TV Western.* New York: Praeger, 1987.

McGee, Mark Thomas. *Faster and Furiouser: The Revised and Fattened Fable of American International Pictures.* Jefferson, N.C.: McFarland, 1996.

McGee, Mark Thomas, and R. J. Robertson. *The J.D. Films: Juvenile Delinquency in the Movies.* Jefferson, N.C.: McFarland, 1982.

McGirr, Lisa. *Suburban Warriors: The Origins of the New American Right.* Princeton, N.J.: Princeton University Press, 2001.

McWilliams, Carey. *California: The Great Exception.* New York: Current Books, 1949.

——. *Factories in the Field: The Story of Migratory Farm Labor in California.* Boston: Little, Brown, 1949.

Maltin, Leonard. *The Disney Films.* New York: Crown, 1973.

Marc, David. *Comic Visions: Television Comedy and American Culture.* 2d ed. Malden, Mass.: Blackwell, 1997.

Marling, Karal Ann. *As Seen on TV: The Visual Culture of Everyday Life in the 1950s.* Cambridge: Harvard University Press, 1994.

Marsh, Dave. *Fortunate Son: The Best of Dave Marsh.* New York: Random House, 1985.

Mast, Gerald. *A Short History of the Movies.* 4th ed. New York: Macmillan, 1986.

Matusow, Allen J. *The Unraveling of America: A History of Liberalism in the 1960s.* New York: Harper & Row, 1984.

Maynard, John Arthur. *Venice West: The*

Beat Generation in Southern California.
New Brunswick, N.J.: Rutgers
University Press, 1991.

Meyers, Barlow. *Walt Disney's Annette:
Mystery at Medicine Wheel.* Racine,
Wisc.: Whitman, 1964.

Miller, Douglas T. and Marion Nowak.
The Fifties: The Way We Really Were.
Garden City, N.Y.: Doubleday, 1977.

Milward, John. *The Beach Boys: Silver
Anniversary.* Garden City, N.Y.:
Dolphin, 1985.

Mitchell, Don. *The Lie of the Land:
Migrant Workers and the California
Landscape.* Albuquerque: University of
New Mexico Press, 1996.

Mordden, Ethan. *Medium Cool: The Movies
of the 1960s.* New York: Alfred A.
Knopf, 1990.

Morgan, Neil. *Westward Tilt: The American
West Today.* New York: Random
House, 1963.

Morris, Charles R. *A Time of Passion:
America 1960–1980.* New York: Harper
& Row, 1984.

Munsey, Cecil. *Disneyana: Walt Disney
Collectibles.* New York: Hawthorne,
1974.

Nachbar, Jack, and Kevin Lause, eds.
Popular Culture: An Introductory Text.
Bowling Green, Ohio: Bowling Green
State University Popular Press, 1992.

Nadeau, Remi. *California: The New Society.*
New York: David McKay, 1963.

Nasaw, David. *Going Out: The Rise and Fall
of Public Amusements.* New York: Basic,
1993.

Nash, Gerald D. *The American West in the
Twentieth Century: A Short History of an
Urban Oasis.* Englewood Cliffs, N.J.:
Prentice-Hall, 1973.

Otfinoski, Steve. *The Golden Age of Rock
Instrumentals.* New York: Billboard,
1997.

Packard, Vance. *The Status Seekers.* New
York: David McKay, 1959.

Parish, James Robert, and Michael R. Pitts.
The Great Hollywood Musical Pictures.
Metuchen, N.J.: Scarecrow, 1992.

Patterson, James T. *Grand Expectations: The
United States, 1945–1974.* New York:
Oxford University Press, 1996.

Pearman, Phil, ed. *Dear Editor: Letters to
Time Magazine, 1923–1984.* Salem,
N.H.: Salem House, 1985.

Perry, Jeb H. *Screen Gems: A History of
Columbia Pictures Television from Cohn
to Coke, 1948–1983.* Metuchen, N.J.:
Scarecrow, 1991.

Phillips, Herbert. *Big Wayward Girl: An
Informal Political History of California.*
Garden City, N.Y.: Doubleday, 1968.

Pynchon, Thomas. *A Journey into the Mind
of Watts.* London: Mouldways, 1966.

Quinlan, Sterling. *Inside ABC: American
Broadcasting Company's Rise to Power.*
New York: Hasting House, 1979.

Rand, Christopher. *Los Angeles: The
Ultimate City.* New York: Oxford
University Press, 1967.

Ravitch, Diane. *The Troubled Crusade:
American Education, 1945–1980.* New
York: Basic, 1983.

Ray, Robert B. *A Certain Tendency of the
Hollywood Cinema, 1930–1980.*
Princeton, N.J.: Princeton University
Press, 1985.

Real, Michael. *Mass-Mediated Culture.*
Englewood Cliffs, N.J.: Prentice-Hall,
1977.

Rice, Richard B. *The Elusive Eden: A New
History of California.* New York: Alfred
A. Knopf, 1988.

Ritter, Kurt, and David Henry. *Ronald
Reagan: The Great Communicator.* New
York: Greenwood, 1992.

Roffman, Peter, and Jim Purdy. *The
Hollywood Social Problem Film:*

Madness, Despair, and Politics from the Depression to the Fifties. Bloomington: Indiana University Press, 1981.

Romney, Jonathan, and Adrian Wooten. *Celluloid Jukebox: Popular Music and the Movies Since the 1950s.* London: British Film Institute, 1995.

Rosen, Marjorie. *Popcorn Venus: Women, Movies, and the American Dream.* New York: Coward, McCann & Geoghegan, 1973.

Rossa, Della. *Why Watts Exploded: How the Ghetto Fought Back.* New York: Merit, 1966.

Santoli, Lorraine. *The Official Mickey Mouse Club Book.* New York: Hyperion, 1995.

Sayre, Nora. *Running Time: Films of the Cold War.* New York: Dial, 1982.

Schickel, Richard. *The Disney Version: The Life, Times, Art, and Commerce of Walt Disney.* 3d ed. Chicago: Elephant Paperbacks, 1997.

Schneider, Cy. *Children's Television: The Art, the Business, and How it Works.* Chicago, Ill.: NTC Business Books, 1987.

Schrag, Peter. *Paradise Lost: California's Experience, America's Future.* New York: New Press, 1998.

———. *Voices from the Classroom: Public Schools and Public Attitudes.* Boston: Beacon, 1965.

Schramm, Wilbur. *Television in the Lives of Our Children.* Stanford, Calif.: Stanford University, 1961.

Schultze, Quentin J., and Roy M. Anker. *Dancing in the Dark: Youth, Popular Culture, and the Electronic Media.* Grand Rapids, Mich.: William B. Eerdman's, 1991.

Schulberg, Budd, ed. *From the Ashes: Voices of Watts.* New York: Meridian, 1967.

Schuparra, Kurt. *Triumph of the Right: The Rise of the California Conservative Movement.* New York: Oxford University Press, 1998.

Schwartz, Stephen. *From West to East: California and the Making of the American Mind.* New York: Free Press, 1998.

Sears, David O., and John B. McConahay. *The Politics of Violence: The New Urban Blacks and the Watts Riot.* Boston: Houghton Mifflin, 1973.

Shore, Michael, with Dick Clark. *The History of American Bandstand.* New York: Ballantine, 1985.

Smith, Dave, ed. *Walt Disney Famous Quotes.* USA: The Walt Disney Co., 1994.

Spoto, Donald. *Rebel: The Life and Legend of James Dean.* New York: Harper Collins, 1996.

Stacy, Jon, and Ryder Syvertsen. *Rockin' Reels: An Illustrated History of Rock and Roll Movies.* Chicago, Ill.: Contemporary, 1984.

Stambler, Irwin. *Encyclopedia of Pop, Rock, and Soul.* New York: St. Martin's, 1971.

Stark, Steven D. *Glued to the Set: The 60 Television Shows and Events That Made Us Who We Are.* New York: Free Press, 1997.

Starr, Kevin. *Americans and the California Dream, 1850–1915.* New York: Oxford University Press, 1973.

Steinberg, Cobbett. *Reel Facts: The Movie Book of Records.* New York: Vintage, 1978.

Stern, Jane, and Michael Stern. *Sixties People.* New York: Alfred A. Knopf, 1990.

———. *Way Out West.* New York: Harper Collins, 1993.

Stone, James C. *California's Commitment to Public Education.* New York: Thomas Y. Crowell, 1961.

Sunset Books and Magazine Editors. *Southern California*. Menlo Park, Calif.: Lane Book Company, 1964.

Teaford, Jon C. *The Twentieth-Century American City: Problem, Promise, and Reality*. Baltimore, Md.: Johns Hopkins University Press, 1986.

A Time for Choosing: The Speeches of Ronald Reagan, 1961–1982. Chicago, Ill.: Regnery Gateway, 1983.

Thomas, Bob. *Walt Disney: An American Original*. New York: Simon & Schuster, 1976.

Thomson, David. *America in the Dark: Hollywood and the Gift of Unreality*. New York: William Morrow, 1977.

Viorst, Milton. *Fire in the Streets: America in the 1960s*. New York: Simon & Schuster, 1979.

Walt Disney's Guide to Disneyland. Anaheim, Calif.: Walt Disney Productions, 1959.

Walt Disney's Mouseketunes, Containing 36 Mickey Mouse Club Songs as Featured on the ABC Television Network. USA: Walt Disney Music Company, 1955.

Watkin, Lawrence Edward. *Walt Disney's Spin and Marty*. Racine, Wisc.: Whitman, 1956.

Watts, Steven. *The Magic Kingdom: Walt Disney and the American Way of Life*. New York: Houghton Mifflin, 1997.

White, Timothy. *The Nearest Faraway Place: Brian Wilson, the Beach Boys and the Southern California Experience*. New York: Henry Holt, 1994.

Wills, Gary. *Reagan's America: Innocents at Home*. Garden City, N.Y.: Doubleday, 1987.

Wise, Nick, ed. *In Their Own Words: The Beach Boys*. London: Omnibus, 1994.

Wood, Jack. *Surf City: The California Sound*. The Life, Times, and Music Series. New York: Friedman/Fairfax Publishers, 1995.

Woolery, George W. *Children's Television: The First Thirty-Five Years, 1946–1981, Part II, Live, Film, and Tape Series*. Metuchen, N.J.: Scarecrow, 1985.

Wright, Betty Ren. *Walt Disney's The Mouseketeers Tryout Time*. Racine, Wisc.: Whitman, 1956.

Wyatt, David. *Five Fires: Race, Catastrophe, and The Shaping of California*. New York: Oxford University Press, 1999.

Young, Nat. *The History of Surfing*. New South Wales, Australia: Palm Beach, 1983.

ARTICLES

"28 People Who Count." *Esquire* 64 (September 1965): 97.

"30 Teen-Agers Arrested: Graduation Parties End in Jail." *Los Angeles Times*, 25 June 1955, sec. 1, p. 1.

"1000 Riot in LA: Police and Motorists Attacked." *Los Angeles Times*, 12 August 1965, sec. 1, p. 1.

"ABC's Chest-Thumping as Trendex on 'Disneyland' Stirs Hope Anew." *Variety* 196 (3 November 1954): 31–34.

"Accessories for the Beach," *TV Guide* 9 (10 June 1961): 20–21.

"After the Blood Bath" *Newsweek* 66 (30 August 1965): 13–20.

Alexander, Shana. "Love Songs to the Carburetor." *Life* 57 (6 November 1964): 33.

———. "Ronald Reagan – For Governor?" *Life* 59 (13 August 1965): 22.

———. "You Don't Shoot Mice With Elephant Guns." *Life* 58 (15 January 1965): 27.

"All Ashore! Beach Party! Fun and Food

Outdoors," *Seventeen* 16 (July 1957): 81, 104.

Alsop, Stewart. "Watts: The Fire Next Time." *Saturday Evening Post* 238 (6 November 1965): 20.

"Ambassador of Goodwill for Police Department." *Ebony* 19 (March 1964): 40–44.

Ames, Walter. "Fans Await Debut of Disneyland via TV Screens Today." *Los Angeles Times*, 17 July 1955, sec. 4, p. 11.

——. "*Mickey Mouse Club* Set for Debut Today as Hour-Long Daily Fare." *Los Angeles Times*, 3 October 1955, sec. 1, p. 34.

Anderson, Nancy. "What Is an Annette?" *Photoplay* 56 (September 1959): 56–57.

Anderson, Totton J., and Eugene C. Lee. "The 1966 Election in California." *Western Political Quarterly* 20 (June 1967): 535–54.

"Annette's Own Story: What Happened to Those Wedding Bells," *Photoplay* 57 (June 1960): 61–63, 84–85.

"Anxiety: Doomsday in the Golden State." *Time* 93 (11 April 1969): 59.

Aquila, Richard. "A Blaze of Glory: The Mythic West in Pop and Rock Music." In *Wanted Dead or Alive: The American West in Popular Culture*, ed. Richard Aquila, 191–216. Chicago: University of Illinois Press, 1996.

——. "Images of the American West in Rock Music." *Western Historical Quarterly* 11 (October 1980): 415–32.

"Are We Listening?" *Commonweal* 82 (3 September 1965): 612–13.

Aronowitz, Alfred G. "The Dumb Sound." *Saturday Evening Post* 236 (5 October 1963): 88, 91–95.

Atwood, William. "How America Feels as We Enter the Soaring Sixties." *Look* 24 (5 January 1960): 11–15.

Avila, Eric R. "The Folklore of the Freeway: Space, Culture, and Identity in Postwar Los Angeles." *AZTLAN: Journal of Chicano Studies* 23 (Spring 1998): 14–31.

Balio, Tino. "Hollywood." *UNESCO Courier* (July–August 1995): 12–15.

"Bang, Bong, Bing." *Time* 74 (7 September 1959): 80.

Bart, Peter. "The California Sound." *Atlantic Monthly* 215 (May 1965): 40, 142.

——. "Hollywood Beach Bonanza." *New York Times*, 13 December 1964, sec. 2, p. 9.

——. "Hollywood Finds Gold on Beaches: Studios Compete for Stars of Teen-Age Surf Films." *New York Times*, 22 June 1965, sec. 1, p. 25.

——. "New Negro Riots Erupt on Coast." *New York Times*, 13 August 1965, sec. 1, pp. 1, 26.

——. "Youths Run Wild," *New York Times*, 14 August 1965, sec. 1, p. 1.

"Baseball: The Gold Rush West." *Newsweek* 50 (2 September 1957): 84.

Baskette, Kirkley. "What Happened When Paul Took Annette Home to His Mother," *Photoplay* 58 (August 1960): 62.

"Battle of Sproul Hall." *Newsweek* 64 (14 December 1964): 44–45.

"*Beach Blanket Bingo.*" *Variety* 238 (7 April 1965): 6.

"*Beach Party.*" *Films and Filming* 10 (September 1964): 22.

"*Beach Party.*" *Variety* 232 (17 July 1963): 6.

"Beachwear: West Coast vs. East Coast." *Look* 22 (8 July 1958): 40–42.

Beardslee, Pat. "Teen-Age Patriots: Los Angeles County 'Torchbearers' Promote Americans' Heritage, Ideals." *American Mercury* 90 (March 1960): 129–30.

Becker, Jules, and Douglas A. Fuchs. "How

Two Major California Dailies Covered Reagan and Brown." *Journalism Quarterly* 44 (Winter 1967): 645–53.

Bierman, James H. "Disneyland and the Los Angelization of the Arts." In *American Popular Entertainment: Papers and Proceedings of the Conference on the History of American Popular Entertainment*, ed. Myron Matlaw, 273–84. Westport, Conn: Greenwood, 1979.

"Big Campus Chess Game." *Life* 48 (2 May 1960): 49–52.

"Big Day for Bards at Bay." *Life* 43 (9 September 1957): 105–8.

Bindas, Kenneth J., and Kenneth J. Heineman. "Image Is Everything: Television and the Counterculture Message in the 1960s." *Journal of Popular Film and Television* 22 (Spring 1994): 22–37.

Biro, Nick. "Sea or No, Chicago Goes Surf." *Billboard* 69 (13 July 1963): 4.

"The Birth of a Mouseketeer." *TV Guide* 4 (16 June 1956): 22–23.

Biskind, Peter. "Rebel Without a Cause: Nicholas Ray in the Fifties." *Film Quarterly* 27 (Fall 1974): 32–38.

Bliven, Bruce. "The California Culture." *Harper's* 210 (January 1955): 33–40.

———. "East Coast or West – Which?" *New York Times*, 12 March 1961, sec. 1, p. 56.

Boddy, William. "The Studios Move into Prime Time: Hollywood and the Television Industry in the 1950s." *Cinema Journal* 24 (Summer 1985): 23–37.

"Bonaparte's Retreat." *Time* 85 (7 May 1965): 54.

Bonfante, Jordan. "Reagan vs. Brown: See How They Run." *Life* 61 (14 October 1966): 42–47.

"Boom in the West." *Time* 66 (18 July 1955): 74.

"Boy, Age 7, Defends His Crockett Cap." *Los Angeles Times*, 30 June 1955, sec. 1, p. 2.

Bradbury, Ray. "The Machine-Tooled Happyland." *Holiday* 38 (October 1965): 100–104.

———. "Not Child Enough – Letters to the Editor." *Nation* 186 (28 June 1958): 1.

Briley, Ron. "Hollywood and the Rebel Image in the 1950s." *Social Education* 61 (October 1997): 325–58.

Broder, David S. "California's Political Free-for-All." *Look* 29 (13 July 1965): 61–64.

Brown, Les. "You Gotta Have a Gimmick." *Variety* 239 (2 June 1965): 35, 48.

Buckley, William F. "On the Right: How Is Ronald Reagan Doing?" *National Review* 18 (11 January 1966): 17.

"Builders and Pioneers of the Dream." *Life* 53 (19 October 1962): 92.

Burdick, Eugene. "From Gold Rush to Sun Rush." *New York Times Magazine*, 14 April 1963, pp. 36–37, 89–92.

Cahn, Robert. "The Intrepid Kids of Disneyland." *Saturday Evening Post* 230 (28 June 1958): 22–23, 118–20.

"Calif. Making Study of TV's Effect on Juve Violence; Medium Rapped." *Variety* 204 (31 October 1956): 25, 44.

"California." *Look* 23 (29 September 1959), special issue.

"California." *Look* 26 (25 September 1962), special issue.

"California Cottons," *TV Guide* 12 (27 June 1964): 24–27.

"California: Democratic Dissidence." *Newsweek* 66 (29 November 1965): 33–34.

"California: Heat on the Beatniks." *Newsweek* 54 (17 August 1959): 36.

"California Lassie, Universally Classy." *Life* 53 (19 October 1962): 119.

"California's Increasing Importance in

U.S." *Los Angeles Times*, 24 July 1955, sec. 1, p. 4.

"California: Spectacular Plus." *Newsweek* 46 (25 July 1955): 32–33.

"California, the Nation's First." *America: A Catholic Review of the Week* 113 (18 September 1965): 275.

"California, There She Blows!" *Nation* 202 (20 June 1966): 732–33.

"California – Too Much, Too Soon." *Esquire* 59 (May 1963): 65–77.

"The California Uprising." *Look* 29 (23 February 1965): 30–35.

"The California Way of Life." *Life* 19 (22 October 1945): 105–16.

"The Call of California." *Life* 53 (19 October 1962), 54–56B.

Cameron, Frank. "I Rode Heartbreak Train." *Saturday Evening Post* 227 (2 October 1954): 38–39.

"Campus Agitation vs. Education." *Life* 58 (22 January 1965): 4.

"A Campus Uproar That Is Blamed on Reds." *U.S. News & World Report* 57 (14 December 1964): 12.

"The Careful Young Men." *Nation* 184 (9 March 1957): 208–9.

"Casual Clothes from California," *TV Guide* 11 (20 April 1963): 20–23.

Champlin, Charles. "The Novel Origins of Gidget." *Los Angeles Times*, 13 September 1986, sec. 5, pp. 1, 10.

"Changes in Today's College Students." *U.S. News & World Report* 56 (1 February 1964): 66–71.

"Choices at Berkeley." *Newsweek* 66 (9 August 1965): 74–75.

Chris, Cynthia. "Beyond the Mouse-Ear Gates: The Wonderful World of Disney Studios." *Afterimage* 23 (November/December 1995): 8–25.

"Chronology of Events." *California Monthly* 75 (February 1965): 34–42.

Ciardi, John. "Manner of Speaking:

Foamrubbersville." *Saturday Review* 48 (19 June 1965): 20.

"Clark Blames Game Show Lemon on California 'Where Everybody's a Hambone." *Variety* 235 (3 June 1964): 64.

Clinton, Farley. "Ronald Reagan: A Light in the West." *National Review* 18 (28 June 1966): 613–15.

Coffin, Patricia. "California Is Bustin' Out All Over," *Look* 23 (29 September 1959): 27–28.

——. "The Great American Weekend." *Look* 20 (10 July 1956): 61–69.

Cort, David. "Our Strangling Highways." *Nation* 182 (28 April 1956): 357–59.

Coy, Kathryn. "Why Did I Ever Let Him Talk Me into Going Steady?" *Photoplay* 55 (May 1959): 62–63.

"Crisis in Race Relations: A Police Chief Talks of Police Brutality." *U.S. News & World Report* 57 (19 August 1964): 33–36.

Cross, Jennifer. "America's Laboratory for Social Change." In *The California Revolution*, ed. Carey McWilliams, 110–25. New York: Grossman, 1968.

Crowther, Bosley. "The Screen: Delinquency." *New York Times*, 27 October 1955, sec. 1, p. 28.

"A Cure for Campus Riots." *U.S. News & World Report* 58 (17 May 1965): 70–72.

"Cut and Thrust: Gubernatorial Primary Preview." *Newsweek* 67 (6 June 1966): 25–26.

Daley, Arthur. "Will the Dodger-Giant Gold Rush Pan Out?" *New York Times Magazine*, 11 May 1958, pp. 34–36.

Dallek, Matthew. "Liberalism Overthrown: 1966 California Gubernatorial Election." *American Heritage* 47 (October 1996): 39–60.

Davies, Lawrence. "Berkeley Report an Issue on Coast." *New York Times*, 15 May 1966, sec. 1, p. 53.

——. "California Issue for '66 Emerges." *New York Times*, 16 August 1965, sec. 1, p. 1.

"Decline of a Hero." *Collier's* 136 (25 November 1955): 102.

Deegan, Robert E. "The Unclosed Frontier." *America: A Catholic Review of the Week* 98 (8 February 1954): 534–36.

De Groot, Gerard J. "'A Goddamned Electable Person': The 1966 California Gubernatorial Campaign of Ronald Reagan." *History* 82 (July 1997): 429–48.

——. "Reagan's Rise." *History Today* 45 (September 1995): 31–37.

——. "Ronald Reagan and Student Unrest in California, 1966–1970." *Pacific Historical Review* 65 (February 1996): 107–32.

Deutsch, Patricia, and Ronald M. Deutsch. "How Los Angeles Eases Racial Tensions." *Reader's Digest* 85 (October 1964): 86–90.

"The Dick Dale Phenomenon." *Billboard* 69 (9 March 1963): 15.

"Disney in TVland." *TV Guide* 2 (23 October 1954): 5–6.

"Disneyland." *Life* 39 (15 August 1955): 39–42.

"Disneyland." *McCall's* 82 (January 1955): 8–11.

"Disneyland." *Woman's Home Companion* 81 (June 1954): 12.

"Disneyland and Son." *Time* 73 (29 June 1959): 54.

"Disneyland as Two-Headed Child of TV." *Variety* 199 (20 July 1955): 2, 52.

"Disneyland Dedication from Coast." *New York Times*, 18 July 1955, sec. 1, p. 42.

"Disneyland Gates Open." *New York Times*, 19 July 1955, sec. 1, p. 22.

"Disneyland, Multimillion Dollar Magic Kingdom, to Open Tomorrow." *Los Angeles Times*, 17 July 1955, sec. 2, p. 1.

"Disneyland Reports On Its First Ten Million." *New York Times*, 2 February 1958, sec. 2, pp. 1, 7.

"Disney's 7-Year ABC-TV Deal: Weekly Series Ties Pix-Video." *Variety* 194 (31 March 1954): 41.

"Disney to Enter TV Field in Fall." *New York Times*, 30 March 1954, sec. 1, p. 24.

Dunne, John Gregory. "Eureka! A Celebration of California." In *Unknown California*, ed. Jonathan Eisen and David Fine, 11–20. New York: Collier, 1985.

Duscha, Julius. "But What If Reagan Becomes the Governor?" *New Republic* 155 (5 November 1966): 11–13.

Dyer, Peter John. "Youth and the Cinema: Part 1: The Teenage Rave." *Sight and Sound* 29 (Winter 1959–1960): 27–30.

"The Dysphoric Generation?" *Newsweek* 66 (16 October 1965): 98.

"Editorial," *California Monthly* 75 (February 1965): 4–5.

"Editorial: A Time for Prayer." *Los Angeles Times*, 15 August 1965, sec. 1, p. 1.

"End of a 'Quiet Summer.'" *U.S. News & World Report* 59 (23 August 1965): 6–8.

"Escalation in California." *Saturday Review* 48 (30 January 1965): 20.

"An Exclusive Interview with Ronald Reagan." *Human Events* 26 (19 February 1966): 9–10.

Eynon, Bret. "Community in Motion: The Free Speech Movement, Civil Rights, and the Roots of the New Left." *Oral History Review* 17 (Spring 1989): 36–69.

"Fair Weather Ahead." *TV Guide* 6 (24 May 1958): 29–30.

Fallows, James. "California Dreaming." *Washington Monthly* 20 (September 1988): 10–19.

Feuer, Lewis S. "Rebellion at Berkeley." *New Leader* 47 (21 December 1964): 3–12.

Field, Mervin D. "The UC Student Protests: California Poll." In *The Berkeley Student Revolt: Facts and Interpretations,* ed. Seymour Lipset and Sheldon S. Wolin, 199–200. Garden City, N.Y.: Anchor, 1965.

"Film Company Seeks a New Locale for Its Teen-Age Movies." *New York Times,* 6 November 1965, sec. 1, p. 18.

"Film Future: GI Baby Boom – Teen Market in Vast Expansion." *Variety* 210 (5 March 1958): 1, 27.

"Film vs. Live Shows." *Time* 63 (29 March 1954): 77–78.

"For Shocked Los Angeles: Now the Morning After." *U.S. News & World Report* 59 (6 September 1965): 34.

Ford, Larry R. "Geographic Factors in the Origin, Evolution, and Diffusion of Rock and Roll." In *The Sounds of People and Places: Readings in the Geography of American Folk and Popular Music,* ed. George O. Carney, 255–69. Lanham, Md.: University Press of America, 1987.

Ford, Larry R., and Floyd M. Henderson. "The Image of Place in American Popular Music: 1890–1970." In *The Sounds of People and Places: Readings in the Geography of American Folk and Popular Music,* ed. George O. Carney, 301–14. Lanham, Md.: University Press of America, 1987.

Fowler, Dan. "Los Angeles: The World's Worst Growing Pains." *Look* 20 (6 March 1963): 21–25.

"Fruits of Fire." *Time* 86 (3 September 1965): 21.

Funicello, Annette. "I'm Just Myself." *Seventeen* 21 (January 1962): 65–66, 117.

Funkhouser, G. Ray. "The Issues of the Sixties: An Explanatory Study in the Dynamics of Public Opinion." *Public Opinion Quarterly* 10 (Spring 1973): 62–76.

"The Fun Worshippers," *Newsweek* 58 (11 December 1961): 88.

Gallup, George, and Evan Hill. "Youth: The Cool Generation." *Saturday Evening Post* 234 (23–30 December 1961): 64–81.

"Get Whitey! The War Cry That Terrorized Los Angeles." *Life* 59 (27 August 1965): 1, 22–30.

"*Gidget.*" *Library Journal* 84 (1 April 1959): 119.

"*Gidget.*" *TV Guide* 13 (11 September 1965): 32.

"*Gidget.*" *Variety* 213 (18 March 1959): 6.

"*Gidget Goes Hawaiian.*" *New York Times,* 10 August 1961, sec. 4, p. 17.

"*Gidget Goes Hawaiian.*" *Variety* 223 (31 May 1961): 6.

"*Gidget Goes to Rome.*" *New York Times,* 12 September 1963, sec. 4, p. 32.

"*Gidget Goes to Rome.*" *Seventeen* 22 (August 1963): 38.

"*Gidget Goes to Rome.*" *Variety* 232 (7 July 1963): 6.

"Gidget Makes the Grade." *Life* 43 (28 October 1957): 111–14.

Gilbert, James B. "Popular Culture." *American Quarterly* 35 (Spring/Summer 1983): 140–54.

Gilbert, Richard. "A Good Time at UCLA: An English View." *Harper's* 230 (April 1965): 75.

"Going Together." *Look* 29 (13 July 1965): 80–85.

Goldstein, Richard. "Drugs on the Campus, Part I." *Saturday Evening Post* 239 (21 May 1966): 40–47.

——. "Drugs on the Campus, Part II." *Saturday Evening Post* 239 (4 June 1966): 34–44.

"Golly Gee! California Is a Strange State." *Ramparts* 5 (October 1966): 11–33.

Gomery, Douglas. "Failed Opportunities: The Integration of the U.S. Motion Picture and Television Industries." In *American Television: New Directions in History and Theory*, ed. Nick Browne, 23–36. USA: Harwood, 1994.

"The Good Life." *Life* 47 (28 December 1959): 12–74.

Gordon, Arthur. "Walt Disney." *Look* 19 (26 July 1955): 28–35.

Gordon, Mitchell. "Walt's Profit Formula: Dream, Diversify – And Never Miss an Angle." *Wall Street Journal* 151 (4 February 1958): 1, 12.

Gordon, Stanley. "California Co-Eds: Beauties from Two Top Campuses." *Look* 23 (29 September 1959): 67–69.

"Gov. Knight to Head List of Guests at Disneyland." *Los Angeles Times*, 30 June 1955, sec. 2, p. 3.

Grafton, Samuel. "When Youth Runs Wild." *McCall's* 90 (April 1962): 76–78, 162–66.

Grant, Barry K. "The Classic Hollywood Musical and the Problem of Rock 'n' Roll." *Journal of Popular Film and Television* 13 (Winter 1986): 192–205.

"The Greatest Triple Play in Show Business." *Reader's Digest* 67 (July 1955): 69–73.

Grevatt, Ron. "Songs for Swinging Surfers." *Melody Maker* 39 (22 August 1964): 7.

"Gripes – Not of Wrath." *Newsweek* 63 (10 February 1964): 80.

Halevy, Julian. "Disneyland and Las Vegas." *Nation* 186 (7 June 1958): 510–13.

Harris, Louis. "Analyzing the Swing to the Right Wing." *Newsweek* 67 (20 June 1966): 32.

Hartt, Juliann. "Kerr Predicts More Student Mob Incidents." *Los Angeles Times*, 7 October 1964, sec. 2, pp. 1, 3.

Hastings, Don. "All Aboard for Disneyland!" *Westways* 47 (July 1955): 4–5.

Hechinger, Fred M. "Berkeley Story." *New York Times*, 4 April 1965, sec. 5, p. 9.

Heirich, Max, and Sam Kaplan. "Yesterday's Discord." *California Monthly* 75 (February 1965): 20–32.

"Here Come the Sidewalk Surfers." *Life* 56 (5 June 1964): 89–90.

"Here's Your First View of Disneyland." *Look* 18 (2 November 1954): 86.

Heylbut, Rose. "Disney Fun with Music." *Etude* 74 (October 1956): 23, 53, 57–60.

"Hi-Fi Citizens." *American City* 71 (July 1956): 18.

Hill, Gladwin. "California: Barbecues and Other Trivia." *Nation* 203 (17 October 1966): 377–79.

———. "Disneyland Gets Its Last Touches." *New York Times*, 9 July 1955, sec. 1, p. 32.

———. "The Never-Never Land Khrushchev Never Saw." *New York Times*, 4 October 1959, sec. 1, p. 11.

Hiyiya, James A. "The Free Speech Movement and the Heroic Moment." *Journal of American Studies* 22 (April 1988): 43–66.

Hodges, Parker. "The Beats Like I Think I Know Them." *Seventeen* 19 (October 1960): 115, 162.

Hodgins, Eric. "What's Wrong with the Movies?" *Life* 26 (16 May 1949): 97–106.

"The Hollywood Scene." *Seventeen* 18 (April 1959): 4.

"Hollywood's Teenage Gold Mine." *Look* 28 (3 November 1964): 60–66.

Holmes, John Clellon. "The Philosophy of the Beat Generation." *Esquire* 49 (February 1958): 38.

Honor, Elizabeth. "Gifts from the Sun – Health and Beauty." *Cosmopolitan* 146 (May 1959): 66–69.

Houseman, John. "Battle over Television: Hollywood Faces the Fifties, Part II." *Harper's* 200 (May 1950): 51–59.

"How Campus Discord Forced a University President to Resign." *U.S. News & World Report* 58 (22 March 1965): 22.

Hughes, H. Stuart. "California – The America to Come." *Commentary* 21 (May 1956): 454–60.

Hulse, Jerry. "Dream Realized – Disneyland Opens." *Los Angeles Times*, 18 July 1955, sec. 2, pp. 1–2.

——. "What Becomes of the Juvenile Delinquent after Court Trial." *Los Angeles Times*, 26 June 1955, sec. 1, p. 8.

Hurup, Elsebeth. "Bridge over Troubled Water: Nostalgia for the Fifties in Movies of the Seventies and Eighties." In *Cracking the Ike Age: Aspects of Fifties America*, ed. Dale Carter, 56–75. Aarhus, Denmark: Aarhus University Press, 1992.

"I Giggle." *Newsweek* 53 (8 June 1959): 104–5.

"The Inheritor." *Time* 89 (6 January 1967): 22.

"Introduction: California." *Look* 23 (29 September 1959): 23.

James, T. J. "New World in the West." *Cosmopolitan* 146 (May 1959): 25–33.

"Janet's Going to the Prom," *Los Angeles Times*, 5 April 1959, sec. 8, p. 1.

Jennings, C. Robert. "The Odd Odyssey of Sandra Dee." *Saturday Evening Post* 236 (22 June 1963): 22–23.

Johnson, David M. "Disney World as Structure and Symbol: Re-creation of the American Experience." *Journal of Popular Culture* 15 (Summer 1981): 157–65.

Johnson, Paul B., David O. Sears, and John B. McConahay. "Black Invisibility, the Press, and the L.A. Riot." *American Journal of Sociology* 76 (January 1971): 698–721.

Katz, Joseph, and Nevitt Stanford. "Causes of the Student Revolution." *Saturday Review* 48 (18 December 1965): 64–67.

Kerr, Clark. "A Message to Alumni from President Kerr." *California Monthly* 75 (February 1965): 94–96.

——. "Student Dissent and Confrontation Politics." In *Protest! Student Activism in America*, ed. Julian Foster and Durward Levy, 3–10. New York: William Morrow, 1970.

"Kids: Built-In Recession Cure." *Life* 45 (16 June 1958): 83–89.

"Kid's Dream World Come True." *Popular Science* 166 (August 1955): 92.

King, Margaret J. "Disneyland and Walt Disney World: Traditional Values in Futuristic Form." *Journal of Popular Culture* 15 (Summer 1981): 116–40.

——. "The Recycled Hero: Walt Disney's Davy Crockett." In *Davy Crockett: The Man, the Legend, the Legacy, 1786–1986*, ed. Michael A. Lofaro, 137–58. Knoxville: University of Tennessee Press, 1985.

"The King at 24." *Newsweek* 62 (26 August 1963): 71.

"King of the Wild Frontier." *TV Guide* 3 (30 April 1955): 5–7.

Kohner, Frederick. "How It All Began." *TV Guide* 13 (11 December 1965): 30–33.

Kopkind, Andrew. "Running Wild: California's Political Rat Race." *New Republic* 153 (30 October 1965): 15–19.

——. "Hooray for the Red, White, and Blue." *New Republic* 152 (8 May 1965): 23–24.

Kuehnl, Neil. "What It's Really Like to Move to California." *Better Homes and Gardens* 39 (August 1961): 56–57.

La Barre, Harriet, and Caroll Seghers. "California – Teenagers' Paradise."

Cosmopolitan 143 (November 1957): 46–53.

"Lady Named Los Angeles Changes Her Face Often." *Los Angeles Times*, 23 May 1960, sec. 1, p. 3.

Langguth, Jack. "Political Fun and Games in California." *New York Times Magazine*, 16 October 1966, p. 28.

"L.A. Traffic Reflects Civic Boom." *Life* 48 (20 June 1960): 74–87.

Leibman, Nina C. "Leave Mother Out: The Fifties Family in American Film and Television." *Wide Angle* 10, no. 4 (1988): 24–41.

Lembke, Daryl E. "801 UC Arrests: Berkeley Rebellion Broken Up." *Los Angeles Times*, 4 December 1964, sec. 1, pp. 1, 3, 8.

Leonard, George B. "The Bored, the Bearded, and the Beat." *Look* 22 (19 August 1958): 64–68.

———. "California: A New Game with New Rules." *Look* 30 (28 June 1966): 29–30.

———. "California – What It Means." *Look* 26 (25 September 1962): 96–104.

———. "Where the California Game Is Taking Us." *Look* 30 (28 June 1966): 110–11.

———. "Youth of the Sixties . . . The Explosive Generation." *Look* 25 (3 January 1961): 16–20.

"Letters." *Nation* 200 (11 January 1965): 4.

"Letters." *New York Times*, 16 April 1961, sec. 1, p. 46.

"Letters to the Editor." *California Monthly* 75 (March 1965): 5–8.

"Letters to the Editor," *Life* 59 (5 February 1965): 21.

"Letters to the Editor," *Life* 59 (17 September 1965): 27.

"Letters to the Editor," *Look* 30 (9 August 1966): 10–11.

Levy, Alan. "Peekaboo Sex, Or How to Fill a Drive-In." *Life* 59 (16 July 1965): 81–89.

Lewis, Richard Warren. "Those Swinging Beach Movies." *Saturday Evening Post* 238 (31 July 1965): 83–87.

"*Life* Visits Dick Dale, King of Surfing Music." *Life* 55 (30 August 1963): 82–83.

Lipsitz, George. "The Making of Disneyland." In *True Stories from the American Past*, ed. William Graebner, 179–96. New York: McGraw-Hill, 1993.

Liston, James M. "The Land That Does Away with Time." *Better Homes and Gardens* 34 (February 1956): 62–63.

Litwack, Leo. "A Fantasy That Paid Off." *New York Times Magazine*, 27 June 1965, pp. 22–28.

———. "The Ronald Reagan Story; or, Tom Sawyer Enters Politics." *New York Times Magazine*, 14 November 1965, pp. 46–47, 174–84.

"The Loneliest Road." *Time* 86 (27 August 1965): 9–10.

"Long Hot Summer." *New Republic* 153 (3 July 1965): 7–8.

Loper, Mary Lou. "They Go Down to the Sea on Surf Boards." *Los Angeles Times*, 29 May 1960, sec. 7, pp. 1–2.

"Los Angeles: And Now What." *America* 113 (28 August 1965): 199.

"Los Angeles: A Race Relations Success Story." *Look* 21 (19 March 1957): 25–29.

"Los Angeles: The Art of Living Bumper to Bumper." *Look* 20 (18 September 1956): 22–23.

"Los Angeles: The Far Country." *Time* 86 (24 September 1965): 23–24.

"Los Angeles: The Fire This Time." *Newsweek* 66 (23 August 1965): 15–17.

"Los Angeles Riots: The Search for Whys." *Senior Scholastic* 87 (23 September 1965): 23–24.

"LSD and the Drugs of the Mind." *Newsweek* 67 (9 May 1966): 59–64.

"LSD: Turmoil in a Capsule." *Life* 60 (26 March 1966): 28–33.

Lubell, Samuel. "Who Will Take California?" *Saturday Evening Post* 229 (20 October 1956): 121–22.

Luckett, Moya. "Girl Watchers: Patty Duke and Teen Television." In *The Revolution Wasn't Televised: Sixties Television and Social Conflict*, ed. Lynn Spiegel and Michael Curtin, 94–117. London: Routledge, 1997.

Lustig, Jeff. "Introduction: Envisioning California." *California History* 68 (Winter 1989–90): 158–259.

"McCone Report." In *Mass Violence in America: The Los Angeles Riots*, ed. Robert M. Fogelson, 3–8. New York: Arno, 1969.

McCurdy, Jack, and Art Beeman. "7,000 in New Rioting, Troops Alerted." *Los Angeles Times*, 13 August 1965, sec. 1, pp. 1, 3.

McFarland, Stephen J. "Understanding the Beach Boys for the Best in Surf Music." In *Back to the Beach: A Brian Wilson and the Beach Boys Reader*, ed. Kingsley Abbott, 22–28. London: Helter Skelter, 1997.

McGregor, Gaile. "Domestic Blitz: A Revisionist History of the Fifties." *American Studies* 34 (January 1993): 5–33.

MacKay, Milton. "The Big Brawl: Hollywood vs. Television." *Saturday Evening Post* 224 (19 January 1952): 17–19, 70–72.

McLellan, Dennis. "This Land Is Your Land: California Adventure, Disney's New Theme Park In Anaheim," *Los Angeles Times*, 11 January 2001, sec. F, p. W1.

McWilliams, Carey. "Reagan vs. Brown:

How to Succeed with the Backlash." *Nation* 203 (31 October 1966): 438–42.

———. "Watts: The Forgotten Slum." *Nation* 201 (30 August 1965): 89–90.

"The Mad Happy Surfers." *Life* 51 (1 September 1961): 47–53.

Maher, Jack. "Hot Rod Trend Catches On." *Billboard* 69 (25 November 1963): 3, 14.

"Manners and Morals: Fried Shoes." *Time* 73 (9 February 1959): 16.

Marine, Gene. "No Fair! The Students Strike at California." *Nation* 199 (21 December 1964): 482–86.

Marling, Karal Ann. "Disneyland, 1955: Just Take the Santa Ana Freeway to the American Dream." *American Art* 5 (Winter/Spring 1991): 169–207.

———. "Imagineering the Disney Theme Parks." In *Designing Disney's Theme Parks: The Architecture of Reassurance*, ed. Karal Ann Marling, 29–177. Paris: Flammarion, 1997.

Maudlin, Bill. "What Gives?" *Collier's* 136 (21 January 1955): 46–53.

"Meet Davy Crockett." *Look* 19 (26 July 1955): 36.

Meinig, D. W. "American Wests: Preface to a Geographical Interpretation." *Annals of the Association of American Geographers* 62 (June 1972): 159–84.

———. "Symbolic Landscapes: Some Idealizations of American Communities." In *The Interpretation of Ordinary Landscapes*, ed. D. W. Meinig, 164–92. New York: Oxford University Press, 1979.

Menin, Aubrey. "Dazzled in Disneyland." *Holiday* 34 (July 1963): 68–75, 106.

"*Mickey Mouse Club*." *Variety* 204 (3 October 1956): 17.

"*Mickey Mouse Club* Review." *TV Guide* 4 (7 January 1956): 20.

Miller, Colin. "The Press and the Student

Revolt." In *Revolution at Berkeley*, ed. Michael V. Miller and Susan Gilmore, 313–50. New York: Dell, 1965.

Miller, Edwin. "Gidget Was Here." *Seventeen* 22 (July 1963): 94–95.

———. "Sandra Dee Out West." *Seventeen* 19 (March 1960): 125–28, 162–65.

———. "The TV Screen: Are You Being Brainwashed by TV to Behave Like a Teen-Age Zombie?" *Seventeen* 25 (May 1966): 97.

Miller, Jim. "The Beach Boys." In *The Rolling Stone Illustrated History of Rock and Roll*, 162–68. New York: Random House, 1980.

———. "13 Years on a Suburban Safari." *Rolling Stone* 7 (21 November 1974): 67–72.

Miller, Michael. "Letter from the Berkeley Underground." *Esquire* 64 (September 1965): 85.

Mitchell, Carleton. "The Fad and Fascination of Surfing." *Holiday* 35 (May 1964): 122–30.

Mitford, Jessica. "The Rest of Ronald Reagan." *Ramparts* 4 (November 1965): 30–36.

Mitgang, Herbert. "The Strange James Dean Death Cult." *Coronet* 41 (25 November 1955): 110–15.

"More Than Restless." *Nation* 199 (21 December 1964): 477.

Morgan, Neil. "The State as a Campus." *Holiday* 38 (October 1965): 78–79, 121–33.

Morris, Gary. "Beyond the Beach: Social and Formal Aspects of AIP's Beach Party Movies." *Journal of Popular Film and Television* 21 (Spring 1993): 2–11.

Morton, Jim. "Beach Party Films." In *Incredibly Strange Films*, ed. Andrea Juno and V. Vale, 146–47. San Francisco: Re/Search Press, 1989.

Moser, Don. "There's No Easy Place to Pin the Blame." *Life* 59 (27 August 1965): 31–33.

Moss, Ian. "*Gidget*." *Films and Filming* 5 (July 1959): 23.

"Movies: End of an Era?" *Fortune* 39 (April 1949): 99–102, 135–50.

Murray, Jim. "Ronald Reagan to the Rescue!" *Esquire* 65 (February 1966): 76–78, 117–18.

"The Nation That Moved West." *Senior Scholastic* 82 (8 May 1963): 6–9, 19.

"New Boom in Surf-Boarding." *Westways* 47 (August 1955): 10–11.

"Newest Travel Lure: Disneyland," *Travel* 104 (July 1955): 16–17.

Nichols, Mark. "Stardom Bound." *Coronet* 47 (January 1960): 61–72.

"No Business Like It." *Time* 88 (16 September 1966): 37.

"No Mothers Allowed." *TV Guide* 4 (1 December 1956): 4–7.

"No Rock, No Mop, But a Big Hit: The Young Americans Look Neat and Sing Sweet." *Life* 69 (13 August 1965): 67–68.

"The Number One State: Blooming, Beautiful California." *Newsweek* 60 (10 September 1962): 28–38.

Obear, Frederick. "Student Activism in the Sixties." In *Protest! Student Activism in America*, ed. Julian Foster and Durward Levy, 11–26. New York: William Morrow, 1970.

O'Boyle, J. G. "Be Sure You're Right, Then Go Ahead: The Early Disney Westerns." *Journal of Popular Film and Television* 24 (Summer 1986): 69–113.

O'Connor, John E. "History in Images/ Images in History: Reflections on the Importance of Film and Television Study for an Understanding of the Past." *American Historical Review* 93 (December 1988): 1200–1209.

O'Neil, Paul. "The Only Rebellion

Around." *Life* 47 (30 November 1959): 115–30.

Oulahan, Richard, and William Lambert. "The Real Ronald Reagan Stands Up." *Life* 60 (21 January 1966): 70–72, 77–78.

"Our Good Teenagers: The Healthy 97 Percent That Count." *Newsweek* 54 (23 November 1959): 69–72.

"Panty Raids? No! Tough Campus Revolt." *Life* 57 (18 December 1964): 46A–46B.

"Paradise Reagan-ed: Voters' Psychology." *Nation* 203 (5 December 1966): 596.

Parales, Jon. "Surfin' Again." *New York Times*, 1 May 1994, sec. 9, p. 5.

"Parkinson's Law." *Time* 87 (27 May 1966): 20.

Parsons, James J. "The Uniqueness of California." *American Quarterly* 7 (Spring 1955): 45–55.

"Pavement Surfing Makes Splash." *New York Times*, 3 March 1965, sec. 1, p. 43.

Perimutter, Emanuel. "Dodgers Accept L.A. Bid to Move to Coast," *New York Times*, 9 October 1957, sec. 1, p. 37.

Phelan, James. "Can Reagan Win California?" *Saturday Evening Post* 239 (4 June 1966): 89–92.

"Physiques Pay Off: Teen-agers Parade in Posture Contest," *Los Angeles Times*, 8 May 1959, sec. 3, p. 1.

"Pied Piper to Millions." *TV Guide* 4 (2 June 1956): 12–13.

"Pinky Pastels Are Flourishing in Los Angeles," *Seventeen* 20 (September 1961): 127.

Poe, Elizabeth. "Nobody Was Listening." In *Los Angeles: Biography of a City*, ed. John and Laree Caughey, 426–31. Los Angeles: University of California Press, 1976.

"Polls Apart." *Time* 86 (24 September 1965): 28.

"Poll Shows Teen-agers Look Westward." *Senior Scholastic* 82 (8 May 1963): 19.

Poppy, John. "California: A Vision of Hell and Heaven." *Look* 30 (28 June 1966): 74.

——. "A Human Cry Behind the Speeches: 'I'm Here.'" *Look* 29 (23 February 1965): 42.

"Population of 6 Million Forecast in County By '60." *Los Angeles Times*, 5 May 1959, sec. 3, p. 1.

Postol, Todd. "Reinterpreting the Fifties: Changing Views of a Dull Decade." *Journal of American Culture* 8 (February 1985): 39–45.

"Premier Annoyed by Ban on Visit to Disneyland." *New York Times*, 20 September 1959, sec. 1. p. 1.

Putnam, Jackson K. "A Half-Century of Conflict: The Rise and Fall of Liberalism in California, 1943–1993." In *Politics in the Postwar American West*, ed. Richard Lowitt, 42–63. Norman: University of Oklahoma Press, 1995.

Raddatz, Leslie. "Sally Field's Actually a Lot Like Gidget." *TV Guide* 14 (28 May 1966): 15–17.

Ransom, James. "Beach Blanket Babies." *Esquire* 64 (July 1965): 90–94, 108.

Raskin, A. H. "The Berkeley Affair." *New York Times Magazine*, 14 February 1965, pp. 24–25, 91.

——. "Where It All Began – Berkeley, Five Years Later Is Radicalized, Reaganized, Mesmerized." *New York Times Magazine*, 17 January 1970, p. 28.

Rawls, James J. "Introduction." In *California: A Place, a People, a Dream*, ed. Claudia K. Jurmain and James J. Rawls, 144–45. San Francisco: Chronicle Books/Oakland Museum, 1986.

——. "Visions and Revisions." *Wilson Quarterly* 14 (Summer 1990): 56–65.

Ray, Bill. "Fever of a Mass Thrust for Knowledge." *Life* 53 (19 October 1962): 96B–98.

"Reagan for President?" *New Republic* 155 (2 July 1966): 4.

"*Rebel*'s Child-Parent Hostility Theme Drawing Lots of Mail." *Variety* 201 (14 December 1955): 2, 71.

"*Rebel Without a Cause*." *Films in Review* 6 (November 1955): 167–68.

"*Rebel Without a Cause*." *Time* 166 (28 November 1955): 104.

"*Rebel Without a Cause*." *Variety* 200 (26 October 1955): 6.

"Recreation: Disneyland East." *Newsweek* 66 (29 November 1965): 82.

"Recreation: Surf's Up!" *Time* 82 (9 August 1963): 49.

"Republicans: Reagan Rides East." *Newsweek* 66 (11 October 1965): 42.

"The Riot." *TV Guide* 13 (28 August 1965): A1.

Robbins, Michela. "The Inside Story of a Girls Reformatory." *Collier's* 132 (2 October 1953): 74–79.

Robinson, Louie. "This Would Never Have Happened." *Ebony* 20 (October 1965): 114–24.

"Rock and Roll: The Sounds of the Sixties." *Time* 85 (21 May 1965): 84–88.

Roddy, Joseph. "The Big Contest Is in California." *Look* 30 (1 November 1966): 41.

———. "California: Ronnie to the Rescue." *Look* 30 (1 November 1966): 51–52.

———. "The Networks Turn to Teen-Agers." *Look* 29 (5 October 1965): 34–38.

Rogers, Warren. "California: Pat Runs Scared." *Look* 30 (1 November 1966): 42.

"Ronald for Real." *Time* 88 (7 October 1966): 31–35.

Rorabaugh, W. J. "The Berkeley Free Speech Movement." In *True Stories from the American Past*, ed. William Graebner, 197–216. New York: McGraw-Hill, 1993.

Ross, Tim A. "The Rise and Fall of the Beats." *Nation* 192 (27 May 1961): 456–57.

Roth, Sanford H. "The Late James Dean." *Collier's* 136 (25 November 1955): 62–63.

Salisbury, Mike. "The Californication of America." *Print* 53 (May–June 1998): 78–86.

"Sally Field: Gidget '65." *Seventeen* 24 (September 1965): 48.

Sampson, Edward E. "Student Activism and the Decade of Protest." *Journal of Social Issues* 23 (July 1967): 1–33.

"San Francisco: Casual, Cosmopolitan." *Seventeen* 18 (September 1959): 129.

"The San Francisco Riot." *Newsweek* 68 (10 October 1966): 28.

Santelli, Robert. "Catching a Wave: An Informal History of New Jersey Surfing." In *Teenage New Jersey, 1941–1975*, ed. Kathryn Grover, 50–54. Newark: New Jersey Historical Society, 1997.

Sargent, Herb. "How to Face the Move to California." *Esquire* 59 (May 1963): 68–70.

Savio, Mario. "California's Angriest Student." *Life* 59 (26 February 1965): 100–101.

———. "Why It Happened at Berkeley." In *West of the West: Imagining California*, ed. Leonard Michaels, David Reed, and Raquel Sherr, 189–94. San Francisco: North Point, 1989.

"Savio Onstage." *Newsweek* 64 (21 December 1964): 71.

Schaftner, Dorothy. "When These Teen-Agers Say: Everybody's Doing It, Everybody Is!" *Good Housekeeping* 144 (April 1957): 38, 212.

Schapiro, Steve. "Golden Girl: A Success Story – or At Least It Ought to Be." *Life* 55 (11 October 1963): 68–85.

Schiesl, Martin J. "Behind the Badge: The Police and Social Discontent in Los Angeles Since 1950." In *20th Century Los Angeles: Power, Promotion, and Social Conflict*, ed. Norman M. Klein and Martin J. Schiesl, 154–94. Claremont, Calif.: Regina, 1990.

"Screen: *Beach Party*." *New York Times*, 26 September 1963, sec. 1, p. 40.

"Screen: Sun and Surf – *Gidget*: The Story of a Teen-Age Girl, Opens." *New York Times*, 23 April 1959, sec. 4, p. 27.

Seabury, Paul. "The Antic Politics of California." *Harper's* 230 (June 1965): 82–89.

Sears, Roebuck and Company Catalog (Spring 1956).

"Seaside Fashions." *TV Guide* 7 (20 June 1959): 28–29.

Semple, Robert B. "21 Dead in Los Angeles Riots." *New York Times*, 15 August 1965, sec. 1, p. 1.

"Senate Committee Reports: TV Has 'Greater Impact' on Children Than Movies, Radio." *U.S. News & World Report* 39 (2 September 1955): 75–76.

"7-Up . . . Where There's Action," *TV Guide* 13 (3 July 1965): 2.

Severson, John. "Riding the World's Giants." *Saturday Evening Post* 235 (14–21 July 1962): 20–25.

"She's the Idol of Little Boys – And Big Ones, Too." *TV Guide* 11 (12 October 1963): 12–13.

"She Sure Doesn't Look Sick." *Life* 55 (25 October 1963): 119–20.

"Shooting the Curl for the Camera." *TV Guide* 12 (5 December 1964): 10–11.

"Shooting the Tube." *Time* 83 (10 January 1964): 57.

"Show Business: How to Make a Buck." *Time* 70 (29 July 1957): 76–78.

"Showing Now and Notable." *Los Angeles Times, Home Magazine*, 2 July 1961, p. 21.

"Sidewalk Surfing." *Newsweek* 65 (5 April 1965): 71.

Siegel, Jules. "Surf, Wheels, and Free Souls." *Saturday Evening Post* 239 (19 November 1966): 32–37.

Smith, Jack. "Politics Stirs New Interest at Colleges." *Los Angeles Times*, 12 June 1962, sec. 2, p. 1.

——. "Silent Generation Finding Its Voice in College." *Los Angeles Times*, 11 June 1962, sec. 2, p. 1.

Smith, Richard Austin. "Los Angeles, Prototype of a Supercity." *Fortune* 71 (March 1965): 99–103.

"So Long, Mickey." *TV Guide* 7 (21 February 1959): 18–19.

"The Spectacular Mr. Disney." *TV Guide* 3 (1 October 1955): 4–7.

"*Spin and Marty*." *TV Guide* 5 (1 June 1957): 28–29.

"Splashy Suits to Swim In." *Life* 46 (25 May 1959): 49–55.

"Sporting Look Well-Suited by the West." *Sports Illustrated* 3 (3 November 1955): 54–56.

"Squaresville, USA, vs. Beatsville." *Life* 47 (21 September 1959): 31–37.

Staehling, Richard. "The Truth about Teen Movies." *Rolling Stone* 3 (27 December 1969): 34–42.

Starr, Kevin. "California, A Dream." In *California: A Place, a People, a Dream*, ed. Claudia K. Jurmain and James J. Rawls, 13–22. San Francisco: Chronicle Books, 1986.

Stegner, Wallace. "California: The Experimental Society." *Saturday Review* 50 (23 September 1967): 28–29.

Steiner, Michael. "Frontier as

Tomorrowland: Walt Disney and the Architectural Packaging of the Mythic West." *Montana: The Magazine of Western History* 48 (Spring 1998): 2–17.

"Stiffening the Spine." *Time* 85 (19 March 1965): 48.

Stone, Irving. "California: A Land to Build a Dream On." *Holiday* 16 (December 1954): 42–61.

"The Story of Ronald Reagan." *U.S. News & World Report* 62 (2 January 1967): 30–36.

"Struggling with the Board of Education." *TV Guide* 13 (13 September 1965): 24–25.

"Surf Boredom: *Gidget Goes to Rome, Beach Party.*" *Time* 82 (16 August 1963): 74.

"The Surfin' Craze." *Senior Scholastic* 83 (20 September 1963): 22–23.

"Surfing: Go East, Golden Boy." *Time* 85 (25 June 1965): 62–63.

"Surfing in Tandem." *Life* 57 (3 July 1964): 68–70.

"Surfing Pizza Style." *Life* 58 (7 August 1964): 47–49.

"Surfing Scene: Coast Craze Adds Hearse." *Billboard* 69 (1 June 1963): 3.

"Surfing: Young Californian Is Expert at New Sport." *Ebony* 20 (April 1965): L109–L113.

Sugrue, Thomas J. "Reassessing the History of Postwar America." *Prospects* 20 (1995): 493–517.

Summons, Jerold. "The Censoring of *Rebel Without a Cause.*" *Journal of Popular Film and Television* 23 (Summer 1995): 56–63.

"Taste of Action – Chesterfield King," *Life* 55 (19 July 1963): 100.

"Teen-ager Makes Her Mark as Glamorous Cover Girl," *Los Angeles Times*, 5 April 1959, sec. 2, p. 3.

"The Teenagers." *Newsweek* 67 (21 March 1966): 75.

"Teenagers – Why They Go Steady, Why They Go Wild – Why They Don't Listen." *Look* 21 (23 July 1957): cover, 21–39.

"That California Way of Life." *Changing Times* 14 (January 1960): 27–32.

"Their Happiness Castle: Insurance by North America," *Life* 43 (18 November 1957): 41.

"This Week in Review." *Time* 64 (8 November 1954): 95.

Thompson, Thomas. "The Sound Flowed Out of the Music Streams." *Life* 59 (21 May 1965): 92–98.

Thompson, William L. "Introductory." *Annals of the Association of American Geographers* 49 (September 1959): 5–6.

"Tidal Wave." *New Yorker* 31 (9 April 1955): 24–26.

"Tinker Bell, Mary Poppins, Cold Cash." *Newsweek* 66 (12 July 1965): 74–76.

"Today's Teenagers." *Time* 85 (27 January 1965): 56–58.

"Topics of the Times: Mr. Disney and His Wonderland." *New York Times*, 22 July 1955 sec. 1, p. 22.

"To Prison with Love." *Time* 84 (11 December 1964): 60.

Treuhaft, Jessica Mitford. "Rebels with a Hundred Causes." *Nation* 192 (27 May 1961): 451–56.

"Trigger of Hate." *Time* 86 (20 August 1965): 13–19.

Trombly, William. "The Exploding University of California." *Saturday Evening Post* 237 (16 May 1964): 22–29.

"Trouble Again at Cal." *Life* 58 (19 March 1965): 43.

"Troubled Los Angeles – Race Is Only One of Its Problems." *U.S. News & World Report* 59 (30 August 1965): 58, 60–62.

Turner, Wallace. "Berkeley Students Stage Sit-In to Protest Curb on Free Speech."

New York Times, 3 December 1964, sec. 1, p. 50.

Turpin, Dick. "California Schools Given First Place in Enrollment." *Los Angeles Times*, 24 April 1959, sec. 3, p. 1.

"A Two-Way Summer Set," *Seventeen* 18 (June 1959): 18.

"Up from Death Valley." *Time* 87 (17 June 1966): 24–25.

"U.S. Again Is Subdued by Davy." *Life* 38 (25 April 1955): 27–33.

"The U.S. Teenager: A Searching Picture and Word Report on the Most Maligned Generation in Our History." *Look* 20 (24 January 1956): 21–32.

Vance, James E., Jr. "California and the Search for the Ideal." *Annals of the Association of American Geographers* 62 (June 1972): 185–204.

——. "Revolution in American Space Since 1945, and a Canadian Contrast." In *North America: The Historical Geography of a Changing Continent*, ed. Robert D. Mitchell and Paul A. Groves, 438–59. USA: Rowman & Littlefield, 1987.

Verge, Arthur C. "The Impact of the Second World War on Los Angeles." *Pacific Historical Review* 163 (August 1994): 289–326.

Wallace, Kevin. "Onward and Upward with the Arts: The Engineering of Ease." *New Yorker* 39 (7 September 1963): 104–29.

"Walt Disney (1901–1966): Imagineer of Fun." *Newsweek* 68 (29 December 1966): 68–69.

"Walt Disney Accused." *Horn Book* 41 (December 1965): 602–11.

"Walt Disney – To Enchanted Worlds on Electronic Wings." *Time* 64 (27 December 1954): 40–46.

"Watts Today." *Newsweek* 66 (13 December 1965): 31.

"Wave of the Future." *Newsweek* 64 (13 July 1964): 59.

Ways, Max. "On the Campus: A Troubled Reflection of the U.S." *Fortune* 72 (September 1965): 130–35, 198–202.

"Weather." *Newsweek* 52 (8 December 1968): 24.

Weatherbee, Linda. "Surf's Up: A New Wave in Sports: Teens Head for the Sea." *Seventeen* 21 (July 1962): 61, 100.

Webster, David Kenyon. "They Ride the Wild Water." *Saturday Evening Post* 230 (14 June 1958): 38–39, 88–90.

"Wee Surf Disk Ripple Building into Big Wave." *Billboard* 69 (29 June 1963): 26, 31.

Weinstein, Raymond M. "Disneyland and Coney Island: Reflections on the Evolution of the Modern Amusement Park." *Journal of Popular Culture* 26 (Summer 1992): 131–64.

Welch, Paul. "Homosexuality in America." *Life* 56 (26 June 1964): 68.

"Welcome to Disneyland." *Los Angeles Times*, 15 July 1955, sec. 5.

"West Coast Activities – Network Makes Big Plans for Opening of Disneyland Park." *New York Times*, 3 July 1955, sec. 3, p. 9.

"The West Coast Surfers: The Look, The Living, the Lingo." *Look* 28 (30 June 1964): 54–57.

"West Coast, Too, Has Its Race Problems." *U.S. News & World Report* 40 (2 June 1956): 36–40.

"When and Where to Speak." *Time* 84 (18 December 1964): 68.

"When Students Try to Run a University." *U.S. News & World Report* 57 (21 December 1964): 43.

"When the Poor Are Powerless." *New Republic* 153 (4 September 1965): 7.

While, Donald F. "I Hate Southern

California." *American Mercury* 82 (June 1956): 19–29.

White, Theodore H. "The Gentlemen from California." *Collier's* 137 (3 February 1956): 38–47.

"Why Negroes Rioted in Watts – An Official Report." *U.S. News & World Report* 59 (20 December 1965): 54.

"Why Republican Hopes Are Rising." *U.S. News & World Report* 60 (20 June 1966): 31–32.

"The Wide World of Disney." *Newsweek* 60 (31 December 1962): 48–51.

Wilson, James Q. "A Guide to Reagan Country: The Political Culture of Southern California." *Commentary* 43 (May 1967): 37–45.

Wilson, Richard L. "California: The Year's Most Important Election." *Look* 22 (28 October 1958): 23–27.

Wolfert, Ira. "Walt Disney's Magic Kingdom." *Reader's Digest* 76 (April 1960): 144–52.

"A Wonderful World: Growing Impact of Disney Art." *Newsweek* 45 (18 April 1955): 60–69.

Woodfield, William R. "Bringing Up Mother." *Coronet* 45 (May 1959): 88–92.

Wright, Alfred. "To the Big Game and to the Barricades." *Sports Illustrated* 24 (3 January 1966): 48–54.

Wright, John L. "Croonin' about Cruising." In *The Popular Culture Reader*, ed. Jack Nachbar, Deborah Weiser, and John L. Wright, 109–17. Bowling Green, Ohio: Bowling Green University Popular Press, 1978.

"Yesterday's Rebels." *Time* 86 (6 August 1965): 49.

York, Neil L. "California Girls and the American Eden." *Journal of American Culture* 7 (Winter 1984): 33–43.

"Your Letters," *Seventeen* 21 (September 1962): 4.

"Youth: Sunset along the Strip." *Time* 88 (2 December 1966): 69.

Zhito, Lee. "Capitol Comeback on Singles Front: Three in Top Ten." *Billboard* 69 (18 May 1963): 1.

——. "Capitol Snags Dick Dale after Hot Bidding." *Billboard* 69 (23 February 1963): 1, 8.

——. "Surfing Craze Ready to Splash Across Country to East's Youth." *Billboard* 69 (29 June 1963): 26, 31.

Zimmerman, Geron. "Walt Disney: Giant at the Fair." *Look* 28 (11 February 1964): 28–32.

DISSERTATIONS AND THESES

Avila, Eric R. "Reinventing Los Angeles: Popular Culture in the Age of White Flight, 1940–1965." Ph.D. diss., University of California, Berkeley, 1997.

Bowie, Patricia Carr. "The Cultural History of Los Angeles, 1850–1967: From Rural Backwash to World Center." Ph.D. diss., University of Southern California, 1980.

Coleman, Barbara Jean. "Fitting Pretty: Media Construction of Teenage Girls in the 1950s." Ph.D. diss., University of Minnesota, 1995.

Fischman, Lisa Anne. "Coonskin Fever: Frontier Adventures in Postwar American Culture." Ph.D. diss., University of Minnesota, 1996.

Nestegard, Elizabeth Anne. "Reading Disneyland: A Historical Look at the Textual Interpretations of the Disney Parks and the Study of American Popular Culture." M.A. thesis, California State University, Fullerton, 1994.

Pendleton, John Philip. "Assault on the American Dream: A History of the Youth Revolt, 1955–1965." Ph.D. diss., University of California, Santa Barbara, 1974.

Scheiner, Georganne. "Are These Our Daughters?: The Image of Female Adolescence in Film, 1920–1970." Ph.D. diss., Arizona State University, 1990.

Simonette, Matthew. "The Walt Disney Programs, 1954–1961, and the Ideological Tools of Progress." M.A. thesis, Marquette University, 1995.

FILMS AND TELEVISION PROGRAMS

The Adventures of Spin and Marty (serial), *The Mickey Mouse Club*. The Disney Channel. 1955–56.

Annette (serial), *The Mickey Mouse Club*. The Disney Channel. 1957–58.

Beach Blanket Bingo. American International Pictures/Goodtimes Video, 1964; video, 1993.

Beach Party. American International Pictures/Goodtimes Video, 1963; video, 1993.

Berkeley in the Sixties. San Francisco: California Newsreel, 1990.

Bikini Beach. American International Pictures/Goodtimes Video, 1964; video, 1993.

"Dateline: Disneyland." Walt Disney Productions, 1955.

Davy Crockett: King of the Wild Frontier. Walt Disney Productions: 1954, 1955.

"Dear Diary – Et Al." *Gidget*. Columbia/TriStar Home Video, 1965; video, 1997.

Gidget. Columbia Pictures, 1959.

Gidget Goes Hawaiian. Columbia Pictures, 1961.

Gidget Goes to Rome. Columbia Pictures, 1963.

Interview, "*Good Morning America*," ABC Television Network (9 October 1979).

"Is It Love or Symbiosis?" *Gidget*. Columbia/TriStar Home Video, 1965; video, 1997.

Jan and Dean: Behind the Music. VH1 Productions, 1998.

Leo, Malcolm. *The Beach Boys: An American Band*. New York: High Ridge Productions/Vestron Video, 1983.

The Mickey Mouse Club. Walt Disney Productions, 1955–59.

Muscle Beach Party. American International Pictures/Goodtimes Video, 1964; video, 1993.

Rebel Without a Cause. Warner Brothers, 1955.

SOUND RECORDINGS

ALBUMS

The Beach Boys, *Good Vibrations: Thirty Years of the Beach Boys* (CD). Capitol Records, 1993.

——. *Surfer Girl*. Capitol Records, 1963.

——. *Surfin' USA*. Capitol Records, 1963.

Jan and Dean, *Folk 'n' Roll*. Liberty Records, 1965.

SONGS

"409." The Beach Boys, words and music by Brian Wilson, Mike Love, and Gary L. Usher.

"All Summer Long." The Beach Boys, words and music by Brian Wilson and Mike Love.

"Be Sure You're Right, and Then Go Ahead." Words and music by Buddy Ebsen and Fess Parker. © 1955 Walt Disney Music Company. All rights reserved, reprinted by permission.

"Be True to Your School." The Beach Boys, words and music by Brian Wilson and Mike Love.

"California Girls." Words and music by Brian Wilson, Mike Love. © Irving Music Inc. (BMI). International copyright secured. All rights reserved.

"California, Here I Come." Words and music by Al D. Jolson, Bud De Sylva, Joseph Meyer, and Jimmy Dale. New York: M. Whitmark & Sons, 1924.

"California Sun." The Rivieras, words and music by Henry Glover and Morris Levy.

"Catch a Wave." The Beach Boys, words and music by Brian Wilson and Mike Love.

"Do What the Good Book Says." Words and music by Jimmie Dodd and Ruth Carrell. © 1955 Walt Disney Music Company. All rights reserved, reprinted by permission.

"Fun, Fun, Fun." The Beach Boys, words and music by Brian Wilson and Mike Love.

"Get Busy." Words and music by Jimmie Dodd and Tom Adair. © 1955 Walt Disney Music Company. All rights reserved, reprinted by permission.

"I Get Around." The Beach Boys, words and music by Brian Wilson and Mike Love.

"Little Honda." The Beach Boys, words and music by Brian Wilson.

"The Merry Mouseketeers." Words and music by Jimmie Dodd. © 1955 Walt Disney Music Company. All rights reserved, reprinted by permission.

"Mickey Mouse March." Words and music by Jimmie Dodd. © 1955 Walt Disney Music Company. All rights reserved, reprinted by permission.

"Shut Down." The Beach Boys, words and music by Brian Wilson and Roger Christian.

"Sidewalk Surfin'." Jan and Dean, words and music by Roger Christian and Brian Wilson.

"Surf City." Jan and Dean, words and music by Jan Berry and Brian Wilson.

"Surfin'." The Beach Boys, Words and music by Mike Love and Brian Wilson.

"Surfin' Safari." The Beach Boys, words and music by Mike Love and Brian Wilson.

"Surfin' USA." Chuck Berry, © 1958 and 1963 (renewed), ARC Music Corp. All rights reserved, used by permission.

"When I Grow Up." Words and music by Jimmie Dodd and Sonny Burke. © 1955 Walt Disney Music Company. All rights reserved, reprinted by permission.

Index